CAPTURE

The Author setting out from Gangtok on the journey into Tibet

Captured in Tibet

ROBERT FORD

With an Epilogue by the author

With a Preface by
His Holiness the Dalai Lama

HONG KONG
OXFORD UNIVERSITY PRESS
OXFORD   NEW YORK
1990

Oxford University Press

Oxford New York Toronto
Petaling Jaya Singapore Hong Kong Tokyo
Delhi Bombay Calcutta Madras Karachi
Nairobi Dar es Salaam Cape Town
Melbourne Auckland

and associated companies in
Berlin Ibadan

First published in Great Britain 1957
by George G. Harrap & Co. Ltd
First published in English by George G. Harrap & Co. Ltd
© George G. Harrap & Co. Ltd 1957
Preface and Epilogue © Oxford University Press 1990

This edition reprinted, with permission
and with the addition of a Preface and an Epilogue
in Oxford Paperbacks 1990

ISBN 0 19 581570 X

Printed in Hong Kong by Skiva Printing and Binding Co., Ltd
Published by Oxford University Press, Warwick House, Hong Kong

THE DALAI LAMA

PREFACE

Robert Ford occupies a special place in the recent history of Tibet. He was not only to be employed by the Tibetan Government, but also to be granted an official rank. His unprecedented appointment as a radio operator was an indication of the value attached to his service and can be seen as a sign that Tibet really was beginning to emerge from its self-imposed isolation. Unfortunately for both Robert Ford and Tibet, appreciation of the need for change was too little and too late, for the country remained ill-prepared to meet the Chinese invasion. As a result, he gained the further distinction of being the only European to suffer capture and imprisonment by the Chinese for his loyalty to Tibet. Although not the first European to be inspired by a sense of adventure and a genuine affection for the Tibetan people to offer them his help, he was the only one to pay such a price. I am grateful to him for his work in Chamdo and regret the trials he faced as a consequence.

Concerning the Chinese invasion of Tibet, an issue about which general understanding is vague at best, his account is of great value, for few others observed it as he did. He presents a frank picture of Tibet as he found it in the last years of independence, expressing his fondness for Tibetans and their unique way of life, but not hesitating to mention what he saw as the shortcomings that contributed to its vulnerability. Similarly, the story of his imprisonment and interrogation by the Chinese communists is revealing, because it clearly shows their inability to accept anything but their own version of events. No matter how often he told the simple truth, they either refused to believe it or could not admit that they did it. I deeply share the sense of relief he felt on being released and pray that all my fellow countrymen in similar circumstances may also obtain their freedom.

Forty years after the events it describes, it is opportune, in the context of recent happenings in China, that CAPTURED IN TIBET should be reprinted now. I have no doubt that people reading it will more clearly understand the tragedy that befell a whole nation and hope that this may yet lead to some redress.

September 18, 1989

To
MY MOTHER
who never gave up hope
and to
MONICA
who gave me a new happiness

Contents

Epilogue

AUTHOR'S NOTE

I have changed a few names and circumstantial details to avoid the possibility of further persecutions as a result of this book

R. F.

Illustrations

NOTE

The photographs by the late Sir Eric Teichman are reproduced by
courtesy of Lady Teichman

I

The Red Peril

THE Chinese were coming. I had just heard them say so.

"The tasks for the People's Liberation Army for 1950," announced Radio Peking, "are to liberate Taiwan [Formosa], Hainan, and Tibet."

I switched off the radio and told my boy Tenné to saddle my pony. Suddenly I felt a foreigner and alone.

"What is the news, Phodo Kusho?" asked Lobsang, one of the two clerks attached to the radio station.

I told him.

"You and Tashi had better think about sending your wives and children back to Lhasa," I added as I went out. "The frontier's less than a hundred miles away. If anyone wants me I've gone to see the Governor-General."

The Germans had been less than a hundred miles away when I heard them say they were going to invade England in 1940, but it had been easy to deride Lord Haw-Haw in a packed N.A.A.F.I. at Cranwell. Now, as the only European in Eastern Tibet, I could not raise even a wry smile at that anonymous voice from Peking. It separated me from all the people of Tibet. I had always laughed when the newspapers called me the loneliest Briton in the world, but this made me feel I was. For I was not down on the list for liberation; the Tibetans were to be liberated from me.

It was the first of January and bitterly cold, and I drew my fur-lined blue silk robe closer as I mounted my pony. Tenné rode in front and set the pace, which was slow. Haste would have been undignified for a Tibetan Government official whatever his mission, and in any case the rough track that passed for the main street of Chamdo was heavily iced. I had become a careful rider since I put myself so far beyond the reach of medical aid that a broken leg would mean death or at least deformity for life.

Some women were shopping at the stalls; others churned butter-tea in front of their wattle-and-daub houses. Children kicked a shuttlecock in the Chinese style. Claret-robed monks walked along telling their beads and murmuring prayers. Old Smiler, the beggar, turned his prayer-wheel and stuck out his tongue, paying me the Tibetan's highest mark of respect. Two men and a woman in sheep-skins proceeded painfully along the icy street in a series of full-length prostrations. They would reach Lhasa in six months if they were lucky, and had a fifty-fifty chance of dying on the way. But they could be sure of rebirth in a higher station next time.

Slowly as we rode, it took us less than five minutes to go through this, the principal town of Kham, the eastern province of Tibet.

The Ngom Chu river, flanking Chamdo on the west, was frozen hard, and heavily laden yaks were being driven across the ice. We used the old wooden cantilever bridge, which still had doors as a reminder of the last time the town was besieged. For comfort I took a second glance at the bullet-marks on them, which had been made when the Tibetans last took up arms. They won that fight and drove the Chinese out, and the bullet-marks were only thirty-two years old.

We rode up the river for a few minutes, and then across a small plain to the Governor-General's Residency. It was a new building made of rammed earth, freshly whitewashed and looking bright and clean. Two eighty-foot poles supported huge prayer-flags on either side of the gateway, and the wind turned a prayer-wheel on the flat roof. Tenné dismounted and led my pony in. Mounted sentries pre-sented arms, and a servant ran across the courtyard to help me at the dismounting stone. Mastiffs snarled and strained at their chains. The steward came out and bowed, and led me upstairs.

Lhalu Shapé, Governor-General of Kham and one of the four Cabinet Ministers who were the chief rulers of Tibet, rose from his cushion as I entered his private room and bowed. He was wearing a bright yellow robe with a red sash. His plaited hair was tied in a double top-knot with a golden amulet or charm-box in the middle, and a long gold-and-turquoise ear-ring dangled from his left ear. On one of his fingers glittered a diamond ring which he wore on the advice of his personal physician to protect his health. He walked across and shook hands.

Butter-tea was served, and as I blew off the scum I made the usual polite remarks. But Lhalu could see I was impatient to tell him why I had come.

"There is news?" he asked.

I told him the news. It was not a complete surprise to either of us, for there had been vague threats from Peking before. But this was chillingly definite.

Lhalu picked up his rosary and began to tell his beads.

"They will not come yet," he said.

I agreed. They could not invade Tibet yet, for they were still five hundred miles from the frontier. It was not much more than a month since Chungking had fallen and Chiang Kai-shek fled to Formosa. Between Chungking and us lay the Chinese province of Sikang, deep gorge country with a Tibetan population and no through road. The Chinese province of Chinghai in the north, where the reigning Dalai Lama had been found, presented similar obstacles, and we were safe at least until the spring. What worried me was whether we should be still as defenceless then as we were now.

"More troops will be sent from Lhasa," said Lhalu. "And modern arms. We shall not let the Chinese cross the river."

The river was the Upper Yangtse, the *de facto* boundary between Sikang and Tibet. I had been told it was difficult to cross, but it was a long line to defend.

"Phodo," said Lhalu, "when does your contract expire?"

"At the end of the third month, Your Excellency."

The third month of the Tibetan calendar ended in the middle of May. My contract with the Tibetan Government dated from my arrival at Bombay in 1948 and was for two years. It was renewable at mutual option.

"Do you think you will want to renew it?" Lhalu asked.

I hesitated. According to Tibetan etiquette the initiative would have to come from me, but I was not going to ask for a further engagement in the present circumstances unless I knew my services were needed.

Lhalu understood.

"We hope you will want to stay," he said. "You know how much we appreciate what you have done in bringing radio to Chamdo. Before you came it took at least ten days for an official dispatch to reach Lhasa even by the fastest courier. Now it takes no time at all. As you know, we did not think of defence when we first offered you this appointment, but I do not need to tell you why it is so important for us to keep this radio link. If you leave it will break down."

I knew that was true. I was training four young Indians as wireless operators and mechanics, but they would not be ready to take full charge of the station by May. Nor was the Government likely to find a suitable relief.

"I don't have to decide yet, do I?" I asked.

"I am not asking you officially, Phodo. I only want to know myself."

"I have been very happy here," I said. "Even if I knew your language better I would not be able to tell you how happy I have been. I want to stay. But I can do so only while Tibet remains independent. I would not work for a Communist Government even if they wanted me to, which is not very likely."

"You must ask Shiwala Rimpoche if you want to know the future," said Lhalu with a smile. "But our spirit of independence is strong. We are not frightened of the Chinese. Did we not show that when we threw their officials out last year?"

Tibet had expelled all Chinese officials from the country the previous July, to assert her independence and neutrality in the Civil War. But the war was nearly over then, and the Chungking Government could do no more than protest.

"They were representatives of the Kuomintang," I pointed out.

"The Communists are even worse. They have no gods, and they would destroy our religion. We shall never let them in.'

"They have a better army than the K.M.T.," I pointed out; "and there is nothing more in China for their army to do. And I have heard rumours," I went on, choosing my words carefully, "of secret negotiations between Lhasa and Peking. I do not believe these rumours, but it seems at least possible that the Tibetan Government will seek a peaceful settlement. Whatever the terms might be, I have no doubt what it would mean in the end."

"The Chinese never keep their word," nodded Lhalu.

"The Communists are more dangerous than all previous Chinese Governments," I said. "And if Tibet falls into their hands it will be very serious for me. I have heard several times from Radio Peking that Tibet is controlled by American and British imperialists."

"What nonsense!"

"Yes, and that is why it worries me. If the Chinese succeed in liberating Tibet, as they put it, they will want to find some evidence of foreign imperialism when they arrive. Your Excellency knows how many Americans there are in Tibet."

"There are none."

"And Britons?"

A monastery in Eastern Tibet
   Sir Eric Teichman

A typical Khamba house
   Sir Eric Teichman

Yak-skin coracles crossing the Upper Yangtse
Sir Eric Teichman

VJ celebrations at the British Mission in Lhasa
The Author is the first on the left.

"Only you and Fox, the radio officer in Lhasa. Two."

"Three including Mr Richardson at the Indian Mission, although he will hand over to an Indian soon. He and Fox are relatively safe in Lhasa. I am the only foreign imperialist in danger of falling into Communist hands. If I renew my contract it must be binding only so long as Tibet remains independent. And if Tibet gives in without fighting I want to be told before the agreement comes into force. I want enough time to get out of the country before the Communists come in."

"I assure you that you will have it, Phodo," said Lhalu emphatically. "I will personally guarantee your safe passage to Lhasa and out of the country."

"Thank you, Your Excellency."

"But," he added slowly, "I do not think it will come to that. We shall try to avert a war, but we have fought the Chinese before, and if we must we shall fight them again." He paused. "If there is fighting will you stay?"

"If I am still under contract, of course I shall stay. But only so long as Tibet resists."

Lhalu smiled.

"At least I can promise you one thing," he said. "There will be no local surrender in Kham so long as I am here."

I was sure that was true. Pro-Chinese Tibetans had put out his father's eyes for witchcraft, and would do the same to Lhalu if they had the chance.

Outside the Residency there was still ice in the shade, but the sun was pleasantly warm. It could burn, too, for in the clear atmosphere of 10,500 feet the ultra-violet rays are strong. The sky was blue, and I could see the great snow-clad peaks, rising to 18,000 feet, many miles away. Nearer Chamdo the hills were bare and eroded, and only a few clumps of firs had escaped deforestation. There were prayer-flags and cairns of stones on the summits, and a thin plume of incense smoke rose from one. This peaceful valley in the high mountains could have been the original Shangri-la, for there was little in it to remind me of the world I had left behind.

Along the river wound the track to Lhasa, five hundred miles to the west: the Holy City, the Forbidden City, the City of Mystery, but to me then a sophisticated city where you could drink cocktails and dance the samba, play tennis and bridge and read newspapers only three weeks old. The rough, narrow track leading to it was our life-line—and if there was an attack from the north it was perilously easy to cut.

Some building was going on in the Residency grounds, and I saw a Tibetan army officer watching some soldiers dressing timber. He might have been a British officer by his uniform, complete with Sam Browne; but there was a charm-box under his topee, and from his left ear dangled the five-inch earring that was compulsory for all Government officials except Fox and me. He saw me and came across.

"What's the news?" he asked, as every official did, every time we met.

I told him the news. It concerned him deeply, for he was Dimön Depön, the officer commanding the Chamdo garrison, directly responsible to Lhalu Shapé, Commander-in-Chief of all forces in Kham.

Depön is usually translated as General, because it is the highest rank in the Tibetan Army. As that seems too grandiose some English writers have reduced him to Colonel, but this also is misleading. The word simply means an officer commanding five hundred men, the largest formation in the Tibetan Army.

There were no badges of rank, so Dimön Depön wore symbolical *dorje* (thunderbolt) emblems on his shoulders instead of pips and crowns. He also wore a fine array of British campaign ribbons, including both the Mons Star and the Africa Star. No Tibetan ribbons had been issued yet, but it looked as if his time might be coming.

"We can beat the Chinese," he said confidently. "Come and look at the troops."

They were exercising on the plain in front of the Residency, forming fours, and from the front they looked like the Gurkhas I had seen in India. They were in the old-style British service dress, but their long single pigtails, braided with red thread, gave them away when they turned round. They also wore earrings—the infallible safeguard against being reincarnated as a donkey—but a much cheaper sort than those worn by Lhalu and Dimön.

The Anglo-Indian influence had come into the Tibetan Army in the nineteen-twenties, when selected instructors were trained by British and Indian officers in western Tibet. Tibetan has no military vocabulary, and the words of command were given in English; and so they were handed down. It was a purely oral tradition, and now they were hardly recognizable, but it was almost eerie to stand in Chamdo and hear orders like "Open order—march!"

Dimön Depön ordered battle practice, and the troops went through the motions of firing their rifles.

"We shall do target practice when we get some more ammunition," he told me. "At present there is not enough to spare. We must save it for the Chinese!"

He was no coward, but he was not a soldier either. He had not been a *depön* for long, and he had no previous military experience. That was normal. The rank of *depön* was just another stepping-stone in the Tibetan hierarchy, and was reserved exclusively for members of the two hundred noble families that constituted the Tibetan official class. As I had been told that my own rank was not honorary, I might be promoted to *depön* myself one day. Lhalu had once been a *depön* in the Royal Bodyguard.

The senior professional officers were the *rupöns*, who were next to the *depöns* in military seniority but in the official hierarchy came nowhere at all. They were lowly officials without hope of advancement who had made the Army their career. There were two *rupöns* under a *depön*, each having charge of two hundred and fifty men. Dimön's *rupöns* were both able and conscientious, and worked hard on training the troops when he was not using them as builders.

Dimön Depön was an excellent architect. The Khambas, as the people of Kham are called, are poor builders, and it was normal to use troops for this work. Dimön had designed the Residency, and the Army had built it. He wanted to build me a new radio station in the Residency grounds.

"Soon we must choose a site and have it tested by the monks for devils," he said. "Did you discuss it with the Governor-General?"

"No," I said, "we were talking about the Chinese."

It was absurd to stay in Chamdo and stake my future on this Drury Lane Army and a lot of prayer-flags. The town had a garrison of five hundred men, and there were another two hundred and fifty in Lhalu's bodyguard. There were not many more than that guarding the whole of the Upper Yangtze. Their heavy arms were four Lewis guns and three pieces of mountain artillery, which were fired once a year to amuse the people. When bullets were precious one could not expect them to waste a shell just for practice. And this was the headquarters of Tibet's Eastern Command! Lhalu had said reinforcements would come from Lhasa, and I knew they had Bren and Sten guns there; but the nominal strength of the Tibetan Army was only 10,000, and what could they do against Communist China?

It was true that the troops were as tough as nails, incredibly brave, well disciplined, and fanatically loyal to their God-King. It was also true that the country was a military paradise for defence. It was useless for tanks or armoured cars or motor transport of any kind; for there were no wheeled vehicles in Tibet, not even animal-drawn carts, and therefore there were no made roads. Bomber aircraft would not be of much use to an invading force, for there was nothing to bomb. The mountain ranges and rivers ran from north to south in both Eastern Tibet and Sikang, making invasion exceptionally difficult from the east. Narrow passes could be held against powerful forces, immense losses inflicted on the invaders. In the past the Tibetans had beaten the Chinese off by rolling rocks down passes, and they could do better than that now.

But the Tibetans would never hold Chamdo. It was situated on a triangular peninsula formed by the Ngom Chu and Dza Chu, the West River and East River, which joined to form the Mekong just to the south of the town. On the north rose the hill on which the monastery stood, and the enemy could come down either side of it.

I looked up at the monastery as I rode back towards the town. It was the largest in Kham, but certainly not the most beautiful: a brown and white red-fringed building, or rather collection of buildings, with a few gilded ornaments glinting on the roofs. Physically and spiritually it dominated the town. It was the biggest landowner in the region, and in Tibet a landowner owned the tenants like serfs. Before I could engage my boy Tenné he had to get a formal release from the owner of the estate on which he was born.

The monastery housed two thousand monks, and they were supported by the three thousand people who lived in Chamdo. The monks did no work and did not even look after their own needs. Half a dozen women spent their lives carrying tubs of water, holding about four gallons each, up that hill from dawn till dusk. They lived at the foot of the hill, quite near the radio station, and I never looked out without seeing them going up or down. Tibetans drink at least fifty bowls of tea a day. Far more women would have been needed if the monks had also washed.

The monastery was quite new, for the old one was destroyed by the Chinese in 1912. They had never been forgiven for that. The only relics of the Chinese occupation were a ruined temple in the town and the neglected graves of their fallen soldiers by the river, one of the very few cemeteries in the country. The frozen ground is too hard for burials, so the Tibetans cut their dead to pieces and

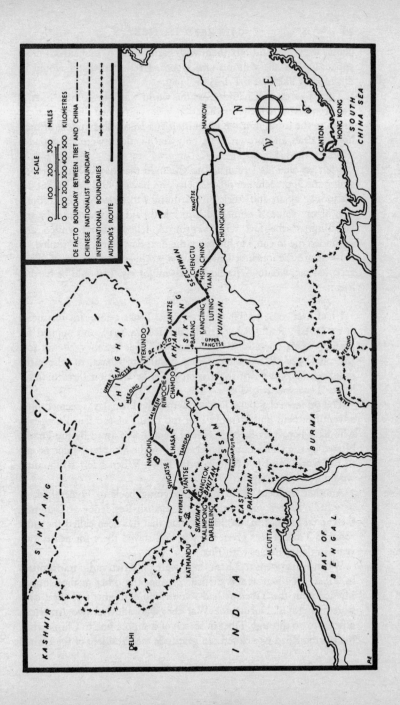

pound the bones and mix them with barley-meal to make them more appetizing for the vultures and ravens. I reflected that I would be disposed of like that if I died in Tibet.

The "fortress of Chamdo," as the world was later to hear of it, is not pretty from whichever direction it is approached. There is some green to the south, but the town itself is a featureless huddle of mud houses, drab and brown. The only fortifications were the wooden doors on the bridges.

I felt an alien as I returned to Chamdo that day. Then a trader, seeing me approach, got off his pony and bowed. Old Smiler put out his tongue again and stuck up his thumbs to show his high estimation of my value; I reminded him I had paid him last month, and he admitted the fact with a grin. A fellow-official smiled and reminded me to come to his party the next day. Every one smiled.

I was not the loneliest Briton in the world—not alone at all. They accepted me, whatever Radio Peking might say. It would be hard to leave.

I had first come to Tibet by accident. I was a sergeant instructor at an R.A.F. Radio School in Hyderabad in 1945, and applied for posting to an operational unit because I was bored with my job. Instead I was offered a temporary posting to Lhasa, to relieve the radio officer at the British Mission while he went on three months' leave. That was Reg. Fox.

The three weeks' pony journey across the Himalayas seemed high adventure then, and I enjoyed all the thrills of the few Europeans who have been privileged to enter Lhasa. I was awed by the Potala, blessed by the Dalai Lama, entertained by the most hospitable people in the world, and fell in love with Tibet. When I left I thought I would never see it again.

Another accident saved me from going back to Hyderabad. A new radio officer was needed at the British Residency at Gangtok, the capital of Sikkim, the Indian state that has been called the anteroom to Tibet. I was given the job, and stayed there for nearly two years in daily contact with Fox.

When I first went to Lhasa there were only two radio transmitters in Tibet. One was at the British Mission, the other at the Chinese Mission; but the Tibetans had some radio equipment of their own stored in crates. During the War they had allowed two American officers to go through Tibet in search of a supply-line to China when the Burma Road was closed. In gratitude the President of the United

States gave the Tibetans three complete radio stations, which they wanted for internal communications. Because of their traditional policy of seclusion they did not want any foreigners to operate them, so they asked Fox to train Tibetans for the work in his spare time. When I relieved him I took over this training as well.

For a variety of reasons the scheme was not a success, and in 1947 the Tibetans reluctantly decided they would have to bring in technicians from outside. They tried to get Indians, as being less foreign than Europeans; but no suitable candidates applied. I tested some of the applicants in Gangtok, to save them the long journey to Lhasa; and, not very hopefully, I applied to the Tibetan Government for employment myself.

My offer was accepted. I went back to England and was released from the R.A.F., and returned to Lhasa in the summer of 1948. I was given a middle rank in the Tibetan hierarchy, and became the first European to receive the Dalai Lama's blessing as a Tibetan Government official.

I shall never forget the last time I walked up to the throne where His Holiness sat cross-legged, wearing his claret-coloured monk's robe and the tall yellow pointed hat that was his crown. He greeted me with a smile, when all other heads were bowed low: for a Buddhist may not look on the face of his God. I presented the traditional white scarf with swastika borders, and then the three symbolical offerings: an image made of butter representing the Buddha's body, a copy of the Holy Scriptures representing his speech, and a miniature temple representing his mind. Then I bowed, and the Dalai Lama placed both hands on my head—a great honour, for this two-handed blessing was normally reserved for officials of the highest ranks. His Holiness honoured me further by presenting me with a small red silk scarf which he had knotted with his own hands. I followed custom by wearing it round my neck for the rest of the day.

There was only one part of the prescribed ritual that I did not perform myself. Had I been a Tibetan I should have been required to prostrate myself three times before the throne. It was impossible for me to do this sincerely—not because I was a European, but because I was not a Buddhist; and my own religion forbade it. It would have been as improper as for a Tibetan to take Holy Communion in a Christian church. This was therefore done for me by another official. He also offered tea to the Dalai Lama on my behalf, first drinking some himself to show that it was not poisoned.

Then I sat on a cushion and was served with rice and butter-tea. I flicked a few grains of rice over my right shoulder as an offering to the gods, and sipped my tea while Tashi and Lobsang and my servants filed quickly past the throne. Junior officials were blessed with the right hand only, and commoners were lightly touched with a tassel suspended from a small rod. The Dalai Lama bestowed his blessings with dignity and majesty, and relaxed only to give me a broad smile of farewell that reminded me that he was a boy of fourteen.

Mainly because of trouble over equipment, I stayed in Lhasa for nearly a year. During that time I built and opened Radio Lhasa, and for the first time Tibet was able to broadcast to the outside world.

It had already been arranged that I should open another station in Chamdo, and some one was needed to take over in Lhasa. As a result of the Transfer of Power, the British Mission had become the Indian Mission, and Fox was expecting to be replaced. He was already working for the Tibetan Government in his spare time, building a new hydro-electric station together with Peter Aufschnaiter, the German agricultural engineer who had reached Lhasa with Heinrich Harrer after escaping from British internment at Dehra Dun.[1] Fox resigned from the Indian Mission and also became a Tibetan Government official. Then I set out for Chamdo.

I left Lhasa in charge of a caravan of twenty riding animals, eighty mules and yaks, ten muleteers, forty porters, and an armed escort of twelve soldiers. Besides all the radio equipment I took four hundred gallons of petrol for the engines. The journey over the mountains took more than two months, and parts of the route had never been reached by a European before. I camped with nomads, dodged bandits, doctored the sick, crossed yak-hide bridges, forded rivers, crossed high mountain passes, and witnessed a miracle performed by an incarnate lama. When I arrived at Chamdo the whole population turned out to stare at my blue eyes, long nose, and especially the ginger beard I had grown on the way. When I appeared clean-shaven the next morning the rumour went round that two Europeans had arrived at Chamdo.

That was only five months ago, but now Phodo Kusho—Ford Esquire—was no longer a curiosity but accepted as a member of the community. I had picked up enough words of the Khamba dialect to be able to talk to the local inhabitants; they invited me freely to their

[1] See *Seven Years in Tibet*, by Heinrich Harrer (Hart-Davis, 1953).

homes, and they had even got used to the marvel of radio. But it was not such a marvel in a land where levitation was commonplace, and holy "wind-men" travelled hundreds of miles in a day.

At 4 P.M. I had my last schedule of the day with Fox. It always did me good to hear his voice, although we could not say anything over the radio that we did not want to be overheard. I knew for a fact that my transmissions were being monitored by the Chinese Communists. But at least I could ask him if he had heard the news from Radio Peking.

"Yes, Bob. Don't worry. It'll work out."

Fox's roots in Tibet were deeper than mine. Born in London, a dispatch-rider in the First World War, he had gone to Lhasa in 1937, just after the British Mission was established. He had been there ever since. Now he had a Tibetan wife and three lovely children with their father's fair hair and their mother's almond eyes. Tibet was his homeland now, and he always said he was there for life.

After a brief chat we switched over to the key. We dealt first with the Government messages, which were in a code that neither of us knew. Then we handled the commercial traffic, which was in a published numerical code. A trader came in to speak to a friend in Lhasa, and before he began I gave him the usual warning that anyone with a radio receiver in Lhasa could listen in. Our service had come under heavy suspicion in the early days, after a Chamdo trader told his Lhasa agent to buy all the calico he could—and every scrap of calico had gone by the time the agent reached the market.

At 5 P.M. Fox put Radio Lhasa on the air. The news was read in Tibetan, then in English by Fox, and finally in Chinese by the Dalai Lama's brother-in-law, a young man from Chinghai. I relayed it to Sikang, Chinghai, and as much more of China as my low-powered transmitter could reach. I was mildly disappointed that no reference was made to the threat from Radio Peking, although I had not really expected an immediate Tibetan reaction.

Later that evening I tried to contact some radio amateur in England. It was only a formality, for bad conditions had made communication with Europe impossible for several weeks. I searched the twenty-metre band for a call-sign begining with G, but without luck; and I knew that if I could not receive I had no chance of being heard with my low power. I spoke to an amateur in Australia, and then closed down.

At 10 P.M. I tuned in to Radio Peking for the news in Tibetan. These broadcasts had only begun recently, and evidently it had not yet dawned on the Chinese that almost all Tibetans are in bed by nine. They rise early because the first part of the day is the most auspicious. So I was the only person in Tibet to hear that broadcast, which was a little more explicit than the version I had heard in English.

"The tasks for the People's Liberation Army for 1950 are to liberate Formosa, Hainan, and Tibet," said the announcer, "from American and British imperialism."

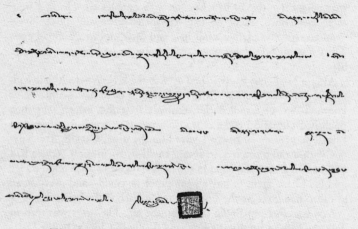

The Author's 'Road-pass' for the Journey into Tibet

2

Moment of Decision

ON the sixth of January the British Government announced its *de facto* recognition of the People's Government of China.

I included the announcement in the daily news summary that I prepared for Lhalu by monitoring the chief radio stations of the world. Soon after I had sent it to the Residency, Rimshi Trokao came in.

"Does this mean that the British have made friends with the Communists?" he asked.

They would all be asking me that. Lhalu would know what *de facto* recognition meant, but probably he was the only one.

Rimshi Trokao was the lay head of the Governor-General's Executive Council—nearly all official posts were held in duplicate, monk and lay—and he was Lhalu's right-hand man. He was over fifty, an old man by Tibetan standards, and had a drooping moustache and a few more whiskers on his chin of which he was very proud. He was able, clever, and shrewd. He kept the Government code, and did all the coding and decoding himself; and there were not many men in Tibet, even in the official class, capable of that.

To that extent he was exceptional. He was typical in that he had never been out of Tibet and was utterly innocent of international affairs.

I tried to explain the meaning of *de facto* recognition. Tibetan has no diplomatic vocabulary, and it had not been easy to translate the term for Lhalu.

"It is a fact that the Communists won the Chinese Civil War," I said. "It is fact that they are now the actual rulers of nearly all China. The British Government has recognized these facts. That does not mean it likes them. It doesn't. But it cannot see any gain in pretending they do not exist."

Perhaps I oversimplified. It was certainly too simple for the tortuous ways of Tibetan politics.

"Britain has helped us to keep the Chinese out in the past," said Rimshi Trokao. "Will they help us now?"

"I am an official of the Tibetan, not the British Government," I reminded him. "I don't know. I imagine it all depends on India. Since the Transfer of Power, Britain no longer has any direct strategic or commercial interest in Tibet. Britain and the other Western Powers are opposed to all aggression and do not want Communism to spread, but the only way to Tibet is through India. I don't suppose the Indians want to see Chinese troops on their northern frontier, but that does not mean they will send their own troops to your help."

I remembered something I had read in one of Sir Charles Bell's books. He said that if the British left India the Indians would not be able to protect Tibet against Chinese aggression even if they had the will. Bell wrote that long before China had an efficient unified army, and now India was not showing much will.

"They can send us arms," said Rimshi Trokao. "They can let others send us arms. Do you think Britain will give us aeroplanes?"

Aeroplanes! He had been looking at the pictures in some of my illustrated magazines.

"Who would fly them if they did?"

"Our soldiers, of course. You could show them how to—you were in the British Air Force."

It was the sort of conversation I could have had with any of the officials. Lhalu also talked about aeroplanes, and had a fantastic idea of basing them on some other country so that the Chinese would not know Tibet had them. The only obstacle he could see was that the monks would not allow aeroplanes to fly over Tibet. They said they would disturb the gods that dwelt in the upper air. There was no getting round this, and the senior Cabinet Minister was always a monk.

I was regarded as an expert not only on aviation and radio but on almost every other subject under the sun, except the Buddhist religion. The Tibetans were ignorant because they had no means of acquiring knowledge. There were almost no Tibetan books, except the scriptures; no newspapers, except a sheet that was published once a week in Kalimpong; no cinemas; and there had been no radio until a year ago. As a result Europeans in Tibet were regarded as experts on everything, and the fact that I had been to an English grammar school made me the only educated man in Chamdo.

The heart of the trouble was that there were no real Tibetan schools. One or two had been started in Lhasa, but they were very elementary and catered mostly for the children of traders. An English school had been founded in Lhasa by a man named Parker during the Second World War, but the monks had forced him to close it after only six months. Most of the officials' sons had private tutors, who were themselves uneducated, and then were trained for Government service in the Finance Office. A few had been educated in India, and they too were regarded as walking encyclopædias by their compatriots. There were none of these in Chamdo.

Lhalu knew more than the other officials because his father was one of the very few Tibetans who ever went to England. Lhalu himself had not been out of Tibet, but he was keenly interested in the outside world and studied the pictures in my illustrated magazines. He wanted to know about tractors and other agricultural machinery and about industrial processes in the West. He was typical of the more progressive Tibetan officials. They knew they were backward, and genuinely wanted to learn and to modernize their country —so long as no harm was done to their religion.

Because of his high rank Lhalu was a lonely man in Chamdo. He was so far above all the other officials that he had no social life at all. He could not even carry on an intelligent conversation in private with Rimshi Trokao, who was bound to agree with everything Lhalu said and to talk only in reverent monosyllables and with much sucking in of his breath. I was not expected to behave in this way, and Lhalu encouraged me to talk freely and naturally, without too much respect for his rank.

I used to go to the Residency every Saturday, usually for lunch and often for the whole day. Naturally he did not discuss Tibetan politics with me, but he asked my opinion on many aspects of defence. I did not presume to say what I thought Tibet should do in her relations with China and other countries. Her foreign policy was her own affair. But the results of that policy concerned me very much.

Early in the New Year we learnt that five separate 'goodwill missions' were preparing to leave Tibet. Their purpose was to demonstrate the country's independence, and presumably in some cases to negotiate for aid. Their respective destinations were Britain, the United States, India, Nepal, and Communist China. The members were appointed. Preparations for departure were made. Then Peking intervened.

The Communist Government said that the proposed missions were illegal, because Tibet was not an independent state but a part of the Chinese People's Republic. This was the traditional Chinese point of view. The Tibetans were invited to send representatives to Peking alone for "the peaceful solution of the question of Tibet." A warning was issued, obviously directed at India, that any country receiving one of the "illegal" missions would be considered as "entertaining hostile intentions against the Chinese People's Republic."

None of the goodwill missions ever left Lhasa.

Peking repeated the "liberation" threat. Lhasa still did not reply.

I listened to every news bulletin broadcast by Radio Lhasa, and I never heard even the mildest expression of defiance. Not once did Tibet say she would defend herself against aggression; not once did she even assert her independence. Every reference to China was conciliatory and polite. I could almost hear the words sticking in Fox's throat.

I began to wonder if my problem might be solved for me. Peking was talking of American and British imperialists using Tibet as a back-door for aggression against China. Perhaps the Tibetans would decide to get rid of me to appease the Chinese. Then we heard that a Tibetan delegation was leaving Lhasa to try to negotiate with the Chinese. Perhaps by May the Tibetans would have given in.

When I thought of this I realized that my motives for wanting to stay were not so unselfish as I would have liked to believe. I did not want to go, because I liked being where I was.

The radio station and my own quarters occupied the upper floor of the old Summer Palace which the Governor-General had used for entertaining before the new Residency was built. It stood outside the town, at the foot of the hill on which the monastery stood, and the grounds were enclosed by a wall. Rimshi Trokao lived in the same compound and was my nearest neighbour.

It was very pleasant and quite park-like, and there were stores inside the compound where I could keep the petrol for the engines. This petrol had been my greatest worry on the journey, for the nomads persisted in using the cans as wind-breakers when they lit their fires and cooked their meals. It was, of course, the first time petrol had ever been taken to Chamdo. The only disadvantage about the station was that it lay on the east of the town while the Residency was on the west. That was why Dimön Depön was going to put up a new building for me.

Besides my boy, Tenné, my establishment consisted of my cook,

Do-Tseten, and my personal bodyguard, a soldier named Puntso. The two clerks, Lobsang and Tashi, lived in the town with their wives and children. Both were very junior officials, and they had been among the Tibetans originally chosen for training as radio operators. I had first met them when I relieved Fox in 1945. They had given up trying to operate and were now simply clerks. They were essential to me, as, although I could now speak Tibetan quite fluently, I had not had time to learn the written language.

Tibetan children were tough. Tashi had brought his daughter from Lhasa, a girl aged nine, and she had ridden her pony without complaint the whole way. Lobsang's children were too young—even by Tibetan standards—to ride by themselves. His elder son, aged five, had sat in front of his father's servant, while the other boy, who was three, was swaddled in a cloth and carried on the back of a porter, like my jar of concentrated sulphuric acid.

The four Indian trainees also lived in the town. They were Indian by nationality only, for all were of Tibetan stock. From the beginning it had been decided that the radio network should eventually be staffed by Tibetans, but I had told the Government that we could not train men who had not had an ordinary elementary education. So Fox had recruited suitable young men in the Indian border states, while I had found a few Muslims who were living in Lhasa. Four of Fox's recruits joined me at Chamdo, while he trained the rest in Lhasa.

I was giving the Indians the full course that I had taught at the Radio School in Hyderabad when I was an instructor in the R.A.F. This included radio theory as well as operating technique, and I reckoned it would take until September to complete their training. To prevent the Indians from coming to Tibet for free tuition and then taking jobs at home, each had signed a contract for five years' service after his training was finished. They had also agreed to go anywhere in Tibet.

At the beginning of February Lhalu asked me if I could cut the course short and get the Indians ready to operate portable radios as quickly as possible. He wanted them to set up stations at garrison posts on the frontier.

"How soon could they be ready?" he asked.

"If I change the training programme I can bring their operating up to standard in a month," I said. "They will still not be trained radio mechanics. It would be better if they began working in pairs."

"Find out how they feel about it," Lhalu told me. "Of course," he added, playing with his rosary, "I shall not send them out until I know whether you are going to apply to renew your contract."

I said I would give him my decision within the month.

"I shan't be sorry to get out of here," said Sonam Dorje, the eldest of the four. "I always said the Chinese could take it in their sleep. If there's going to be a war I'd rather be on the frontier than cooped up in Chamdo."

Sonam Dorje was of mixed Nepali-Tibetan descent, and had been educated at Darjeeling High School. He had been in the Indian Army and fought in the Burma campaign. He was a few years older than I was, in his early thirties, and still had something of the soldier about him, even in his gaily coloured Tibetan robe.

Wangda, the second oldest, was also ready to go. Wangda was ready to do anything. He was happy-go-lucky and devil-may-care, quite fearless, a great humorist and a born story-teller. He also came from Darjeeling and had taught English in the Chinese school there. In Chamdo he had acquired a wife.

"Tsering will come," he said. "She's a Khamba—I'll need her as my bodyguard."

Of course she would go. In Tibet a woman always went with her husband. The troops had their wives and children with them right on the frontier, and no one dreamed of suggesting they might be evacuated.

Dronyer, who came from Kalimpong and had worked in Tibet for a trader, said he could do with a move. He was of much the same type as Wangda, and these two were later to help keep my spirits up when there was little to joke about.

Sonam Puntso, the youngest of the four, simply said he would go. He was my star pupil, and one of the nicest lads I ever met. Quiet and serious, quick-witted and intelligent, he was easily the best operator and already well advanced in radio theory. He was Sikkimese, and I had played football against him when he was a schoolboy in Gangtok. He was only nineteen; at twenty-six I felt for him a sort of paternal responsibility.

I changed the training programme, putting up a station in the courtyard and making them concentrate on operating procedure. I had to abandon radio theory, and gave them a compressed course on maintenance and simple fault-finding. Sonam Puntso would be ready to take a station out within the month. He was the last of them I wanted to send to the frontier.

But I was by no means sure that any of them would need to go.

The Tibetan delegation had arrived in India. The Chinese had invited it to go to Peking. Radio Lhasa was still noncommittal. There were rumours of Communist activity in Sikang. A thin crackle of rifle fire told me that Dimön Depön had received his ammunition, but there was still no sign of troop reinforcements or modern automatic weapons.

Then everything stopped for the Tibetan New Year.

Or rather everything started for the New Year.

Preparations began some days before, and I was involved when Tharchi Tsendron came and asked if he could have my aerial masts taken down and fitted with new prayer-flags. Tharchi was a young monk official in charge of labour and public works, and he had helped me greatly in converting part of the Summer Palace into a radio station. He had also become my closest friend in Chamdo. He was always anxious to see that I was properly protected by the gods, and now he wanted prayer-flags on the aerials as well as the poles. I drew the line at that and told him he would have to put the new prayer-flags on the masts without taking them down, but I agreed to having an incense-burner on the roof.

The huge poles outside the Residency were taken down and re-erected with new prayer-flags, and more new flags festooned the roof-tops of Chamdo. Monks began to come in from the outlying villages, and more women were engaged to carry water up to the monastery. Housewives baked New Year cakes, ordinary work almost ceased, and military training was suspended while the troops helped in the preparations for the holiest day in the Tibetan calendar, the first day of the first month.

On New Year's Eve I went up to the monastery to watch the traditional lama dances. Lhalu was there, seated on a throne in his finest regalia, and I took my place with the other officials. Opposite was a lama band of drums and cymbals and nine-foot horns. There was the famous Black Hat dance, which commemorates the assassination of a wicked Tibetan king in the ninth century; the Skeleton Dance, in which the monks wore huge grotesque masks, hideously deathlike, and were dressed to look like animated corpses; and the Warrior Dance, for which the performers appeared clad in long robes, wearing helmets, and carrying swords and shields. All was in honour of the Buddha, who was going to defeat the Chinese.

I went to bed early, for I had to get up again before dawn. I also had to put on a European suit. Ironically the only occasions when I could not wear Tibetan clothes were when I attended functions as a Tibetan Government official; for my short hair and unpierced ears made it impossible for me to appear properly dressed.

My suit was poor protection against the cold and uncomfortable to ride in, and I was glad when we reached the top of the hill. We rode into the courtyard of the monastery, where other officials were already dismounting from their ponies, which wore bright saddle-cloths and had silver and gold filigree on their saddles. We stood chatting until a servant rode in and announced the approach of the Governor-General.

Two incense-burners were lighted on either side of the entrance to the main hall of the monastery, and we lined up in order of rank. There were about twenty Lhasa officials, and I was sixth. Tharchi Tsendron was just below me, and Tashi and Lobsang were at the lower end of the line.

Mounted soldiers of the Governor-General's bodyguard rode in, followed by trumpeters and Lhalu's personal standard-bearer. Then came more soldiers, Lhalu's equerry, and then his chief steward and two servants; and then the trumpeters blew a fanfare as Lhalu came in himself, resplendent in a dragon-patterned robe of fur-trimmed yellow silk and brocade, and wearing a fur-trimmed hat. He was followed by more servants and about forty soldiers.

Two servants held his pony while others helped him to dismount, and we bowed our heads as he walked along the line. Then he entered the monastery, and we followed slowly, still in order of rank.

The main hall, lit only from the roof and by a few butter-lamps below the images, was hung with huge silk and brocade banners and paintings. We walked up one side, and Lhalu sat cross-legged on a high cushion at the end. We also sat down, and the thickness of our cushions was so graded that our heads were in a continuous descending line. Monks took their seats on the opposite side of the hall, headed by Shiwala and Pakpala, the two incarnate lamas. Pakpala Rimpoche looked across at me curiously as I sat cross-legged in a European suit with a wooden tea-bowl on my lap. He was only nine.

Two theologians came out and began a religious disputation. I had seen them practising this for weeks outside the radio station. Each in turn threw off his outer robe and, with bare arms pounding palm into fist and slapping thighs, drove his points home with exaggerated poses and gestures. Few understood what they were saying. According to Tharchi Tsendron, their theology was too profound for anyone except the Dalai Lama himself.

Then a drum-and-fife band struck up, and in trooped thirteen boys in blue and red flowered robes and tam-o'shanters. Each carried a small battleaxe. They performed a jerky, stylized dance with some acrobatics, of such antiquity that its meaning had long been forgotten.

Tea was served, and servants brought in the New Year gifts of meat and bread. They were placed on low tables in front of us, and we each received a whole sheep's carcass that had been blessed by the incarnate lamas. There was more theological disputing, the boys danced again, and more tea was served; and the cycle was repeated a third time. Then we all rose and, led by Lhalu, walked in procession before the huge gilt images of the Buddha at the head of the hall. The Tibetans touched the base of each image with their foreheads, and presented ceremonial white scarves to the biggest. Then Lhalu led the way out of the hall.

Incense was still burning and the monk musicians were playing their clarinets and trumpets and conch-shells as we returned to the courtyard; the troops presented arms and the trumpeters blew a fanfare as Lhalu mounted his horse. All Chamdo was assembled outside the courtyard when he rode out. He went to each of the private chapels of the two Rimpoches, and we followed in turn to present scarves, receive blessings, and drink more butter-tea.

The rest of the day was spent in visiting and receiving calls. I went first to Lhalu, with a white scarf and presents, and then to the other officials senior to myself and to my friends. Afterwards I returned to my own quarters, where junior officials came with scarves and presents for me. It was a moving experience, and it made my kinship with the Tibetans complete.

But their gods were not my gods, and as the New Year celebrations went on I began to feel an outsider. It was all pageantry to me, but to them it was the very breath of life. And this year it had an added significance; it was their defence against the Chinese.

The celebrations had never been on such a large scale before. More prayer-services were held, more incense-burners lit, more prayer-flags were put up than ever before. Soldiers were relieved of military duties to join civilians in making the circuit of the Holy Walk round the monastery; their extra prayers might make all the difference between victory and defeat.

This was not confined to Chamdo. The same fervour was being shown in Lhasa and all over the country. Everywhere there were more dancing monks, bigger butter-images, brighter butter-lamps.

c

Prayer-wheels were turned unceasingly, rosaries were never still, and all hearts and hopes were turned to the gods. Except mine. '

I was not the loneliest Briton in the world. I was the loneliest Christian.

I was completely alone. The Indians were also Buddhists, and Wangda's wife was devout.

A yak strayed into the compound and walked about in my vegetable garden. I sent Tenné to drive it off. It came again, and I sent a message to the owner to keep it under control. It came a third time, and to teach the owner a lesson I told Tenné to keep it for the night. I forgot I would have to feed it.

Tsering reminded me. She was angry.

"My father is a yak," she said. She even knew in which part of Tibet he was grazing.

Lobsang and Tashi assured me it was true. An incarnate lama had told Tsering that her father had been reborn as a yak. They knew that the lama was a very wise and holy man. Then they asked for a morning off as they wanted to help in casting out some devils.

I respected the Buddhist religion, as the Buddhists respected mine. They are the most tolerant people in the world and never try to proselytize. But the Tibetan form of Buddhism is mixed with the earlier animist religion of the country, and I could not respect belief in magic and ghost-traps; at least, I could not respect the belief that they would defeat the Chinese.

Was it absurd to stay? Was it absurd to throw in my lot, perhaps at the risk of my life, with people who relied not on their own efforts but on a distorted form of a religion in which I did not believe?

I felt moody and depressed when I went up to the monastery on the fifteenth of the first month to watch the Festival of the Images. Huge figures made of coloured butter had been rigged up on scaffolding, some of them forty feet high. At dusk they were lit up by thousands of tiny butter-lamps, throwing them into relief. Lhalu inspected the images, all of which had been made in monasteries, and awarded a prize for the best. Then Khambas came into the courtyard brandishing torches of tightly bound bundles of grass that had been soaked in paraffin, and ran round and round the images, making them look fantastic and grotesque. It was a thrilling sight.

"The gods will give us victory," Lhalu told me the next day.

I said nothing.

"Phodo," he said gently, "I do not think you understand. We do not appeal to the gods out of fear. We turn to them with hope and confidence. The Chinese have more soldiers. The Chinese have better arms. Therefore, if we fight they should win. But the Chinese have no gods. Our gods are our best weapon, and with their help we shall win."

I was still silent. There was nothing to say.

"Have you heard the story of my father's downfall?" Lhalu asked suddenly.

I had heard one version. Lhalu's father had been Commander-in-Chief under the thirteenth Dalai Lama, and was said to have tried to set himself up as dictator during the struggle for power after the God-King's death. He had been overthrown, and, as the Buddhist religion does not allow capital punishment, blinded and imprisoned in the dungeon below the Potala. He had been kept there for five years, and had died soon after Lhalu secured his release.

"When the Great Thirteenth departed to the Heavenly Field," said Lhalu, "some men of power wanted to betray Tibet to the Chinese. My father opposed them, and sent defiant messages to Chiang Kai-shek telling him to leave us alone. Then he was lured by his enemies to the Potala, where they arrested him. They said afterwards that they found two pieces of paper in his boots. They said that he managed to swallow one, but they seized the other and found the name of a Cabinet Minister written on it. Then, of course, my father was convicted of trying to kill him by witchcraft, and his eyes were put out. But the story was false."

I thought it sounded a little far-fetched.

"My father never practised witchcraft," said Lhalu. "His enemies practised witchcraft against him. They have practised witchcraft against me. When that failed they used bullets."

I had also heard the story of the attempt to assassinate Lhalu, which had been made shortly before he left for Chamdo, while I was still in Gangtok. He had been riding to his home outside Lhasa at dusk, and his horse had been shot under him.

He told a servant to bring the robe he had been wearing at the time.

"Look," he said, holding it up. "You see the holes? Those bullets passed clean through my body without leaving a mark. Now I will show you why." He revealed a small bundle wrapped in silk. "These are prayers," he said. "They have been blessed by the Presence"—that is, the Dalai Lama—"and I always wear them next to my skin. Not only have they protected me, but they have brought about the downfall of my enemies."

He was referring to Kapshöpa, one of the men who had brought about the downfall of Lhalu's father. Kapshöpa had been made a Cabinet Minister in 1945, and I had been a guest at one of the parties he gave to celebrate the occasion. Recently he had been deposed and degraded for intrigues with the Chinese. He had escaped the usual punishment of a public flogging by paying a heavy fine; but he had been forced to submit to public ridicule by riding out of Lhasa dressed in white clothes on a yak. All his estates had been confiscated, and he had been banished to southern Tibet.

"The gods have saved my life, so is it surprising that I look to the gods for help against the Chinese?" said Lhalu. "You also have a God. Do you not seek His help?"

"Yes," I said. "But we have a saying in England that God helps those who help themselves."

"A very good saying!" said Lhalu. "Very good indeed. I think so too. We are helping ourselves. More troops and arms are being sent to Chamdo. Bren guns and Sten guns will come in three days' time."

To my surprise they came—and suddenly everything changed. The Tibetan delegation was still in India and had refused the invitation to go to Peking. The leaders of the delegation said they would meet the Chinese on neutral ground. They also said their purpose was to negotiate a non-aggression treaty based on Chinese recognition of Tibet's independence. I had a letter from a very reliable source in Lhasa telling me that the Government was determined not to yield. A new radio station, operated by two of Fox's trainees, was set up at Nagchu, the garrison town protecting the only direct track from Chinghai to Lhasa. Radio Lhasa still did not tell the world that Tibet would defend herself if attacked, but now I was sure she would. And she was not going to rely on the gods alone.

Instructors were sent with the Bren guns, and the first practice crackles of those weapons were the sweetest music I had heard since I arrived in Chamdo. The Tibetan Army began to look a little less like something out of the Middle Ages.

Then the crackling stopped, and a little later there were shouts in the courtyard below. Tenné came running upstairs to tell me that one of the soldiers was seriously hurt.

He was nearly dead.

He had been brought in on an improvised stretcher with his knee-cap blown off. He was not groaning—Tibetans have an unbelievable capacity for bearing pain—but I gave him a shot of morphia after stopping the bleeding with a tourniquet. Then I had to make the ghastly decision whether to amputate.

I had no surgical instruments or experience, but I was the best doctor in Chamdo because I was not a Tibetan Buddhist and had learnt first aid in the Boy Scouts. The only professional doctors in Tibet were the medical monks, and the most highly prized medicine was the Dalai Lama's urine. I had brought a medicine chest to Chamdo, and used most of the contents in treating the local population as well as I could. I had set fractures, stitched wounds, and cured diseases I could not diagnose with penicillin. But I had never amputated.

Lack of instruments was no excuse for inaction. All over Tibet I had seen men who had been deprived of an arm or a leg for theft, and they looked healthy enough. Penal amputations were done without antiseptics or sterile dressings, and at least I had these. If removing this man's leg would save his life I had to chop it off. And at least there was not much left to chop.

I did not think he would live anyway, but I decided to do it. Then his breathing changed, there was a rattle in his throat, and he was dead.

I wiped off my sweat and loathed myself for my feeling of relief. Then I imagined what it would be like after a battle, and the thought kept me awake that night. There was not even a pretence of a medical service in the Army, and I was the only person in Chamdo with the faintest idea of treating casualties.

The next morning I went to Lhalu and told him I wanted to renew my contract.

Of course it was not just cause and effect. I did not decide to stay to save lives, when I had hardly any drugs and dressings and was not even a trained medical orderly. Amateur doctoring came into it, but it was only one of the things.

When I am asked why I stayed I can give a dozen reasons, and each is true but none is the whole truth. I stayed because it would have been cowardly to run away; because I thought the Tibetans needed help and were worth helping; because I felt responsible for the Indians; because I liked and respected Lhalu. I stayed because I had a well-paid, interesting job and knew I could not get anything as good in England. I stayed because I preferred a life of adventure to nine-till-six drab routine. I stayed because I liked Tibet, or because I enjoyed life in Tibet and wanted it to go on.

I did not stay because I was unaware of the risks. I knew the danger when I took the first step on the road that was to lead to that filthy prison in Chungking. And I knew that this was the moment of decision. Whatever happened now I was committed to staying so long as the Tibetans resisted the Chinese. If they surrendered I would have to try to get out as best I could.

But I still do not know what I would have done if Shiwala Rimpoche had been able to tell me what lay ahead.

3

The Khamba Levies

RATHER optimistically I suggested that my new contract should be for five years, again renewable at mutual option. I also asked Lhalu to write for six months' leave in 1951 if conditions should permit. He sent my proposals to the Foreign Office in Lhasa, and repeated his promise to get me out of the country if the Chinese were allowed in.

"Now I can send stations out to the frontier," he said.

"All the Indians can operate adequately now," I said. "But they're not fully trained mechanics, and it would be better if they could start off in pairs."

I need not have worried about this, for there were no portable stations for them to take.

The story of the radio equipment is long and tortuous. First of all the engines sent by the Americans did not generate enough power to work the stations, because of the rarefied air. New engines were asked for, and this time it was suggested that they should be diesels. I was told that diesels had arrived, and I arranged for the supply of diesel oil while I was in India, only to find petrol engines when I got to Lhasa.

The engines had been dismantled and crated and carried by porters over the Himalayas, and when I put them together I found that some of the parts had got lost on the way. Only one engine was complete, and that was used for the radio station in Lhasa. Spare parts for the others were ordered, and I took one incomplete engine to Chamdo. If I had relied on getting the spare parts I would not have been on the air yet. But fortunately I had bought two portable radio transmitters and receivers in India, and the engines originally sent by the Americans were powerful enough for these. In Lhasa I offered to put my own equipment at the disposal of the Government

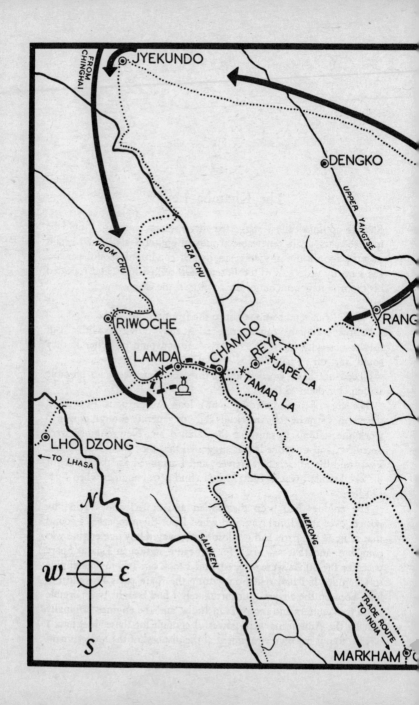

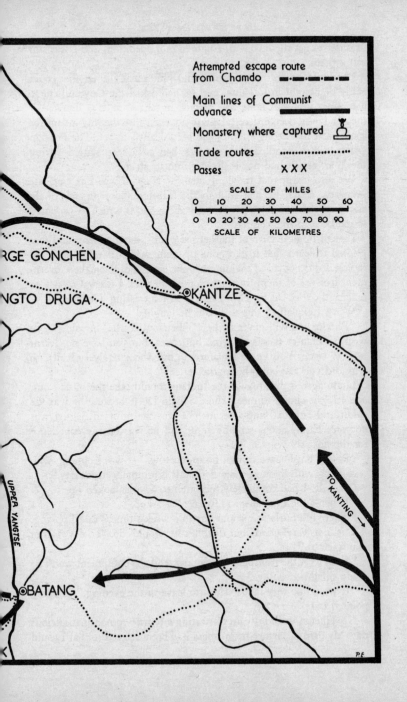

Attempted escape route
from Chamdo ▪—▪—▪—▪—▪

Main lines of Communist
advance ▬▬▬▬▬

Monastery where captured

Trade routes ••••••••••••••••

Passes × × ×

SCALE OF MILES

0   10   20   30   40   50   60

0 10 20 30 40 50 60 70 80 90
SCALE OF KILOMETRES

RGE GÖNCHEN

NGTO DRUGA

⊙KANTZE

UPPER YANGTSE

⊙BATANG

TO KANTING →

P.E.

in order to get the link with Chamdo into operation, and I was still using them.

I had told Lhalu that portable radio equipment and engines could easily be bought in Calcutta, and he had asked the Government to get some. Fox said none had arrived in Lhasa, and he doubted if they had even been ordered; he was not even sure that my indent for spare parts for the big engines had been dealt with yet. The Foreign Office, which handled such matters, had only been started during the War, and it had not really got into its stride.

We also learnt that the equipment at Nagchu was Fox's private property, which he had sold to the Tibetan Government. Lhalu asked me if I would sell my two portables, one of which he proposed to send out to the frontier.

I asked Fox the current market price for the equipment, and was pleased to learn that it had gone up quite a lot since I bought the radios. I did not mind making a profit, as I had given the Government free use of them for nine months. Besides, I needed money to replace the medical supplies I had used for treating Tibetans.

When I explained this to Lhalu he laughed.

"Phodo, you will never make a Tibetan after all," he said. "You wear Tibetan clothes, you drink butter-tea, but you have not learnt how to trade. You knew I wanted to buy those sets very badly, so why did you ask only the market price?"

Lhalu agreed that two of the Indians should take the station out, and left the choice to me. I chose Sonam Dorje because he was the eldest and Sonam Puntso because he was the most efficient. I was not very happy about sending him, and he was on my conscience for the next six years.

"Phodo Kusho, we cannot go to-morrow." It was Lobsang, who was going with them as their clerk. "It is an inauspicious day."

Oh, hell! I had completely forgotten to have it looked up.

"When's the next auspicious day?" I asked.

"There is a fairly auspicious day in a week's time," said Lobsang. "It is not very good, but I think it would do. To-day is not inauspicious."

"I can't get the transport to-day now, and the equipment won't be ready till this evening."

"It would be very inauspicious to leave in the evening," Lobsang pointed out.

No Tibetan would dream of starting a journey on an inauspicious day. My own departure from Lhasa had been delayed so that I could set out on an exceptionally auspicious day, although later I suspected some mistake was made over this. The Tibetan calendar is full of auspicious and inauspicious days, but I could never find out which they were. It is a lunar calendar, like the Chinese—and one year, thanks to an intercalary month, I had thirteen pay-days—but they have made it complicated by omitting some inauspicious dates and duplicating dates that are auspicious. We seemed to have run into a bad patch. I went to report the matter to Lhalu. Perhaps they could get a special dispensation from him or one of the incarnate lamas.

"It is very unfortunate," he said when I had told him. "I am anxious that the station should go out as quickly as possible. But it cannot be helped. They will just have to wait a week."

If I had respected him less I would have asked if the Army proposed to wait for an auspicious day before launching a counter-attack; but even that could have happened in Tibet. I felt irritable when I rode back to the radio station, and my temper was not improved by the sight of Lobsang full of smiles.

But he had found a way out.

"I am going to ride out now," he said. "I shall pretend that I am starting the journey, and go a few miles out of Chamdo. Then the evil spirits will not watch for me to-morrow."

His wife was doubtful if it would work. She said she was not sure that the spirits were fooled so easily. And would it apply to the rest of them? To the Indians and her and the children—for, of course, they were going to the frontier too. But Lobsang persuaded her, and then hurried to set out while the sun was still rising in the sky; for all descents are inauspicious, and that is why all important things should be done early in the day.

The party left the next day according to plan. At least the journey was successful, and a few days later they radioed their arrival. They were stationed with a District Governor, and official coded messages were exchanged.

The radio station was set up at Dengko, and its importance can be seen from the map. There were very few tracks in Sikang, and the Chinese Army was almost bound to come along the main east-west trade-route from Kangting to Chamdo. If it came all the way, so that the attack was from the east, it would be easy for the Chamdo troops to retreat to Lhasa. But before the track reached the Upper Yangtze another route branched out to the north-west. This route ran past Dengko, but still on the other side of the river, and up to Jyekundo, in the province of Chinghai. Jyekundo was almost due north of Chamdo, and from it a force could drive southward and cut the Chamdo-Lhasa track. Then we would have no means of escape except by fighting our way out.

Dengko was only two days' march from the point where the Kangting-Chamdo trade-route forked to the north-west. It was also near enough to Jyekundo to get news if the Chinese sent troops from the north through Chinghai. It was the ideal centre for collecting and transmitting intelligence of troop-movements on the other side of the frontier.

We knew now that the Chinese were marching through Sikang. Reports were brought by traders, and were usually so garbled and mixed up with omens and miracles that it was impossible to separate truth from romance; but there was no longer any doubt that the People's Liberation Army was coming our way.

A radio amateur in Australia told me I had been reported missing.

The rumour had evidently been started deliberately by a pirate station in Peking which was operating on my frequency and using my call-sign. I contacted him myself one night, and when I challenged him he shut down at once. His location was deduced by an Australian in Hong Kong who had a directional aerial. What his purpose was I never discovered, but he certainly succeeded in worrying my parents. I was worried for their sake when I was told I had been reported missing in the British Press.

Of course I had written letters, but the mail was very slow. Postal arrangements were complicated by the fact that Tibet was not a member of the Universal Postal Union. I had to put each letter in three envelopes—the outermost one addressed to a Tibetan friend in Lhasa, the next to another friend living near the Tibet-Sikkim border, and the third to the letter's destination in England. The outer envelope bore no stamp as it was carried by Government courier. The next needed a Tibetan stamp—not on sale in Chamdo, of course—which was valid only in Tibet. The third envelope needed an Indian stamp.

At the very best a letter from Chamdo took five weeks to reach my home in Burton-on-Trent, travelling by air from India. But that was exceptional. Since the radio link had been established the number of couriers going to Lhasa had been greatly reduced, and sometimes my letters were lying about for weeks in the Foreign Office before some one remembered to pass them to my friend.

I knew that newspaper reports about my part of the world were often alarming and almost always inaccurate, as they were based on rumours picked up outside Tibet, and I was very anxious to let my parents know I was safe. The bad radio conditions lasted longer than usual, and Fox was unable to help. Night after night I sat over my radio, trying desperately to contact England. Then at last I heard a weak call-sign with the prefix G.

It was a general call from G5 JF, and as soon as the transmission stopped I gave out my own call-sign, AC4 RF. There was no reply. My power was too low for my transmission to be heard in England.

G5 JF was picked up by a Swiss amateur, and I listened to their conversation. Finally G5 JF said:

"Am on the air every Wednesday, 1630 G.M.T. My position, Burton-on-Trent. CUAGN. [See you again.]"

Burton-on-Trent!

Four-thirty P.M. G.M.T. was 10 P.M. Tibetan time, and I was waiting at my radio long before then the following Wednesday. Sure enough, G5 JF came on with a general call. Again I replied at once, my hand trembling on the key as I almost willed the dots and dashes through the ether.

G5 JF picked me up.

He was a tailor named Jefferies, and Wednesday was early-closing day in Burton-on-Trent. He knew me by repute, for he also had read in the Press that I was missing. He promised to tell my parents that I was safe, and we arranged to speak again the following Wednesday.

Conditions were better then, and after making contact Jeff went over on to voice.

"Can you operate phone?" he asked me.

"I can, but my power's too low for you to hear. I can hear you all right, though," I tapped out.

"I've got a surprise for you," said Jeff. "Hold on a moment." Then I heard another voice say:

"Hullo, Robert."

It was my father.

I was so overcome with emotion that I doubt if I could have replied if I had been able to use phone. I tapped out an answering message, and at the other end Jeff transcribed, and my father spoke again. In this way we exchanged news.

The following Wednesday I heard my mother's voice.

After that it became normal for my parents to ring me up on Wednesdays. They were never able to hear my voice, but all they wanted was to know I was safe. For me their voices were everything.

I told some of the Tibetans that I could hear my parents talking from England, but they were not greatly impressed. They could not really understand how far away England was.

On April 16 the Chinese Communists invaded Hainan. Five days later the Nationalists claimed a tremendous victory, and from experience of their claims in the Civil War I concluded that they had suffered a heavy defeat. The capital of Hainan was evacuated the following day, and less than a week later it was all over.

Radio Peking's May Day message was a little shorter than the one I had heard on New Year's Day. Otherwise it was unchanged:

"The tasks of the People's Liberation Army for 1950 are to liberate Formosa and Tibet."

Three weeks later I heard Radio Peking offer Tibet "regional autonomy" and religious freedom if she would "achieve peaceful liberation." She was warned that she was "certain to be liberated in any event." She was also warned not to count on geographical difficulties or American or British help. The Tibetan Government was again invited to send delegates with full negotiating powers to Peking.

Gyalo Thondup, a brother of the Dalai Lama, went to Formosa to confer with Chiang Kai-shek. The Tibetan delegation in India was now in Calcutta, preparing to fly to Hong Kong to meet the Chinese Communists there. It was not prepared to go to Peking.

Pandit Nehru said that he supported Tibet's claim to self-government but recognized that China was entitled to "a vague sort of suzerainty" over her. India let it be known that Tibet could not expect her to provide military aid.

Radio Lhasa said nothing.

In Chamdo there were reports that advanced units of the People's Liberation Army were approaching the Upper Yangtze. We also heard rumours that they were recruiting Khambas in Sikang.

I could not imagine that many Khambas would join the Communists, for on both sides of the Upper Yangtze they hated the Chinese.

This river was a purely political boundary, and it cut right through the old Kham as the Pyrenees divide the Basques. Like most of Chinghai in the north, Sikang had once been part of Tibet; and almost the whole population was still of the Tibetan race. I could not distinguish a Tibetan Khamba from a technically Chinese Khamba from Sikang. But it was very easy to distinguish any Khamba from a native of central or western Tibet.

The Khambas were tall and broad-shouldered, strong and hardy, and the least Mongoloid-looking of all the Tibetans I had seen. Their noses were more angular, sometimes almost Aryan in appearance. They had their own dialect and culture, and a distinctive form of dress. They wore a fuller, wider gown, which they pulled up to their knees and tied at the waist; underneath they wore baggy trousers and leather-topped boots. Their hair was plaited in the usual single pigtail, but it was threaded through jewelled rings, and a long tassel hung down at the end.

Lhasa people regarded the Khambas as wild, lawless, and uncouth. When Radio Peking switched its Tibetan broadcasts to a more suitable hour it still had no audience, for the news-reader spoke with a Khamba accent. I admired the Khambas for their independence and relative lack of servility. Even old Smiler did not stick his tongue out as far as the Lhasa beggars, although he practised the same spiritual blackmail. It was meritorious for a Buddhist to give to a beggar, and anyone who failed to make a regular contribution was threatened with a curse.

Lhasa officials regarded service in Kham as a form of exile, and they all longed to return to the capital. Yet competition for their appointments was keen, and at the end of their tour of duty—which was normally three years—they were compulsorily relieved. The reason was that the service was extremely lucrative. The officials had no salaries but were entitled to take as much profit on taxes as they could.

The collection of taxes in Tibet was simple and economical. The Governor-General was told how much he was expected to raise from the whole of Kham. He added what he considered a fair profit, and divided the total among the various District Governors. Each District Governor added his profit and told the petty chiefs and headmen under him how much each of them would have to produce. They collected as much as they could and pocketed the surplus. This was the normal system throughout Tibet. The only properly salaried officials were Fox and me.

For the taxes they paid the Khambas got nothing in return except the protection of the Army, and that lived off the land. Yet there was no general resentment. It had always been like this, and the people knew nothing else. Tibet was under-populated, and there was work for all and enough food for every one. And most Khambas, for all their spirit of independence, were bound inseparably to the Lhasa Government by their worship of the Dalai Lama.

This worship extended across the Upper Yangtze, but there were no Lhasa officials to collect taxes there. Instead the people were squeezed by the Chinese.

"They will never fight for the Chinese," old Khenchi Dawala told me. "You know what the Chinese did in Batang? They used our Holy Scriptures for soling their boots."

I always thought of Khenchi Dawala as the Grand Old Man of Chamdo. He was over seventy—a tremendous age for a Tibetan—and the only inhabitant who could remember having seen a European before. He had met Eric Teichman, a British Consular Officer in China who had come to Chamdo in 1917 and stopped a war single-handed.

Although a monk, Khenchi Dawala had fought in that war. He had fought so bravely that he had been rewarded with the high rank of *khenchi*, which made him senior even to Rimshi Trokao. For a Khamba his position was unique. After the Governor-General he took precedence over every Lhasa official.

"The Chinese destroyed our monasteries and murdered incarnate lamas on both sides of the big river," he said. "And they call us barbarians and treat us as inferiors. That is why we hate them. And that is where the British are different. You respect our religion and treat us as equals. That is why we like you."

I had good reason to be grateful to Sir Charles Bell and the other British Political Officers who followed him into Tibet. Khenchi Dawala was old enough to remember the Younghusband Expedition of 1904, when we first entered the country; and the hard fact is that, whatever the provocation, we fought our way in. It was as humane an expedition as any military campaign can be; but Tibetan soldiers, assured by the monks that they were protected by magic from foreign bullets, were killed by British troops. The memory of that tragedy was effaced by subsequent British actions, and I did not even hear it mentioned until I was in a Chinese gaol.

"What the Chinese call Sikang is part of Tibet," said Khenchi Dawala. "All the people are Tibetans. They will not help the Chinese against their own brothers."

"Will they help Tibet?" I asked.

"You mean, will they fight? That," said Khenchi Dawala, "depends on the brothers Pangda Tsang."

The three Pangda brothers were the most loved and most feared of all the Khambas, and their wealth and power were immense. The eldest, usually called by the family name alone, lived in Lhasa and was the biggest trader in Tibet. He was also the largest transport contractor, and he had brought in the radio equipment given by the United States. I had not met him in Lhasa, because he had been away on an official trade mission—the first that ever left Tibet. It had recently returned after a two years' tour round the world. I had been through Pangda Tsang's richly stocked warehouses when I searched Lhasa for the missing radio equipment.

His two brothers, Topgye and Rapga, lived in Sikang. Topgye had already fought against the Chinese. He had also fought against the Tibetan regular army, as leader of a minor Khamba revolt against the Lhasa Government. He had retreated across the river, taking captured mountain guns and rifles and ammunition; and his brother in Lhasa had been compelled to pay reparations on his behalf. That was in the nineteen-thirties, but Topgye and Rapga were still exiled in Sikang. And there they ruled like feudal barons.

The Chinese had never really conquered Sikang. They had kept the Tibetan Army out, and put governors in the larger towns; but vast areas of the province were under no central control. It even included a self-contained kingdom, called Derge, which was almost autonomous; and in the south-east, not far from the Upper Yangtze, the Pangda brothers ruled as kings from their mountain stronghold of Po, near the town of Batang. It was said that they could mobilize a force of several thousand Khambas in a few days.

Since the fall of Chungking, Sikang had been virtually free from Chinese control. Some of the Chinese local governors had declared for the Communists, others had fled; there was no effective rule by Peking. In the Po district the Pangda brothers ruled unchallenged. Farther north, the Communist Army was advancing along the narrow, difficult trade-route to Tibet. The Communists did not know the country, and there were no reliable maps. As their line of communication lengthened they became mortally vulnerable to guerrilla attacks. If Pangda Topgye gave the word . . .

"Pangda Topgye," said Khenchi Dawala, "will demand his price."

His price would be some sort of autonomy for Kham—on both sides of the river. Topgye and Rapga were Khamba nationalists, loyal to the Dalai Lama but ambitious to rule their own people without interference from the Lhasa Government.

D

I wondered if the price was too high; or if the Lhasa Government could afford not to pay.

On our side of the river Lhalu decided to recruit Khambas for an auxiliary corps.

Not all the Lhasa officials were happy about this. Some had made themselves unpopular by squeezing too hard, and they feared that they might be forging a weapon that could be turned against them. But Lhalu's own prestige among the Khambas was high. He had proved a lenient Chief Magistrate, imposing reasonable fines and punishing by ridicule rather than by amputations and public floggings. The range of penalties was limited in the absence of prisons.

Lhalu had also shown some interest in the welfare of the people. He had built a water-conduit from the river, and had even asked me if the waters of the Mekong could be harnessed to a hydro-electric station like the one in Lhasa. He was possibly the first Governor-General of Kham who wanted to leave Chamdo a better place than he had found it.

The Governor-General's word was law, and his order was obeyed; but it was Khenchi Dawala who saw that it was properly enforced. He spoke as a Khamba and used all his prestige to bring men in from the outlying villages. Their first parade was a heartening sight. There were no uniforms for them, and they brought their own arms. Every Khamba carried a rifle on his shoulder, and a long sword at his waist; for this was the bandit country. In other parts of Tibet the word Khamba was synonymous with robber, and with good reason; for when a Khamba went out of his own territory he usually went to rob. They looked like bandits as they walked about in their swaggering, swashbuckling style.

Lhakpa the trader was typical. He lived in a village about two miles downstream, and he had invited me to his home several times. He was rich enough to have built a house of rammed earth. It was warmer than wattle-and-daub, but more easily burgled. The thief simply cut a hole in the wall. Lhakpa showed me where one had tried to get into his house.

"Did you catch him?" I asked.

Lhakpa laughed.

"I caught him in my sleep," he said.

Like all Khambas, Lhakpa always kept his right hand on the hilt of his sword. Now he explained that he slept with his sword by his side.

"And what did you do?"

There was a flash of steel as Lhakpa unsheathed his sword and brought it down a few inches from my ear.

"No more robbers have come here," he said.

Lhakpa was an authority on robbers and bandits, and knew more than anyone about their hide-outs and customs. I often wondered how he had got the capital to start up in trade.

Dimön Depön was nominally responsible for training the Khambas, but there was not much he or the *rupöns* could do with them. They were hopeless at forming fours, and such good shots that target practice was really a waste of ammunition. They wasted some more in the late afternoons, when they livened up Chamdo by riding round the town firing shots into the air, flourishing their swords, and letting out blood-curdling screams. The girls were kept indoors, and some of the Lhasa officials also kept out of the way.

They would obviously not be a disciplined force like the regular troops, but as irregulars and in hand-to-hand combat they could be invaluable. Of course there was some friction between the regulars and the Khambas, who were put in a separate camp; and one day it came to a head. It was the usual cause. One of the regular soldiers had taken liberties with a Khamba girl.

It could have happened anywhere. It did happen in England during the War, when American and other Allied troops went out with English girls. We also had our squabbles and a few fights. It was never worse than that, because we had military police. There were no military police in Tibet, and what began as a personal quarrel looked like developing into a minor civil war.

By the time I heard about it the Khamba levies were massing outside the regular troops' barracks, waving their swords and taunting the soldiers to come out. Dimön Depön was not there, and the *rupöns* ordered their troops to fix bayonets. A fight looked certain when Khenchi Dawala appeared.

He rode up unarmed, and the Khambas fell silent and made way. "Who will win if we fight each other?" he asked. "I shall tell you—only the Chinese. Go back to your camp. Do not be impatient —you will have some fighting soon."

Without a murmur the Khambas sheathed their swords and went.

Khenchi Dawala's promise of fighting was more soundly based than they knew. He had come from the Government offices, where mounted messengers had just brought the news that the Chinese were only one day's march from the river.

During the last few days the radio traffic from Dengko had been very heavy. On the day after the brawl Sonam Puntso told me he had an urgent message as soon as he came on the air. He began to tap it out, but he did not finish. Suddenly he broke off, and telegraphed in clear:

"The Chinese are here."

Then there was silence. Dengko radio had closed down for good.

4

Arms and the Monks

I TOLD Wangda to keep on calling Dengko, and rode to the Residency to report the news. Lhalu looked grave but gave no sign of alarm. He murmured a brief prayer and then went into action.

He summoned his senior secretary and immediately dictated a message to Muja Depön, who commanded five hundred men at a garrison town on the Chinghai frontier, five days' march north-west of Chamdo.

"Bring your troops at once," he told Muja. Then he dismissed the secretary, and a few minutes later I heard a messenger ride away.

Next he summoned Dimön Depön and told him to send scouts to Dengko at once. They were to ride day and night.

"Unless we retake Dengko we cannot stay in Chamdo," Lhalu told me. "But do not worry. According to my information the Chinese force cannot be very large. That is why we must wipe it out before it can be reinforced."

Here was Lhalu the man of action—cool, practical, decisive, and completely unafraid. I could hardly recognize the man who had told me how the gods had saved his life.

"I suppose you want me to keep this secret, Your Excellency," I said.

He smiled.

"You have been in Tibet long enough to know that secrets are hard to keep, Phodo," he said. "It will be all over the town in a few hours. Now I must see Shiwala Rimpoche. Every effort must be made to win the help of the gods."

That did not lessen my respect for Lhalu. I thought he had put first things first, and the gods would be powerful allies in keeping up morale.

As I rode back to the radio station I instinctively looked up at the hills, as if I expected to see Chinese troops appear. But I knew that even if Lhalu had misjudged their strength we were not in immediate danger. They were still over a hundred miles away, and it would take them a few days to reach Chamdo even if they were unopposed.

They were not going to be unopposed. Later that day detachments of regular troops set off up both the East and the West rivers. Guards were set on the bridges. The water was no longer frozen, and neither river was easy to ford.

The troops looked in good heart. The two *rupöns* organized their deployment, while Dimön Depön remained in nominal command. He also seemed to grow in stature now that the test had come. He might not be an efficient officer, but there was no doubting his courage.

The Khamba levies were held back until Muja arrived. They were to join him in the attack on Dengko.

Old Khenchi Dawala took charge of the fortifying of Chamdo.

I rode with him to the north side of the monastery, and he showed me where he had fought in 1917.

"We were the attackers then," he said, as he began living the battle over again. "The Chinese held the town and the ruins of the monastery, which they had destroyed five years before. We fought our way up the hill, and that is how they will probably come now. Whoever holds the monastery holds the town."

Both attackers and defenders had fought behind stone *sangars*, or barricades, instead of trenches, and relics of these still lay on the hill.

"I had my men here," said Khenchi Dawala. "This is where we broke through: the Chinese had a *sangar* there, and we got round it on the far side. We must put up another *sangar* there to guard against that."

Under his directions fresh barricades were built from the ruins of the old. Chamdo was not going to be taken without a fight.

Lhalu asked me what I thought of the defences of the town.

"Phodo, you have fought in a war," he said. "What else do you think I should do?"

"Put some Bren guns in the hills and dynamite at the bridges," I said.

"We have no dynamite."

No dynamite! No explosives of any kind!

"What will you do if you have to retreat and want to destroy arms and ammunition?" I asked.

"Break and burn. There is no other way."

But he put Bren guns behind Khenchi Dawala's *sangars*, and Chamdo was as much of a fortress as it was ever to be.

The news that the Chinese had crossed the river had spread as quickly as Lhalu expected, and Chamdo was busy strengthening its spiritual defences. More prayer-services were held in the monastery, more devils were cast out, more incense was burnt, and the two Rimpoches went into the mountains to meditate and pray. Every one prayed, both personally and by turning prayer-wheels and putting out more prayer-flags. They did not pray as we pray, asking God for specific favours. They had only one prayer, and it consisted of four words: *Om Mani Padme Hum*, meaning "Hail to the Jewel in the Lotus"—that is, to the Buddha. It was inscribed in tiny Tibetan characters on every prayer-flag and on pieces of daphne-bark paper which were packed tightly into prayer-wheels. The gods were believed to be moved by the numbers of prayers they received, and during the next few days literally millions of prayers were sent up from Chamdo, by one means or another, into the upper air where the gods lived.

Not a moment was wasted, and Rimshi Trokao was murmuring the prayer very rapidly, over and over again, when he came into the radio station to ask me my transport requirements in the event of evacuation.

"This is only an emergency plan," he said. "I do not know what I shall be able to supply, for I need a great deal of transport for the attack on Dengko. But His Excellency has told me to prepare for evacuating Government officials and troops and supplies in the event of a direct threat to cut the route to Lhasa."

I told him what I would need for my staff and myself and the radio equipment. He asked me to be ready to destroy what would have to be left behind.

Rimshi Trokao might not have known what *de facto* recognition meant or how aircrew were trained, but I doubt if anyone was better equipped for the difficult task of collecting ponies and yaks and mules from the villages round Chamdo. He also gave me a feeling of confidence.

Of course the proper strategy would have been to evacuate Chamdo at once—to move the headquarters of the Eastern Command farther west, where it could not be by-passed, and to leave only a detachment to protect Chamdo. It was obvious that if the Chinese succeeded in breaking through as far as Chamdo they would easily be able to go round it to the north and cut the Lhasa route. Small, mobile bands of irregulars would be invaluable behind the enemy lines, but the only sensible way to fight in this war was for the main force to retreat on Lhasa.

The obvious place for Eastern H.Q. was Lho Dzong, several days' march to the west, which guarded the only bridge across the wide, swift-flowing river Salween. It could not be outflanked; and from Lho Dzong to Lhasa the country was wild and rugged, with an average elevation of 12,000 feet and passes of up to 17,100 feet, snow-bound for most of the year.

I had not come by this track, simply because it was considered too difficult for a caravan loaded with equipment like mine. It would be much more difficult for an army to force. I had gone to Chamdo by a longer route, travelling first northward to Nagchu and then westward through the border region between Tibet and Chinghai. This was the only alternative route to Lhasa from the east or north. It was less difficult, but still highly favourable to defence.

"We cannot leave Chamdo yet," said Lhalu. "If we did we should lose the support of all the Khambas, in both Tibet and Sikang. We should be leaving their largest monastery to the mercy of the godless Chinese, and they would feel they had been betrayed. Our levies would melt away, and perhaps even turn against us. Pangda Topgye would come to terms with the Chinese."

Of course he was right. It might seem military suicide, but politically there was no other course.

"You must remember," Lhalu went on, "that until the Chinese captured it forty years ago Chamdo was the capital of a semi-independent state. Lhasa troops helped to drive the Chinese out ten years later, and the people wanted us to stay to protect them from the Chinese. That is all we have to offer them in return for the taxes they pay. If we run away without a fight they will never want us back."

But Lhalu was a realist. He knew that the longer he stayed in Chamdo, the more favourably impressed the Khambas would be. He did not think they would expect the Lhasa troops to stay and fight to the last man when by retreating they could live to fight another day.

The plan, therefore, was to hold Chamdo until the track to Lhasa was almost within the reach of the Chinese. Then we would evacuate and, if necessary, fight our way out. As the first Chinese troops to reach the road would probably be only an advance party it should thus be possible to escape military defeat without the sacrifice of political expedience. It was risky, but it could be done. Its success depended primarily on keeping the track open as long as possible and on obtaining quick and accurate information about the movements of the Chinese.

"I have sent reinforcements to Riwoche," said Lhalu.

Riwoche was the key. To cut the track from the north the Chinese would almost certainly have to come down from Jyekundo, in Chinghai. From there only Riwoche stood between them and our life-line to Lhasa.

I had passed through Riwoche on my way to Chamdo.

It was the prettiest little town I saw in Kham. Situated on a tributary of the Upper Salween, it was well wooded and wonderfully green—as, perhaps, Chamdo had been before deforestation and soil-erosion ruined it. It had a population of about five hundred, and three monasteries full of monks.

There was a caravan track northward to Jyekundo, and it would need skilful defence. It was not likely to get it so long as Changra Depön was in command.

He was one of the poorest types of officer produced by the Tibetan social system. He was a playboy, well suited to party-life in Lhasa and entirely out of his element in Kham. He had come for what he could make out of it, and did not even pretend to show any interest in his troops. He was the exact opposite of Muja Depön, whom I had also met on my journey. He made even Dimön Depön seem a good leader of men.

It was at Riwoche that I saw the miracle performed by an incarnate lama. He had gone for a walk outside one of the monasteries, and left the imprint of his foot on a stone. I was given the great honour of being allowed to hold it, and Tashi and Lobsang were thrilled and ecstatic. I was introduced to the incarnate lama, and felt somewhat embarrassed. It seemed out of order to congratulate a lama on a miracle, yet it might be thought rude if I ignored it. So I just bowed and said I had seen the stone, and then looked rather silly. He returned my bow and looked modest.

The District Governor's wife was most excited about it, for she had been one of the first to see the stone. Later she said she had actually seen the miracle performed. I arranged for her to speak by radio to her parents in Lhasa, and she was grateful but too preoccupied to be impressed by my little conjuring tricks, although she had never seen a radio before. I had the same experience throughout the journey. People were intrigued, and looked for the man in the box, but I was never credited with any magical powers. This made me sceptical about those travellers' tales of Europeans who were acclaimed as white magicians or even gods when they demonstrated a few scientific toys to remote peoples with religions of their own. Belief in miracles does not seem to need or even spring from apparent physical evidence.

Lhalu was deeply impressed when I told him about the miracle.

"That is very auspicious," he said. "It surely means that the gods are looking after Riwoche." But he still sent reinforcements.

I wished he would relieve Changra Depön of his command, but it would have been impertinent to say so. Instead I pointed out that it would be an advantage to have a radio station at Riwoche. As long as we had to rely on messengers, if the town fell while we were in Chamdo the Chinese would have cut the Lhasa route before we heard the news.

Four days after Dengko radio went off the air the scouts returned from their ride of two hundred and twenty miles.

Their news reassured us about the strength of the Chinese but was depressing for me. They said the radio equipment had been taken across the river, but they could get no news of the Indians or Lobsang and his family.

Three days later Lobsang appeared. His escape story was good.

"I looked out of the window in the radio station," he said, "and there they were. Hundreds of them, pouring into the courtyard. I told Sonam Puntso, who was on the key, but he went on tapping, and that's why he was caught. They had already got Sonam Dorje on the way in. I hid in a cupboard, and they never looked in. Then at night I crept out, and ran away."

He stopped as if he had finished his story.

"You didn't run all the way to Chamdo," I said.

"No, I went to my house to get my pony."

"What about your wife and children?"

"They were inside. Chinese soldiers were patrolling outside, and we waited till they passed. Then we came away."

"Who did?"

"My wife and myself and our children and my servant and a porter to carry the little one."

It was fantastic. Although only a junior official, Lobsang was well worth catching; yet he had escaped under the noses of the Chinese, with his whole household, including a three-year-old child swaddled up on a porter's back.

"Didn't you bring your household goods?" I asked.

"No," he said sadly, "we had no transport for them."

But I did not feel like joking. Perhaps Lobsang was right, and Sonam Puntso would have escaped too if he had not stayed to warn me that the Chinese had arrived. At any rate, both he and Sonam Dorje were prisoners now, and I felt responsible. I comforted myself with the thought that the Chinese would soon realize that they were harmless and knew nothing of military value, and would soon send them back to India, where they had originally come from. I did not know the Communists then, which was just as well for my peace of mind.

Lhalu told me to ask Wangda and Dronyer how they felt now about taking radio stations out. As we had only one working set there was no question of anyone going yet, of course, but Lhalu had asked Lhasa for more equipment, and also some of the operators Fox had trained. He said he was going to send stations to Dengko, Riwoche, and Gangto Druga, in the east. If he could get a fourth he would send it to Markham Gartok, south-east of Chamdo.

Both Dronyer and Wangda were still ready to go. So was Tsering.

I spoke to Tashi and Lobsang again about sending their wives and children back to Lhasa. They promised to think about it, but I could see they thought the suggestion odd. All the other Lhasa officials still had their wives with them. Lhalu had his wife, who was nursing a baby a few months old. It is true that it was quite a big thing to organize a caravan to Lhasa, and women and children could not travel alone for fear of bandits. But it was never even suggested that they should go.

"One thing, Phodo Kusho," said Lobsang. "I shall never start a journey on an inauspicious day again."

"You think you didn't fool the evil spirits, then?"

"I think I shall never hear the last of it from my wife."

Ten days after the fall of Dengko Muja Depön arrived.

He left most of his troops camped outside Chamdo, and stayed the night in one of the ground-floor rooms of my house. These rooms were normally used to accommodate visiting officials. I was glad to see Muja again and to invite him in for biscuits and butter-tea.

On my journey from Nagchu to Chamdo I had passed through all the garrison towns protecting Tibet from Chinghai. There were not many, and in most the troops looked idle and bored. Muja's were the exception. They were smart and well disciplined and looked like soldiers. He kept them busy and organized regular exercises, and every man under him knew the country all round.

Muja himself was a real soldier, not just an official in uniform. He was about forty-five, and had been a *depön* for several years; and he took his duties seriously. He was brisk, energetic, and confident, although very much alive to the dangers of the situation. He was also one of the very few *depöns* who could command the respect of the Khamba levies. Although a Lhasa noble himself, he was a little like them in his carefree, swashbuckling way. I told him I thought he must have been a Khamba in one of his previous existences.

"They're fine people," he said. "And they'll make fine troops."

They certainly looked pretty fearsome when they went on parade, and were issued with amulets blessed by the Rimpoches to wear round their necks. Khenchi Dawala gave them a pep talk, reminding them that the Chinese were godless and wanted to destroy their religion. Then Muja took over. His own men were models of smartness, but he realized that the Khambas were not the right sort for spit-and-polish. He took them as he found them, and they took him as a man after their own heart.

Two hundred Khambas went with Muja, bringing his total force to seven hundred. According to the latest reports from Dengko, the Tibetan force would be slightly superior in numbers, although the Chinese could still be reinforced before the attack was made.

Rimshi Trokao produced all the transport required. With Muja at their head, the troops rode off.

Tharchi Tsendron came to see me about radio security. In addition to his other duties Lhalu had appointed him Security Officer for Chamdo.

"His Excellency says there must be no more telephone conversations," he said.

I was very pleased to hear it. When traders came to talk to Lhasa they usually brought their wives and children and friends, and they all wanted to crowd into the radio room to watch and listen. Moreover, it was almost impossible to get them to come on time. Clocks and watches were almost unknown in Chamdo.

Naturally conversations had to be booked and arranged in advance, so that the other speaker in Lhasa arrived at Fox's station at the same time. There were not many clocks or watches there either, so to bring them together was always difficult. The only means I had of telling them when to come was to advise them to be at the station when the sun was over the peak of a particular mountain—and this was no good when the sky was overcast. Often they came too early, and then I had them and their whole retinues hanging about outside.

"His Excellency also wants you to check all messages in the commercial code," said Tharchi Tsendron.

Tibetan cannot be put straight into Morse because there are thirty-six letters in the alphabet. Therefore, when the service was started each Tibetan letter was assigned a two-figure number, and copies of this letter-number code were printed and put on public sale. There was also a copy in the radio station, and we made it a rule that anyone wanting to send a radio telegram should turn it into numbers before he handed it in. Similarly the message was delivered in numbers at the other end, and the recipient had to turn it back into letters.

I told Tashi and Lobsang to check the incoming telegrams, and they soon found that some turned out to be simply a collection of letters that did not make any obvious sense. Clearly secret codes were being used. Tharchi Tsendron investigated, and the reason was not as sinister as it seemed. Some of the traders, fearing their messages might be intercepted by business rivals, had made up codes of their own.

I told these traders that they had no need to worry, as no one outside the radio service was capable of receiving Morse.

"We know that," said one trader guilelessly. "It is your staff that we are worried about. Surely they trade too?"

Lhalu summoned me to the Residency with a message asking me to bring my maps.

They were Government of India survey-maps, over thirty years old and not very accurate: I had been able to make some corrections on my journey from Lhasa to Chamdo. But they were the only detailed maps of Tibet that had ever been made.

The Tibetan Army had no maps, but relied entirely on local knowledge. A Tibetan map had been made of the track from Lhasa to Chamdo, and Lhalu had brought a copy: it could not have helped him much, for it showed the route in a straight line. He also had a hand-drawn map of Kham, copied from a Government of India map, but with the place-names in Tibetan instead of English. This was useful, but it was on a much smaller scale than mine.

"I have been thinking about how you will get out of the country if we are cut off by the Chinese, Phodo," said Lhalu.

I had been thinking about it too. There was a route to the south which led to Assam, and if we were unable to get through to Lhasa I intended to ask Lhalu to let me and the Indians make our own way out. Of course it was understood that if the track to Lhasa was still open, or if we had a chance of fighting our way through, we would go with the other officials, taking our remaining portable radio.

Earlier in the year some American missionaries who had been in Batang had been given permission by the Tibetan Government to cross the Upper Yangtze and go to Assam. Similar permission had been given to a Scottish missionary, George Patterson, who had been with the Pangda brothers at Po. They had all made the journey safely.

"I shan't take this route unless there is no other way," I said, after we had gone over the route on my map.

"I appreciate that," said Lhalu quietly. "Of course you know that you can leave the country now if you like."

My contract had expired four days before Dengko fell, and the new one had not yet come from Lhasa for me to sign.

"Thank you, Your Excellency," I said. "I am very willing to continue to serve under the terms of the old contract until the new one is signed."

Lhalu did not ask me to put this in writing. There was a mutual trust between us, and I respected him more than ever for giving me the chance to leave honourably, at least in a technical sense, when I was probably needed more than ever before.

Lhalu had another bright idea. He wanted to arm five hundred of the monks.

Taking life, human or animal, is strictly forbidden by the Buddhist religion; but, as in most religions, precept and practice do not always coincide. The monks ate yak-meat, and monks had taken up arms in the past. Only three years earlier an incarnate lama had tried to murder the Regent—not by witchcraft but with a time-bomb—and a whole monastery had supported his cause. The post of Commander-in-Chief of the Tibetan Army was held in duplicate, and the monk C.-in-C. was the senior of the two. That valiant old warrior Khenchi Dawala was a monk.

Khenchi Dawala thought it was a good idea. He took out his old Khamba sword, which he kept in a gold and silver scabbard studded with turquoise and coral, and said he was willing to fight too.

"Of course monks should fight," he said. "It's our war more than anyone's. The Chinese do not seek merely to take our country —they want to destroy our religion. The last time they came to Chamdo they destroyed our monastery. We built a new one—and if they come again they will destroy it like the last one. These Communists are even worse than Butcher Chao; they boast that they have no gods. If we let them come they will destroy every monastery in Tibet. They will probably kill all the monks, too," he added warningly.

In spite of Khenchi Dawala's eloquence, the monks did not like Lhalu's idea. Nor did Dimön Depön, although he did not dare say so; when Lhalu had an idea every official had to pretend to support it, for he was the Governor-General.

The monks agreed that the Chinese had to be beaten, and they were very willing to play their part too. But they said that only the gods could give Tibet victory—which was unanswerable—and they were doing their bit by praying. They would pray twice as hard, or rather twice as often, and that would be more use than taking up arms. If they were to spend even part of their time as soldiers thousands of prayers would be lost.

Lhalu consulted Shiwala Rimpoche, who also thought the monks should be armed but suggested he should seek spiritual advice. At one time this would have involved a journey to Lhasa, but now he could do it by radio telephone. I was told that Lhalu and Shiwala Rimpoche were coming to the radio station to speak to Trijang Rimpoche, Spiritual Adviser to the Dalai Lama.

I had to arrange this carefully with Fox. Obviously Trijang Rimpoche must not be kept waiting in Fox's studio; on the other hand it would be improper for Lhalu to be subjected to a long delay. So it was carefully timed, and at the appointed hour Shiwala Rimpoche rode up to the radio station. Shortly afterwards Tenné ran up to say that the Governor-General was arriving. Shiwala and I both went down to meet him.

Lhalu had been to the radio station before, to speak to his mother in Lhasa; but until we had sent the second radio to Dengko I had usually taken it to the Residency so that he could speak from there. This saved all the ceremonial that was obligatory for a visit by the Governor-General.

He was preceded as usual by his equerry, standard-bearer, steward, and servants. His trumpeters played a fanfare, and troops of his personal bodyguard presented arms as he rode into the courtyard and was helped to dismount. We escorted him upstairs, and he sat in the seat of honour. On occasions like this our relationship was purely formal.

We had timed it correctly, and in a few minutes Fox told me that Trijang Rimpoche had arrived in his studio. I asked Lhalu to speak, and he approached the microphone reverently and placed a ceremonial white scarf and a package of paper money on the table in front of it. Then he bowed his head as if to receive a blessing.

"What's holding you up, Bob?" Fox and I had separate microphones, and his voice sounded almost blasphemous.

"His Excellency is offering a white scarf and a present," I said in a hushed voice, feeling like a B.B.C. commentator in Westminster Abbey. "His Excellency is awaiting Trijang Rimpoche's blessing."

"Trijang Rimpoche accepts the white scarf and the present," Fox replied after a few moments, also almost intoning the words. "He is giving Lhalu Shapé his blessing."

When I had translated, Lhalu came away from the microphone, and Shiwala Rimpoche went through the same procedure. It was his first visit to the radio station, and he seemed to be in some doubt whether to offer his scarf and present to the microphone or the loudspeaker; but Lhalu had set the precedent, and a new addition was made to Tibetan radio protocol.

Trijang Rimpoche had been Shiwala's own tutor, and there was affection as well as reverence in Shiwala's voice. Finally he asked the question about the monks.

Of course he did not ask bluntly whether or not they should be armed, for security had to be observed. The interview had been arranged beforehand by messages in the Government code, and both the question and answer were put in a form that made them sound innocent to anyone who was eavesdropping. Shiwala simply asked what the monks should do in the present religious crisis, and Trijang said they should pray harder and also obey the wishes of the Governor-General. The meaning was that they should be armed.

But before anything more could be done about it messengers from Muja rode in with the news that Dengko had been recaptured and all the Chinese there killed.

5

Two Britons in Kham

DIDN'T you take any prisoners?"

Lhakpa, the trader turned soldier, stared as if he did not know what I meant.

"Prisoners?" he repeated. "What would we do with prisoners? Where would we keep them? Who would feed them?"

"But didn't some of them surrender?"

"We never gave them the chance." The Khamba was telling me the story in the radio station, standing with legs apart and his hand still on the hilt of his sword. "A few of them jumped into the river and were drowned. As for the rest——"

His sword was unsheathed in a flash, and I felt the wind as it whistled down about an inch from my ear. I flinched, and Lhakpa laughed. Khambas have a great sense of humour.

From other reports I learnt that it had not been quite as easy as that. Muja had sent scouts forward first, and then attacked with his regular troops, holding the Khamba levies in reserve. There had been some hard fighting, and one of his *rupöns* and several men were killed. But the Chinese were already hard pressed when Muja called in the Khambas for hand-to-hand fighting, and then it was soon over. I learnt also that Muja was not at all pleased by the complete absence of prisoners. He had hoped to get some information.

I thought that perhaps it was just as well that Sonam Puntso and Sonam Dorje had been taken by Chinese rather than Khambas.

Neither Radio Peking nor Radio Lhasa reported the fall or recapture of Dengko. Not a word about the incident ever reached the international Press. China did not want to advertise her aggression or defeat. Tibet still hoped for peace. About a month later I heard All-India Radio from Delhi broadcast an unconfirmed report that

E

Chinese troops had entered Tibet, but this was neither confirmed nor denied by either Lhasa or Peking.

Muja stayed at Dengko, and most of the Khamba levies remained with him. Their success stimulated recruiting, and Lhalu abandoned his plan to arm the monks. The Khambas were obviously more useful, and now they were issued with Army rifles so that they could use the standardized ammunition.

Reinforcements of Lhasa troops continued to trickle in, and Lhalu sent some of these to Riwoche. The immediate threat had passed, but the danger that Chamdo would be by-passed increased daily. The Chinese did not need Dengko in order to reach Jyekundo. They could continue to march to the north-west by the caravan track on the other side of the Upper Yangtze. They could also come down from Chinghai, to the north. I felt that we were sitting on a barrel of gunpowder that might explode at any time.

I spoke to Lhalu about medical supplies. I pointed out that if there was fighting, at least some wounded soldiers could be made fit for duty again if we had only dressings and bandages, which could be bought cheaply in India. He promised to ask the Lhasa Government to send some, but he was not very hopeful about it. There was no allowance for medical supplies in the Army budget. Meanwhile I received some bandages and iodine from the last remaining European missionary in Sikang, an Englishman named Geoffrey Bull.

Bull has told his story in a fine and moving book, *When Iron Gates Yield*.[1] He went to China with Patterson, and, like all missionaries, they wanted to enter Tibet. Of course the Lhasa Government would not let them in. The nearest they could come was Sikang; and at Kangting, the capital of the province, they met the Pangda brothers, who invited them to their mountain stronghold at Po. This brought them to within a few days' march of the Upper Yangtze and, therefore, of Tibet.

Patterson had left for Assam in January, to get fresh medical supplies. In the following month Bull received permission from the Lhasa Government to follow the same route through south-eastern Tibet. Both his application and the reply came through Chamdo, and I had translated his letter to Lhalu. By then he had heard of me, and sent a personal letter to me with it. I was thrilled to hear from a fellow-Briton in the same part of the world. Although not in Tibet, Bull was actually nearer to me than Fox.

[1] Hodder and Stoughton, 1955.

In spite of the situation Bull decided to stay in Po; and at the end of March he went to help a small group of Chinese evangelists in Batang, three days' march north-east of Po. He found the town virtually without any civil government, but with local Communists more or less in control. They had insulted the American missionaries before they left. Their power was limited, however, and they were biding their time until the People's Liberation Army arrived. Bull and his Chinese co-workers bravely established themselves in the old Mission-house and held services in Tibetan and Chinese.

I had little chance to communicate directly with Bull, but I heard news of him from the Governor of Markham Gartok, some eighty miles south-east of Chamdo and facing Batang and Po across the Upper Yangtze. The Governor's name was Derge Sé, meaning the Prince of Derge, the self-contained Kingdom in northern Sikang. Derge Sé was exiled from his kingdom, which was ruled by his mother, and in Tibetan service he held the rank of Depön. He had written to me soon after I arrived in Chamdo—in English.

He had told me he had met the two Americans who had explored Tibet for a supply-line to China during the War, and he hoped he would meet me soon. He invited me to stay with him at Markham Gartok. Meanwhile he asked me to correct his letters and send them back, as he wanted to improve his English. I sent him books and magazines, and afterwards we corresponded regularly.

Derge Sé had learnt English in Tibet. He had been a pupil at an English school run by Frank Ludlow at Gyantse, between Lhasa and Sikkim. The school had been opened in 1923 and lasted for two years; then Tibetan foreign policy took a turn towards closer co-operation with China, and the school was closed down. Twenty years later, when the policy had changed again, Ludlow was in charge of the British Mission in Lhasa.

I was never able to meet Derge Sé, who was undoubtedly the most educated man in Kham. He was one of the very few of Ludlow's pupils who had kept up his English after the school closed, and by all accounts was one of the most progressive officials in the country.

There was another of Ludlow's former pupils in Chamdo itself. His name was Horkhang Sé, and he was the lay Finance Minister. He had also been given English lessons by Mr Richardson, officer in charge of the Indian Mission in Lhasa, but he had almost forgotten the language when I arrived in Chamdo.

I had to go to the Finance Office in Chamdo to hand over the money taken at the radio station for private telegrams and telephone calls. Lobsang and Tashi kept the books, and every telegram and call was recorded and backed with a receipt with a cancelled stamp. After I had been there six months I took the money with the books and receipts to Horkhang Sé.

Horkhang Sé stared at all this in amazement.

"You've gone to a lot of trouble," he said.

"It was no trouble," I told him. "Will you check the accounts?"

"I'll send for the counting machine," he said.

It was not a machine at all. It turned out to be a huge tray divided into compartments, which contained pieces of broken glass, pebbles, bits of pottery, dried berries, chips of wood, and other small articles that could be used as counters. These represented variously units, tens, hundreds, thousands, and so on—for Tibet was sufficiently advanced to have adopted the metric system. At the bottom of the tray was a large empty compartment in which the sums were worked out.

The monk Finance Minister and all the clerks came to help Horkhang Sé. I was so interested that I did not notice at once that they had turned over two pages of the accounts together, and before I could point this out Horkhang Sé had finished the sums and announced that my figures were perfectly correct.

"But there's no need to go to so much trouble again," he said, as he certified the figures and gave me a receipt.

"It's only the totals that matter," added the monk Finance Minister, who had somehow managed to stay in Chamdo for ten years and was famous for his squeeze.

The Finance Office in Chamdo did not differ greatly from the Government offices I had gone to in Lhasa. Official letters and other documents were filed in the same way as in the Foreign Office—tied in bundles and suspended down pillars and doorposts like a lot of prayer-flags. This system was one reason for the frequent delays in my mail. No one could accuse Tibet of too much bureaucracy, and inter-departmental memos were not filed at all. They were 'written' with bamboo pens on slates that had been surfaced with powdered chalk, the surplus chalk being scratched off as the clerk wrote. The slates had raised edges, so that they could be stacked together without the writing being rubbed off. The slates were the property of the office in which the memo originated, and therefore had to be returned when it had been read. That was why they were used. No record was kept, and no one could have his memoranda used in evidence against him.

I became quite friendly with Horkhang Sé, and he even offered to find me a temporary wife.

I was not far from getting one under my own steam.

Her name was Pema. She was about seventeen, perhaps less. I met her through her stepfather, a junior official named Khona.

It all began when I asked Lhalu if some one could monitor the news-broadcasts from Peking in Chinese.

Preparing the daily news summary was taking up a great deal of my time, for I had to monitor all the main stations of the world that normally broadcast in English. Radio Peking was one of the most important, and I said I thought it would be better, besides reducing my work, if it was monitored in Chinese.

Lhalu agreed, and Khona was ordered to come to the radio station every day when the news in Chinese was broadcast from Peking.

He had learnt Chinese in Nanking where he had worked in Tibetan service. His loyalty was above suspicion, for he hated the Chinese.

"They call us barbarians, and they treated me like an inferior," he said. "They were always boasting of their great culture, and they said we have none."

He was a small, quiet, mild-mannered man. Like many other Lhasa officials, when he came to Chamdo he took a temporary wife. She was a big, buxom Khamba, and he did what she said. The status of women was high in Tibet compared with other Asian countries, and henpecked husbands were not uncommon. But Pema was kind to her step-father, and seemed sorry for him. She was a very pretty girl. I found she was also a flirt.

I sat next to her at a party at Khona's house. Our conversation was on international lines.

"Are you married?" she asked.

"No."

"Have you a sweetheart?"

"No."

"What do you think of Khamba girls?"

"I think they are very beautiful."

I did, too, as I looked at her rosy-cheeked oval face, full lips, and clear black almond eyes. Her lips smiled invitingly, her eyes flashed, and she stroked her cheek.

This gesture had a precise meaning. There was a prescribed etiquette in flirting, as in everything else in Tibet. Young couples did not begin by holding hands. Instead, when the man caught the girl's eye he pulled the lobe of his ear, or, if he was a Khamba, and therefore did not wear his hair in a top-knot, rubbed the crown of his head. If the girl returned his interest she stroked her cheek. If she was not interested she gave him the universal brush-off of looking away and raising her chin. I was sure I had not touched my ear or the crown of my head, and Pema was being very forward indeed.

Her step-father, who happened to be looking our way, frowned and suggested some Khamba dancing.

The Khambas are famous for their dances all over Tibet. I had already got the rough idea, and joined the circle. Pema was beside me.

The dance always began slowly, and we walked round, singing. Soon it livened up, and finally it became boisterous. We sang furiously, stamped our feet, and rushed round the room. Sometimes the circle broke, but Pema held my hand very tight.

"Do you like Khamba dancing?" she asked afterwards.

"Yes, very much."

"Come here one afternoon, and I will teach you all the steps."

I did not dare look at her, for I was very conscious that Khona had his eyes on us.

He was having a bad time. His temporary wife was permanently occupied with another Lhasa official, of a rank higher than himself. His step-daughter seemed equally interested in me. I felt embarrassed when I said good-bye, and apprehensive when he came to the radio station the next day. But he was very friendly, and a few weeks later he invited me to another party.

I was more apprehensive than ever, although I had not seen Pema since the previous party. But I need not have worried. Khona's temporary wife was not there—I learnt later that she had gone to live with the more senior official. Pema was our hostess.

"You know Pema, my wife," Khona said by way of introduction. She smiled at me demurely. I had lost my chance.

I had other chances, and I was regarded as unconventional in remaining celibate. By our standards sexual morality in Tibet was lax, and it was even laxer in Chamdo than in Lhasa. No doubt this was due partly to the widespread practice of Lhasa officials, and of the troops, of taking temporary wives. But I suppose this was inevitable in a country where both polygamy and polyandry were allowed.

Polygamy was obvious, for a quarter of the males were monks. Polyandry was usually a matter of keeping a family estate in one piece. A woman could be required to marry all her husband's younger brothers. No complications about paternity arose from such unions, as the offspring were the legal children of the first husband, his brothers being only uncles. It was for reasons of inheritance, too, that in polygamous unions the wives were often sisters.

In Lhasa I knew one high-ranking official whose son had a one-third share in his stepmother. She was a commoner, and already had a husband when the official married her. He did not want to leave her all his money, so he brought in his son as third husband. In another case it was the bride who demanded the hand of her husband's son, making it a condition of the marriage. She was very rich and brought a large dowry, and did not want to risk losing it all when her husband died. The son was already engaged to another girl, but for his father's sake he broke it off and agreed to acquire a wife and stepmother simultaneously.

This does not mean that Tibetans commonly practised free love or that their women were 'easier' than ours. Tibetans showed the normal human instincts, including jealousy and possessiveness. The girls expected to be courted, and Pema was exceptionally forward in taking the initiative with me. Their clothes were much less provocative than those of European women, completely concealing the figure. The story that hospitable Tibetans offered wives or daughters to overnight guests was not borne out by my experience.

Whatever my moral outlook might have been, there were sound practical reasons for my keeping celibate. Although the other officials teased me and incited me to take a temporary wife, I think they respected me more because I did not. I think there would have been resentment if I had; for I was a foreigner, after all. It would have been different if I had married a Tibetan girl, as Fox did; but by then he had already decided to make Tibet his home for life. I intended to return to England, and it would have been cruel to take a Khamba girl with me. I was therefore careful to avoid possible emotional entanglements.

There were other reasons for remaining chaste. One was the tremendous incidence of venereal disease. It was rife all over Tibet, and especially bad in Kham. Medical ignorance and lack of hygiene were such that only the climate saved the country from epidemic disease, and it did not prevent the spread of syphilis and gonorrhœa. Men and women in various stages came to me for treatment, and there was nothing I could do. It was utterly depressing to have to turn away afflicted babies. I tried to disseminate some knowledge, and discovered that most of the Khambas did not know how the disease was spread. They had been brought up to believe that all sickness was caused by evil spirits, and it was impossible to teach them the germ-theory of disease. They were so uninformed that they still thought the earth was flat.

The rain was late in coming, and that was an inauspicious sign. Special prayers were said, and services were held by experienced rain-bringing monks. A little temple by the river was kept specially for this purpose. In the town Lhalu issued the usual order to the people to water the streets. Buckets were brought up from the river, and some of the officials' wives kept a full one handy to empty on me when I rode past their houses. All building was forbidden: a person building a house was bound to pray for dry weather, and his prayers would cancel an equivalent number of prayers for rain.

The rain came—and then there was hail. This was indeed a bad omen, and there were others too. The top of a famous stone monument in Lhasa crashed to the ground. The water in one of the holy lakes was seen to boil. Two-headed animals were born. One of Rimshi Trokao's ponies ate aconite and died, and even I had to admit that this was an exceptional event. There was some long grass behind our houses, where his ponies used to graze. On my arrival I had put mine there too, and he had warned me to take them away as there was aconite in the grass. His ponies avoided it because they were locally bred. But now it was a Khamba pony that ate the monkshood and died.

There was even more ominous news from Sikang. Communist troops were nearing Batang, and Bull had to return to Po. On his way he ran into an advance unit of the People's Liberation Army. It was going in the same direction, to try to persuade Pangda Topgye to come to terms with Peking. Bull was not scared. He still would not flee to Assam, but stayed in Po and even tried to convert the Communist officers to Christianity. He was a free-lance missionary, and could leave at any time: his courage was inspiring.

Radio reports from Delhi told me that the Tibetan delegation in India had still not made contact with the Chinese. It had refused repeated invitations to go to Peking, and insisted that negotiations should be carried out on neutral ground. The delegation now proposed a meeting in Hong Kong, and booked passages from Calcutta on an aircraft of B.O.A.C. But the British Government refused them visas because of the "delicate situation" at Hong Kong, and the delegation returned to Delhi. The Indian Government had recently established diplomatic relations with Peking, and a new Chinese Chargé d'Affaires was expected in the Indian capital. The Tibetan delegation decided to try to negotiate with him when he arrived.

A fortnight later—on June 25—I heard the news that war had broken out in Korea.

I felt a new surge of hope when the United Nations at once went to South Korea's aid. The United Nations Organization was Tibet's best hope now that Britain had no further direct interest and India had shown she was not prepared to help on her own.

"It means that America and Britain and the other free nations are helping a small country against Communist attack," I told Rimshi Trokao when he asked me what the news meant. "Of course it is much easier for them to send troops to South Korea than it would be to Tibet. But even India is sending an ambulance unit, and she might be prepared to allow the passage of United Nations troops if she was sure they would win. It all depends on how quickly they drive the Communists out of South Korea."

My hopes began to fade when the North Koreans continued their advance, and it looked as if the United Nations forces might be thrown out altogether.

"How can we rely on foreign help now?" one of the less resolute of the Lhasa officials asked me. "If they cannot save the South Koreans from the North Koreans, what can they do for Tibet against China?"

I had no answer, for I was asking myself the same question. I had hoped for a quick victory that would show the readiness and strength of the United Nations and deter the Chinese from aggression. I still think that if this had happened Tibet could have saved her independence, and I might have been there to-day. I was not a complete fool to stay in the face of the Chinese promises to "liberate" Tibet. Those who stayed on Formosa heard the same threats at the same time, and they are still there.

But in July something else happened that was to settle my fate. I could not know this then, but I had an uneasy premonition when Lhalu told me the news.

"Phodo," he said, "I am going to be relieved."

6

The Red Lama

THE news that Lhalu was going came to me as a shock. I had known that he was due to be relieved in July, when his three years' tour of duty expired. If times had been normal all the Lhasa officials would have gone then, except presumably the monk Finance Minister, who seemed to be immovable. Their reliefs should have been appointed in May. But the Lhasa Government had told them that they would have to stay at their posts while the crisis lasted, and it was generally assumed that the most important official of all would also stay.

"It is a Cabinet decision," Lhalu told me.

I was sure he had not asked to be recalled. He may not have minded returning to Lhasa—the exile was worse for him than for any of the others—but I knew he was not the sort of man to run away from danger.

Lhalu said that apart from his personal staff—his equerry and secretaries—most of the other Lhasa officials would stay in Chamdo.

This was no consolation for me. All local decisions of importance were made by the Governor-General alone, and his Executive Council merely carried out his orders. He was too superior in rank to be able to ask other officials for their opinions, and none would dare give them unasked. I was the only person he could converse with naturally without loss of dignity.

The political folly of recalling Lhalu was not my business, but I feared it might affect me very much. Lhalu had been one of my reasons for deciding to renew my contract and stay in Tibet. This was not only a matter of personal affection: I had been impressed by his ability, and especially his determination to resist the Chinese.

My new contract had not yet come from Lhasa, so technically I could still leave. My agreement to continue service under the terms of the old contract was only verbal, and a personal arrangement between Lhalu and me. The same applied to Lhalu's promise to inform me in advance if the Tibetan Government should come to terms with the Chinese. In my mind the one was conditional on the other, and I decided to ask the new Governor-General for a similiar promise before I gave my word to stay. If the new contract arrived before he did I would have to ask Lhalu for a more official undertaking before I signed.

Meanwhile a Communist incarnate lama came to Chamdo, and I entertained him with tea.

His name was Geda, and he came from a monastery in Sikang. He came as the official representative of the Chinese Communist Government, with instructions to go to Lhasa to negotiate with the Tibetan Government.

On the face of it a lama could not be a Communist. Buddhism and Marxism are incompatible in every way. Even the idea of equality of opportunity is heresy to the Buddhist, as Tharchi Tsendron once explained to me.

"The law of Karma says that as you sow, so shall you reap," he said, "not only in this but in all future lives. A man who leads a pious life will be rewarded by rebirth in a higher station. A man who is wicked will be punished by rebirth in a lower station."

We were not talking about Communism. He was explaining to me why our ideas of social democracy could not be used in Tibet.

"Isn't there any envy or resentment against the position of the nobility?" I asked.

"Envy and resentment are wicked," he said. "Anyone who felt like that would suffer for it, for it could count against him in his next incarnation. But in fact we have more equality of opportunity than you. Anyone can be reborn in a higher station—indeed, he is bound to be—if he gains enough merit in this life."

But the greatest cause of opposition to Communism was that i was godless and even opposed to religion. A Communist cannot be a Buddhist any more than he can be a Christian.

But in Tibet, as in England, a few persons professed to be able to reconcile the two opposites; and in one respect a Tibetan Red lama was slightly less incongruous than an English Red dean. A Tibetan did not become an incarnate lama out of choice: he was discovered to be one while he was still a child. The monks also were entered into the church when they were boys, and not because they had felt a calling for the ministry as, presumably, an Englishman must have done to become a dean.

The Buddhist Church was reactionary, but it had also shown revolutionary tendencies in the past. This was because it ruled the country jointly with the two hundred noble families, the one serving to check and balance the other. The ruling class was occasionally reinforced by the ennoblement of commoners, like our House of Lords, but the main check was the fact that any peasant's son could aspire to a political career by becoming a monk. Inevitably there was some friction between lay and monk officials, and therefore the principle of opposition to aristocratic government had a certain appeal to the monks.

It evidently appealed to Geda Lama, who had helped the Chinese Communists in the Civil War.

He came to Chamdo by the trade-route from Sikang, and stayed in a house in the town while he waited for permission from the Tibetan Government to go on to Lhasa. One day Horkhang Sé brought him to the radio station to hear the news from Peking.

He was a typical Khamba in appearance, with a noticeably angular nose; but in manner he was mild and quiet and reserved. He seemed to be uneasy in my presence—but he took the opportunity to see all he could. He watched me closely when I tuned in the radio, and when he thought I was not looking at him his eyes darted round the room.

I gave him tea and cake, but did not try to make polite conversation. He was equally silent, and after he had heard the news he thanked me and left. He did not come to the radio station again. But I had not heard the last of Geda Lama.

Lobsang told me that Geda's steward had invited him to tea and tried to pump him about the radio station.

"I did not tell him anything, Phodo Kusho," he said.

"Good. Do you know if his servants have tried to get anything out of Tenné or Do-Tseten?"

"No, his servants are all girls."

"Girls?"

"Yes, Phodo Kusho. He came with just his steward and three Khamba girls. They go to his room in the evenings to sing to him."

I suppressed a desire to make a bawdy remark. Lobsang was no prude—none of the Tibetans I met were—but one did not make dirty jokes about an incarnate lama. Not even if he was a Communist working for the Chinese.

The attitude of the Tibetans to Geda Lama was interesting. Every one knew what he was and why he had come to Chamdo, but they treated him with all the respect and reverence due to a lama. This was not just a matter of being polite. To the common people he was a spiritual leader in spite of his politics, and they regarded him as the protector of the religion which they believed his masters were trying to destroy. I do not think all the officials were so naïve, but it was made clear to me how easily the Communists could rule if they once gained control of the Church.

Geda's steward came once or twice to send telegrams to Lhasa. He handed them over in clear, and the clerks put them into the commercial code for him. They looked perfectly innocent. He also saw all he could of the radio station, and later he invited Tashi to his house and tried to pump him. Tashi was as reticent as Lobsang, and they both resisted the temptation to seek Geda Lama's blessing. Many people, including some of the Khamba levies, went to him to be blessed.

Geda himself went almost every day to the Residency, and once or twice I ran into him there. Lhalu did not mention his name to me, but from other officials I heard rumours that Geda had been refused permission to go to Lhasa. On his arrival the Government radio traffic increased, but after about a week it was back to normal. Then Geda stopped going to see Lhalu. He still did not go back to Sikang, and as he seemed to expect to stay some time in Chamdo he asked for a more suitable house.

He was given one of the rooms reserved for travelling officials on the ground floor of the old Summer Palace, directly under the radio station. I saw him arrive with his steward and the three Khamba girls. They were young and rosy-cheeked, and far too pretty for me to have allowed in my establishment. They did not look as if their presence would make celibacy easier, but perhaps Geda liked to prove his strength of character by rising above temptation. I did not hear them singing to him in his room.

But there was enough singing for me at the Government summer parties.

These official parties were an annual institution, and they could not be cancelled even by the threat of a war. It is true that Lhalu reduced the season from two weeks to one because of the situation, but what annoyed me was that during that week nearly everything came to a standstill. As a Government official I was obliged to attend on at least two days myself. I did not mind, for I had no part in the anti-invasion preparations; but it was galling to see all those who were responsible feasting and enjoying themselves as if they had not a care in the world. This was even worse than the New Year celebrations, for there was not even a pretence of a religious sanction.

Lhalu had at least cancelled the annual theatre, as many of the parts were normally played by soldiers. I was relieved to see that military training was going on, and I doubted if it suffered much from the fact that Dimön Depön was too much occupied with the parties to take part.

It was now pleasantly warm during the day, and Tibet was not at all like the roof of the world. There was no snow except on the highest peaks. Because the air is dry and thin Tibet can be very hot as well as very cold, and sometimes the difference between day and night temperatures is as much as eighty degrees. The summer is short, but can be hot while it lasts, the temperature sometimes rising to ninety in the shade.

There was Khamba dancing on the lawn in front of the Residency, and Lhalu invited me to watch with him and his wife from his private room. Then we had a great feast, served in bowls of solid gold and silver and eaten with silver and ivory chopsticks. There were over twenty courses, including expensive Chinese delicacies like sea-slugs and sharks' fins. In spite of the Communist march through Sikang there was little interruption to Sino-Tibetan trade.

The drink was *chang*, a rather flat and yeasty beer made from barley that looks like cloudy lemonade. It was served by two girls, specially chosen for their beauty, and magnificently dressed and bejewelled. One carried a huge solid silver bowl, chased with gold filigree, and the other a silver jug with a white scarf round the handle. They served us strictly in order of rank, and before drinking we went through the traditional ritual of offering *chang* to the gods. This was done by dipping the third finger of the right hand into the *chang* and flicking a few drops upward with the thumb. The third finger was considered the cleanest as it was said that babies are born with it in their nostrils.

Chang is not to be drunk like English beer, and I had learnt in Lhasa that at big parties of this sort it was wise never to drink until you were forced—and not always then. As soon as a glass was half-empty the *chang* girls filled it up without asking, so I kept mine fairly full. Then they came up with beguiling smiles to coax me into drinking, and they were hard to resist. *Chang* girls were chosen for their powers of persuasion as well as their beauty, and when all else failed they sometimes resorted to force. I have seen *chang* girls sticking pins into senior officials who drank too slowly. This was regarded as great fun, and it was reckoned bad manners to stay cold sober. A state of intoxication showed the host that the guest found his *chang* so good that he was unable to abstain. If a guest drank himself into such a stupor that he could not rise he was presented with a white scarf as a compliment.

The Lhalu brand of *chang* was one of the most famous in Tibet, and Lhalu had had barley sent specially so that it could be brewed in Chamdo. But it was for his guests, not for himself. He was a teetotaller. This did not stop him from encouraging his guests to get drunk, and he had the gift of being gay without needing alcoholic stimulation.

I saw Pema at the parties, still in the rôle of Khona's wife. Geda also attended, and was treated with the normal deference due to an incarnate lama. But he was quiet—monks were not allowed to drink alcohol—and none of the officials seemed to make any move to be friendly. Khenchi Dawala avoided him. I could imagine what he thought of a lama who was working for the Chinese.

In the middle of the party season another visitor came to Chamdo from Sikang. It was Rapga, the youngest of the Pangda Tsang brothers.

Pangda Rapga often came to the radio station to hear the news, not only from Peking and Lhasa but also from Delhi, London, and New York. He could speak and read English, and knew far more about international affairs than any of the officials at Chamdo. He was easily the best-educated Khamba I met, but I could never make him out.

He was quiet and studious, and a keen Tibetan classical scholar; it was said that he knew more about the Buddhist scriptures than most incarnate lamas. Yet in 1944 he had been expelled by the British from Kalimpong, in Bengal, after it was rumoured he had been found distributing bulletins decorated with the hammer and sickle. He had been running some sort of organization opposed to the Lhasa Government, and was reported to have been getting money from the Chinese.

Bull, who knew him better than I did, says that both he and his brother were sincere Khamba nationalists, and there was no mystery about the reason for Rapga's visit to Chamdo. As he was still an outlaw he had demanded and received from the Lhasa Government an assurance of safe-conduct before crossing the border; and his purpose now was to try to negotiate a treaty with a view to establishing a common front against the Chinese. He and his brother were not prepared to give their services for nothing, but demanded a promise of some kind of autonomy for Kham. In return they would use their private army for guerrilla operations in Sikang.

Lhalu did not tell me of the negotiations that went on between Pangda Rapga and the Lhasa Government. I had no doubt that the Pangda guerrillas could do immense damage to the Chinese in Sikang, but I lost much of my optimism when I heard that Pangda Topgye had gone to Kangting, the provincial capital, for talks with the Communists. He had left Po a day or so after Rapga set for Chamdo. Topgye had still refused the Communists' invita to go to Peking, but the fact that he was meeting them half-way looked ominous. I had the feeling that the Pangda brothers were ready to come to terms with whichever side seemed more likely to help them keep their power as medieval barons.

Rapga brought two letters from Bull, one for Lhalu and the other for me. Bull had at last left Sikang and crossed the river into Tibet. Rapga had left him at Markham Gartok, where he was staying with Derge Sé. From there it would have been easy for him to take the southward route to Assam.

But Bull would not go. He had always wanted to come to Tibet, and now he was in the country he did not want to leave. He longed to go to Lhasa, to preach the Gospel of Christianity in the Holy City itself. I did not see eye to eye with Bull over converting Buddhists, but I admired him for his courage. I admired him still more when I read that he was applying for permission to come to Chamdo in order to help treat the wounded in the event of fighting.

Lhalu could not give him permission to come, and he passed the request on to the Lhasa Government. I feared it would be refused. But I was glad to have Bull on the same side of the river as myself, so that there were two of us in eastern Tibet. If I had to leave by the southern route myself I thought we might make the journey together, for I was sure now that Bull was determined to stay till the last minute. Meanwhile he was in good hands with Derge Sé. He was as hospitable to Bull as the Pangda brothers had been, in spite of Bull's very open ambition to convert Buddhists to Christianity.

Pangda Rapga had come in time to attend on the last day of the

The river Mekong south of Chamdo
Sir Eric Teichman

The gorges of Eastern Tibet
Sir Eric Teichman

A Tibetan artist at work on a religious banner

The golden roof of the great temple in Lhasa

Government parties, when the drum-and-fife band of the Governor-General's bodyguard played the tunes that had been originally brought into Tibet by a bandmaster of the Indian Army. They were mostly British regimental marches with some wrong notes. I had heard these before, and the mistakes then had been the same. Tibetan bands played entirely by ear, and if a mistake was repeated often enough it got into the unwritten score.

The party season ended with the band playing *God Save the King*. It was not the custom to stand while this was played, so I had the unusual experience of having to remain seated while the National Anthem was played. It was the Tibetan as well as the British National Anthem, and had also been brought in by the Indian Army bandmaster.

Geda Lama was present as well as Pangda Rapga, and they treated each other with distant courtesy. They had met before in Sikang, but they steered clear of each other while they were negotiating separately with the Lhasa Government with very different ends in view.

That was Geda Lama's last public appearance before he was murdered.

I did not suspect that he had been poisoned when I first heard that he was ill. Tashi brought me the news.

"Will you see him, Phodo Kusho?" he asked.

"Has he asked for me?"

"No, but he seems very ill. There is something wrong with his inside."

I had made a point of never offering medical help without being asked, and I was especially reluctant to treat an incarnate lama. I knew that if one died on my hands I might be blamed. Geda being a Communist envoy created further unpleasant possibilities, and I hoped I would not be asked.

The next day Tashi told me Geda was worse. Then I heard that a physician from the monastery was coming to see him, and I thought it might well be his case rather than mine.

This medical monk was reputed to have cured many sick people with herbs, and at least I knew he was a good vet. He had treated a Khamba pony of mine with excellent results. Soon after I bought the pony it went lame in the left foreleg. Its fetlock was swollen, and I had no idea what to do. I told Lhalu about it, and then wished I had not, for he insisted on sending his physician to treat the pony.

F

I thought he would use magic charms, but to my surprise he just nicked the pony's fetlock in two places. The next day the pony was walking about. A week later it went lame in the right foreleg, and the doctor repeated the treatment with the same result. After that the pony was always in perfect condition.

I lacked the ability to diagnose internal disorders, and had few drugs to use for treatment. At Riwoche I had treated the sister of an incarnate lama with stomach powder for a complaint that turned out to be nothing worse than wind, but from Tashi's reports Geda Lama seemed to have more serious trouble than that. I thought he might do better with the herbs of Lhalu's doctor than anything I could give him.

But Geda only got worse. I saw the medical monk and asked about his patient, and he told me the herbs had failed and Geda's only hope now lay in prayer. He was given a good deal of that. About twenty monks came down from the monastery with drums and cymbals and bells, and they chanted over Geda for two days. They were still chanting on the second evening when I went to bed.

The next morning Tashi told me Geda Lama had been cremated at dawn.

7

Border Question

CREMATION was the normal method of disposing of the body of an incarnate lama, but it was not usually done so soon after death. Normally time had to be allowed for the dead man's spirit to escape. That was the first thing that roused my suspicions.

I soon discovered other curious circumstances about Geda's death, and I felt very thankful that I had not offered him medical aid. I am afraid that is all I can say here. It took all my self-control to keep my knowledge to myself during long and merciless interrogations, and I am not going to reveal it now. I have good reasons for believing that Geda was murdered, and I think I know who killed him. I hope he will never be found out.

Geda's steward and the three pretty girls went back to Sikang, and the Chinese did not make any further attempts to send a representative through Chamdo to Lhasa. Pangda Rapga stayed. Hong Kong radio reported that the People's Liberation Army was advancing towards the Tibetan border, but that news was months out of date. We knew the Communists had reached the Upper Yangtze at several points. They had not tried to cross the river again, and Muja still held Dengko. I had no idea how far they had gone to the north-west, but I gathered that Riwoche was not yet in immediate danger. I was disturbed to hear that in the south they had reached the river opposite Markham Gartok. My emergency escape-route to Assam passed Markham Gartok on the west, but if the town fell it could quickly be cut. I hoped Derge Sé was as good as he seemed from his letters.

There was still no reason to expect that Tibet would get military aid from outside. In Korea the United Nations forces remained on the defensive, and even if India co-operated Tibet would be much harder than Korea to help. And Indian co-operation looked very unlikely now.

About this time Pandit Nehru said publicly that the Indian Ambassador in Peking had spoken informally to the Chinese Government about Tibet. He had pointed out that India considered it desirable that the matter should be settled peacefully. It was understood that the Chinese had replied—also informally—that they had no intention of forcing the issue but were willing to negotiate for a settlement.

But on August the first Radio Peking told me that Chu Teh, the Commander-in-Chief of the Communist Army, had repeated the Army's promise to "liberate" Formosa and Tibet.

Although Khona still monitored Radio Peking, I listened regularly to the news in English and Tibetan. I learnt that I was still the enemy. There was no criticism of Tibet's feudal system, no promise of land reform, no appeal to the workers to rise and throw off their chains. It was simply a matter of getting rid of American and British imperialism. Tibet was told that if she did this China would respect her rights and allow her regional autonomy within the Chinese Republic. She was also promised that there would be no interference with her religion.

Several officials came to the radio station one day to hear a talk from Peking by a very learned and respected monk named Sherap Gyatso. He had been in one of the largest monasteries in Lhasa until fourteen years ago, when he went to China and began working for the Kuomintang. Now he had gone over to the Communists, who had rewarded him with the appointment of Vice-Chairman of the Provisional Government of Chinghai. That such an eminent Buddhist theologian should support Communism had some effect on the Tibetans, and after the broadcast Tharchi Tsendron asked me if I thought the Chinese would really respect the Tibetan religion this time.

"I think Communists will follow whatever policy they consider to their best advantage," I said. "Of course they may decide that destroying monasteries would not help them to colonize Tibet."

But the Communists had no success in trying to win support for their candidate for the new incarnation of the Panchen Lama.

The Panchen Lama, or Tashi Lama, was the second great spiritual leader in Tibet. His seat was at Shigatse, about two hundred miles west of Lhasa; and it had not been occupied for twenty-seven years.

The Panchen Lama was a spiritual leader only. Except in a few

small districts round Shigatse, all temporal power was in the hands
of the Dalai Lama. In the past various Chinese Governments had
tried to change this without success. The Communists were now
continuing the policy not only of the Kuomintang but of the Manchu dynasty before the Chinese Revolution.

When the Chinese invaded Tibet in 1910 the Dalai Lama fled to
India and remained there for over two years. The Chinese officially
deposed him and ordered a new Reincarnation to be sought: but the
people of Tibet remained loyal to their exiled God-King, and none
was found. The Chinese then invited the Panchen Lama to take his
place. Wisely he refused, although he went to Lhasa and was said
to have sat on the Dalai Lama's throne.

The Dalai Lama returned to Lhasa in 1912 after the Chinese had
been thrown out, without the help of the Panchen Lama. There was
a long quarrel between the two spiritual leaders, and in 1923 the
Panchen Lama fled to Chinghai and accepted Chinese protection.

The thirteenth Dalai Lama died in 1933, and until the next Reincarnation was found Tibet was without both its traditional spiritual
leaders. The Tibetans wanted the Panchen Lama to return. He was
willing to do so—with an escort of three hundred Chinese troops.
One of the main objects of the British Mission that went to Lhasa in
1936 was to try to persuade him to return without the troops, and it
was ready to go to Jyekundo to meet him if necessary. Nothing
came of this because the Panchen Lama was firmly in the hands of
the Chinese.

In 1937 the Panchen Lama died. Within the next few years two
boy candidates for his Reincarnation were found. One was in
Chinghai, and sponsored by the Chinese (Kuomintang) Government. The other was in Lhasa. In the view of the Lhasa Government
both remained candidates, as they had not passed the religious tests.
The Kuomintang Government said the Chinghai candidate was the
true Reincarnation, and the Communists took him over. They even
made him Chairman of a "Provisional Government of Tibet" in
readiness to take over the throne if they gained physical control of
the country and the Dalai Lama fled.

"We would never accept him as our ruler," Khenchi Dawala told
him. "When the Great Thirteenth was in exile our loyalty to him
was not affected in the slightest degree. When the Chinese insulted
him and deposed him it only increased our hatred of the Chinese."

Every one, both monks and laymen, told me the same. They all
wanted a new Reincarnation of the Panchen Lama to be installed,

but outside Shigatse no one was prepared to accept him as a temporal ruler. Nor was there any general belief that the Chinghai candidate was the true Reincarnation.

I heard a talk on the subject given by an anonymous official on Radio Lhasa.

"There are two candidates," he said. "No one knows for certain which is the true Reincarnation, for neither has passed the tests. In my opinion"—he was careful to emphasize that he was not speaking for the Government—"the candidate in Lhasa will prove to be the true one."

And this timid statement was the nearest Radio Lhasa ever came to defying the Chinese.

I was still relaying the transmissions, and I had listened to every news-bulletin and talk that had been broadcast. I had still not heard a single reply to Peking. No one had said that Tibet did not want to be liberated. There had not even been a denial that Tibet was controlled by American and British imperialists.

"How can you expect help when you don't even say you want to be helped?" I said to Tharchi Tsendron when he asked me whether I thought the United Nations would come to Tibet's aid. "You haven't even told the world that you will defend yourselves if you are attacked. Surely it isn't surprising that the world thinks you're going to give in?"

"We shan't give in," he said. "But we don't want to fight if we can avoid it. We don't want to provoke the Chinese to attack."

"If Communists want to attack they'll invent the provocation," I said.

"Then we shall appeal for help."

"Then it will be too late. You haven't even told the world you consider yourselves independent now."

"Surely we showed that when we expelled the Chinese officials last summer?"

"You showed your neutrality in the Chinese Civil War, that's all. At least, that is how it was interpreted by other countries."

"But aren't we showing it now by refusing to go to Peking? Our delegation has been in India since the beginning of the year, trying to negotiate with the Chinese and always refusing to go to their country."

I tried to think of a Tibetan equivalent for 'sitting on the fence,' and then thought better of it. I had always been careful not to interfere in Tibetan politics, and I would not have said as much as I did if Tharchi had stopped throwing questions at me. But he still persisted.

"What do you think we should do then?" he asked.

"There are only two things you can do," I said. "Either proclaim that you are an independent state and determined to remain so, or go to Peking and get the best terms you can. Either would be better than just sitting and waiting to be swallowed up."

"But surely every one knows Tibet is an independent state?"

That was the trouble. Every one did not know. Under international law the question of Tibet's sovereignty was ambiguous and confused.

The fact of Tibet's independence was beyond doubt. Except for two short periods of Chinese rule, both of which were ended by a national revolt, Tibet had been an autonomous state for centuries. Under the Manchu dynasty the Chinese had exercised a vague and remote suzerainty, based on a personal relationship between the Chinese Emperor and the Dalai Lama; but that had ended with the Chinese Revolution of 1911. Since then Tibet had been completely independent.

In 1913 Tibetan, Chinese, and British representatives met at Simla and initialled a convention under which Tibet recognized Chinese suzerainty on condition that China recognized Tibetan autonomy; in other words, nominal suzerainty in exchange for practical independence. But they could not agree on the frontier, and in the end the Chinese refused to sign. Tibet continued to enjoy *de facto* independence, and China continued to claim a suzerainty that she was unable to enforce. She also denied Tibet's right to autonomy. Even in Formosa, Chiang Kai-shek maintained that Tibet was simply a province of China. It was the one subject on which he and Mao Tse-tung agreed.

Britain recognized Tibet's independence, and so did most other countries—unofficially; officially the question never arose. For Tibet never sought recognition, never wanted to exchange ambassadors or open diplomatic relations, held herself aloof from all other nations.

"Doesn't that show that all we want is to be left alone?" said Tharchi Tsendron. "And isn't that our right?"

"Yes, Tharchi," I answered. "Morally there is no argument. I was talking about whether you are likely to get any help. That Tibet deserves help is obvious. I don't think I should be staying here if it wasn't."

·   ·   ·   ·   ·   ·

"You are not in Tibet at all. Chamdo is in China. I've looked it up in an atlas."

If I heard that once I heard it a hundred times. And it was very hard to convince British and American radio amateurs that their atlases were wrong.

"But it's a new atlas. It was published this year."

"I didn't say it was out of date. I said it was wrong."

"But it's my son's school atlas. He's learning geography with this."

"Then he's learning it wrong."

Their interest was not just academic. Many of them were trying to qualify for a "Worked All Zones" certificate that was issued by an American radio magazine to any amateur who could prove that he had been in contact with every zone in the world. For this purpose the world was divided into forty zones, and Zone 23 was the whole of Tibet. It was the hardest to work. As Fox was not doing much amateur radio now—he was a very sick man—radio 'hams' were at first jubilant when they made contact with me. Then they looked Chamdo up in their atlases, and became reproachful or annoyed.

I sent a message to the Radio Society of Great Britain and the Radio Relay League in America pointing out that the atlases were wrong.

"What's your authority for saying Chamdo is in Tibet?" one contact asked me.

"I'm in Chamdo, and I'm employed by the Tibetan Government. I'm the first European to stay here for over thirty years. The last was Sir Eric Teichman, and the boundary-lines on his maps are still pretty well right. Yours were always wrong."

"Who put them in, then?"

"The Chinese."

Chamdo had always been part of Tibet, although for one brief period (1910–18) it had been under Chinese military occupation. Before then the Sino-Tibetan frontier had changed frequently, but it had never come as far west as Chamdo.

Chamdo had fallen to the Chinese when they invaded Tibet in 1910, and it had come under the rule of a Frontier Commissioner named Chao Erh-feng. Khenchi Dawala still remembered him by his nickname of "Butcher Chao," which he had earned for his habit of ordering wholesale executions. He had been butchered himself, by his fellow-countrymen, in the Revolution of 1911, when the

Chinese were thrown out of Lhasa and most of Kham. But they succeeded in holding Chamdo until it was liberated in 1918 after the Chinese had engaged in fresh aggression against Tibet with disastrous results for themselves.

"We could have liberated the whole of Tibet then," said Khenchi Dawala, referring to the provinces of Sikang and Chinghai. "Lord Teichman stopped us from going on."

Mr Teichman, who was later knighted, had admitted this himself. As British Consular Agent in Western China he was asked to mediate by the Chinese, and he urged restraint on the Tibetans for their own good. In another month they could have reached the border between Sikang and the province of Szechwan, but the Chinese were not likely to let them stay there for long. Single-handed Teichman stopped the war, and the Tibetans withdrew to a line running through Batang. In the 1930's the Chinese pushed them back to the west bank of the Upper Yangtze, thus approximately restoring the boundary that had been effective, with various changes, ever since 1727. This was still the *de facto* boundary in 1950. There was no *de jure* boundary. That was the trouble.

At the Simla Conference the Tibetans had claimed the whole of Sikang. The Chinese claimed up to the limit of Butcher Chao's advance in 1910, which had reached to within a few days' march of Lhasa. The British proposed a compromise, which would have given Tibet complete autonomy as far as the Upper Yangtze and a degree of nominal control in Sikang. The Lhasa Government was willing to accept this. The Chinese refused.

Ethnologically the Tibetan claim was beyond dispute. The Chinese claim was based solely on the temporary success of Butcher Chao's aggression in 1910. The British proposal was based on the situation as it was.

After the talks broke down the Chinese recognized their own claim and published their map for the whole world to see. The Tibetans had no maps that were even publishable. China had diplomatic relations with the other nations of the world. Tibet had not. The Chinese map was followed by map-makers in other countries, including Britain, and that is why the atlases were wrong.

All of which was difficult to explain to the numerous radio amateurs who told me I was not in Tibet.

Lhalu began to talk to me about the future.

"Is Rugby a good school, Phodo?" he asked.

"I believe it is very good. It is one of the most famous schools in England."

"Did you go there?"

"No, Your Excellency." I tried to explain the difference between a public school and a grammar school.

"You know that my father took four Tibetan boys to Rugby?"

"Yes, I met Kyipup in Lhasa."

Kyipup was the only survivor of the four sons of Tibetan nobles whom Lhalu's father had taken to England in 1913 at the suggestion of Sir Charles Bell. After leaving Rugby each of the boys had been trained in a profession. Kyipup had taken surveying, and on his return to Tibet he had been given the task of developing the telegraph system. There was only one telegraph line in the country, running from Lhasa to Kalimpong, in Bengal, and it had been built by the British.

Kyipup is dead now, so I cannot hurt his feelings when I say he was not one of the most intelligent Tibetans I met. He failed with the telegraphs, and was then appointed City Magistrate and Chief of Police. He had such a nervous, apologetic manner that it was hard to think of him in a position of this sort, and he did not hold it for long. One of his duties was the erection of poles for the New Year which, like those outside the Residency at Chamdo, were made of a number of tree-trunks bound together with yak's hide and rose seventy or eighty feet high. If one fell down in Lhasa the City Magistrate lost his job, and that is what happened to Kyipup. Then he went into the Foreign Office, and acted as interpreter and guide for English-speaking visitors. He also sometimes read the news in Tibetan on Radio Lhasa, and he was the speaker I had heard talking on the Panchen Lama. I knew him quite well, and it was he who had prostrated himself on my behalf when I had my last audience with the Dalai Lama.

"The experiment was not a great success," said Lhalu.

That was not entirely the boys' faults. One of them, a monk named Möndö, had shone at cricket and showed some aptitude for mining engineering, which he studied after leaving school. Tibet is rich in minerals, including gold, and they had never been exploited. Möndö came back and began prospecting. At once the local abbot protested that he was upsetting the spirits and would cause the crops to fail.

Möndö did not want to be blamed for a possible bad harvest, so he moved to another district and began digging there. The same thing happened. After a few more attempts he abandoned prospecting and went into Church politics, in which he was much more successful. But he upset Lhasa by riding a motor-cycle he had brought from India, and one day the noise made a frightened mule buck a high official. Möndö was degraded and put in charge of a remote district in western Tibet. Later he returned to Lhasa, but he did not ride his motor-cycle again. Nor did he try any more prospecting. So far as he was concerned, as Lhalu said, the Rugby experiment was not a success.

"My father said that Ghonkar was the best of the boys," Lhalu told me. "I wish he was still here now."

I did, too. Ghonkar had gone to Woolwich, and was expected to remodel the Tibetan Army. But for political reasons he had been posted to a frontier station in Kham, and he died young. I had heard a rumour that he had fallen in love with an English girl and been forbidden to marry her by the Dalai Lama, and that he had died of a broken heart or some other more sinister cause.

The fourth of the Rugby boys, Ringang, was the only one who achieved anything in Tibet. Being the youngest, he spent longer than the others in England, and took a course in electrical engineering. When he came back to Lhasa he built a hydro-electric power station at the foot of a mountain stream and laid a power-line to the city and to the Dalai Lama's Summer Palace. All the equipment had to be brought over the Himalayas by porters or on mules.

It was a tremendous undertaking for a Tibetan—and it worked. Except for a few months in the winter, when the stream was frozen, it provided the city with electric light. But nothing was spent on maintenance, and after Ringang died the plant fell into disrepair. When I was in Lhasa it produced only enough power to drive the machines in the Mint. It was to replace this that Fox and Aufschnaiter were building a new hydro-electric station on much more ambitious lines.

"I want my two boys to be engineers," said Lhalu. "I want them to go to Rugby, too. I shall take them there myself. Perhaps you will come with me, Phodo?"

I would have loved to take Lhalu to England, although I think he might have been a little disappointed. When he looked at the pictures in my illustrated magazines he was always pleased to find ceremonial events like Trooping the Colour.

"You are just like us when you are at home," he said. "Why don't you wear bright clothes like this when you come to Tibet?"

Lhalu wanted to travel round the world. He wanted me to go with him.

"When I return to Lhasa," he said, "I shall organize a new Trade Mission and lead it myself. It will go to England, America, all over the world. I hope you will be able to come if you can leave the radio by then. I wish you had gone on the last one."

The last Trade Mission, which had been abroad for nearly two years, had been a flop; at least, from Tibet's point of view. No doubt Pangda Tsang and some of the other members had done good business, but it had failed in its real object, which was to gain economic and political help. It had only been called a Trade Mission so as not to annoy the Chinese. They had been annoyed, all the same. The Mission had arrived in Washington unannounced, and the Chinese Embassy (Kuomintang) at once protested against the admission to the United States of "Chinese subjects with false passports."

"The Mission failed because none of the members could speak English properly or knew anything about the outside world," said Lhalu.

I thought the Mission had failed because its members had been too timid to open international relations on their own account.

"You know both worlds, and if you come with me as a Tibetan Government official you can do even more for us than you are doing now. With you in it the next Trade Mission will be a success."

I thought that with a man like Lhalu as the leader it could be a success. I only hoped it was not too late.

I found one compensation in the fact that Lhalu was going to leave Chamdo. He was likely to stiffen the Cabinet in Lhasa, and it needed stiffening.

It was becoming more and more obvious that the Lhasa Government was pitifully weak. I could see clearly that the people had more spirit to resist than their rulers. But Tibet had always been like this when the Dalai Lama was a minor, and a number of officials were jockeying for power.

From what I had seen and heard of the Fourteenth Reincarnation I gathered that he was exceptionally able and intelligent, and had the makings of a ruler of the same calibre as the Great Thirteenth. His minority would end soon; but again I feared it might be too late.

Meanwhile I was waiting to learn what sort of a man would be sent to Chamdo.

"Ngabö Shapé is to be the new Governor-General," Lhalu told me at last.

This cheered me up a bit. I had met Ngabö at parties in Lhasa. I had not known him well, but I was impressed by his seriousness and I had heard he was efficient. He was also said to be brave and resolute and to have no love for the Chinese. Moreover, he had already done one tour of duty in Kham, as lay Finance Minister. At least the Government had chosen a man who knew the country, which was of vital importance as he would automatically become Commander-in-Chief of all forces in the province.

Ngabö had not been a Shapé when I met him, and no vacancy in the Cabinet had arisen. The Governor-General of Kham did not have to be of Cabinet rank, so in creating a fifth Shapé the Government was underlining the present importance of the appointment. I thought that was another good sign.

Ngabö left Lhasa at the beginning of August. The journey would take him over a month, and handing over would take nearly as long. It was unlikely that Lhalu would leave until the end of September. If the invasion had not begun by then it seemed probable that it would be postponed until the following year. It would be too late for the Chinese to have a chance of reaching Lhasa before the winter brought them to a halt.

In the evening of August 15 I was in my office writing a letter when I felt my chair moving. As I stopped writing I heard an ominous creak from the beams. I looked up and saw the walls heaving, and dust fell down on me from the ceiling. Then the whole building trembled, and I was running out of the office for my life.

"Get outside!" I shouted to the servants. "Quick! Run! It's an earthquake!"

8

Before the Storm

WE got clear of the house, and I ran to knock up Rimshi Trokao. He was already on his way down.

"The gods!" he exclaimed.

It seemed more like devil's work to me. For this was no ordinary earthquake: it felt like the end of the world.

We went and stood in the open, clear of all buildings.

"Listen!" said Rimshi Trokao.

So the rumbles were not my imagination. Was it thunder? But there was no lightning, and it was anything but stormy weather. Gunfire, then? The series of dull explosions sounded like distant artillery. Perhaps the Chinese had chosen this moment to attack, but it seemed a strange coincidence. Yet what else could it be?

"The gods!"

That was sufficient explanation for every one else, and as it happened they were right. At least, the rumbling was part of what we call an Act of God. I did not know it then, but I was hearing the noise of the earth's crust cracking up.

"Look!" said Rimshi Trokao.

A great red glow appeared in the cloudless sky to the south-west. That could not be the Chinese. I realized it was all part of this earthquake, already remarkable for its violence and the fact that there had been no premonitory tremors.

"Phodo Kusho! A house has fallen down! Some one is hurt! Please come."

I told Puntso to bring my pressure-lamp and told Tenné to come with me. Three or four houses had collapsed, but the people had got out in time. The casualty was a girl who had been pinned under a falling beam. She was conscious and groaning, and as she was a Khamba that meant she was in great pain. The beam had caught her leg—an almost certain fracture. I told Tenné to bring splints, bandages, morphia, blankets, and my camp-bed. Then we had to jack up the beam to get her out. Part of the roof still hung above us, and the earth would not keep still. I was sweating with more than exertion when we at last drew her clear.

It was not as bad as I had feared. There was a break, for certain, but her leg had not taken the full weight of the beam. At least it was a simple fracture, and not of the femur. I diagnosed a break in the shaft of the tibia. The fibula seemed all right. As a first-aid job it would have been easy, but I had to set the break.

Do-Tseten helped. He had cooked for the doctor at the Indian mission, and could act as a medical orderly at a pinch. I gave the girl a shot of morphia, treated for shock, and set the fracture as gently as I could. Then I put on the splints.

A woman came out of one of the other damaged houses, carrying a baby. It had been by the fire when the roof crashed in, and the pot had fallen over and scalded the baby's arm. I told the woman to bring the child to the radio station, and treated the scald with penicillin ointment. Only then did I realize that the tremors had ceased.

There were no more casualties. Chamdo had got off lightly, considering the violence of the tremors. I wondered if there were more to come. I felt sure that this would be regarded as a terrible omen and start a panic of prayer.

There I was wrong.

Tharchi Tsendron came early the next morning, and I expected to be asked all about seismology. But he was too pleased for that.

"Did you smell it?" he asked.

"Smell what?"

"It was like burning matches. Not at first, but a few hours later."

The rumblings and the glow began to make a little more sense.

"Sulphur," I said. "Like a volcanic eruption."

"The gods were showing their strength," said Tharchi.

As soon as I had finished my schedule with Fox I went to see my patients. Both were doing well.

"When can I get up?" the girl asked.

"Not for several weeks. You mustn't touch these pieces of wood or move your leg." I examined it and thought I had not done too badly. With luck and care—but that would be difficult—she would be able to walk again without too bad a limp.

She was a pretty girl. I knew most of the people of Chamdo, and I had not seen her before.

"Are you married?" I asked.

"No. I have come to get a husband."

"Where are you from?"

She named a village a few miles outside Chamdo.

"Do you want to be taken back to your parents?"

"I have no parents."

"Other relatives, then? Or have you some here?"

"I have no relatives. They have all been killed."

They had all been killed in a blood-feud, she told me. It had been going on for generations, and now all the family except herself had been wiped out. She had been lucky to get away alive.

"That is why I want a husband," she said.

"To protect you?"

"No, to give me children so that they can kill them."

I was horrified. If I had left her alone she might have been too badly deformed to get a husband, and then the blood-feud would have died out.

I traded on what I had done for her.

"Why don't you forget it?" I said. "If your children kill them they will kill your children."

"You don't understand," she said.

The woman with the scalded baby was looking after her. I told her what to do. The baby was comfortable, and the mother cheerful although her home had been wrecked.

"The gods have shown their strength," she said.

I went to see Lhalu. I could have taken the words out of his mouth.

"Phodo," he said, "the gods have shown their strength."

It was all perfectly logical. The gods had caused the earthquake, and they would not have done that for nothing. It was a big earthquake, so they were showing their strength. The Chinese had no gods, so this could not be for their benefit. The gods had shown they would help Tibet, and no army could stand up against such might.

"You see the power of prayer," said Lhalu. But he was no fool. "This is a signal for us to redouble our efforts. We must pray more, and be more than ever ready to resist the Chinese."

Morale was higher than it had been since the beginning of the year. I was pleased about that, but my own morale was low. I was hearing the reports of the earthquake from Delhi.

Apparently it had been one of the five biggest earthquakes ever recorded, and it had literally changed the face of the earth.

Khamba dancing at a summer picnic party

Potato-planting in Tibet

Chamdo: East and West Rivers and the monastery on the hill overlooking the town

*Chamdo and
the West
River valley*

Sir Eric Teichman

*Cantilever
bridges at
Chamdo*

Sir Eric
Teichman

Mountains had become valleys, and *vice versa*: one mountain had fallen into the Brahmaputra, changing its course, and hundreds of villages were inundated. Landslides and floods had caused immense loss of life. The gods seemed to have a funny way of showing they were on our side, and it was not at all auspicious for me.

The epicentre of the earthquake was on the border between Tibet and Assam, about two hundred miles from Chamdo. It was directly on my emergency escape-route. And the reports made it clear that the route had gone. I might as well try to find my own way over the Himalayas.

I was alarmed about Bull, for it was his only way out. There was no radio receiver at Markham Gartok, so I wrote to him and Derge Sé giving them a summary of the news. Then I went to see Lhalu.

"Unless Bull is allowed to come to Chamdo," I said, "he is almost bound to fall into the hands of the Communists. He is a missionary, and they are not kind to men who preach religion."

"If he came to Chamdo," said Lhalu, "and the Chinese also came, where would he go then?"

"He could withdraw with us."

"And where would we go? Which way could we go?"

He had made his point. The only way Bull could leave Tibet now was through Lhasa. A Christian missionary was the last person to be allowed in the Holy City.

"If he was allowed to come," Lhalu said, "do you think he would refrain from trying to convert our people to his religion?"

"Yes," I lied.

"You know that I cannot give him permission myself," said Lhalu. "But I will ask the Government again. I will explain the new situation, and recommend that permission should be given."

It was better than nothing, but I had little doubt what the answer would be. If Tibet was invaded Bull was almost bound to be captured. By comparison my own position was very good. But only by comparison.

"Phodo," Lhalu said, when I saw him shortly after passing some Government messages to Rimshi Trokao for decoding, "you were right. The earthquake was inauspicious. The gods were showing their anger and displeasure."

Shiwala Rimpoche had made a mistake. The monks in the Potala had placed an exactly opposite interpretation on the earthquake, and Lhasa was heavy with gloom. So was Chamdo, as soon as the correct

G

interpretation was known. The jubilation ceased at once, there were long faces everywhere, and all the people prayed harder than ever.

Lhalu ordered defence preparations to be intensified.

On August 26 there was another tremor, but no damage was done. Then the earthquake was forgotten when Ngabö arrived.

Lhalu had already vacated the Residency and moved to Shiwala Rimpoche's house, a few miles down the river. He sent his equerry and some of the junior officials to Lamda, the last stage before Chamdo, to welcome Ngabö and escort him in. Every official in Chamdo except Lhalu himself was expected to ride to the willow grove just outside the town, where the usual reception tent was pitched. Every official went, except me.

I doubt if an official had ever before failed to appear on such an occasion on a plea of duty, for his most important duty was to attend. But I had to keep my radio schedules with Fox, and was granted a special dispensation. I sent Tashi to present a white scarf on my behalf, and then I saw the long caravan ride past my house and through the town. As soon as Ngabö reached the Residency I rode over with presents and another white scarf and paid my first call. I apologized for not having gone to meet him, and he smiled and said he understood very well.

He was a tall and stately man, long-jawed and with a dignified but cheerful face.

"The Government greatly appreciates your decision to stay," he said. "If you need any help do not hesitate to come to me."

"As you probably know," he went on, "during the period of taking over there will be a number of parties and other receptions. I hope you will come to as many as you can, but I shall understand when your work keeps you away."

It seemed a good start. I did not think I could ever be as friendly with Ngabö as I had been with Lhalu—he was more formal and made me more conscious of our difference in rank—but at least he seemed thoughtful and understanding. And I took him at his word, for I was too busy to attend many receptions.

Ngabö had brought another portable radio station, and he told me to get it ready to send out. Unfortunately no operators had come with it, and I had to consider whether to put it in the hands of Dronyer or Wangda or both. They were now pretty good operators and reasonable mechanics, and at a pinch either could have taken charge of a station. Both were ready to go. Tsering was no problem:

if Wangda went she would go too. I did not like the idea of sending one of them alone, but on the other hand I wanted to have some one at Chamdo to relieve me in case of an emergency. I decided to shelve the problem until the time came.

Meanwhile Fox was going on sick leave. He was now nearly crippled with rheumatoid arthritis, and he was going to Calcutta for treatment. About a year earlier two Americans had visited Lhasa, the Lowell Thomases, father and son. I had spoken to them on the radio telephone. After returning home they arranged for a supply of the new drug cortisone to be sent to Calcutta by air for treating Fox. Now he was riding painfully across the Himalayas, having left the best of his trainees in charge of the station at Lhasa. They were not very quick operators, so I took on more work by having all traffic channelled through me.

There were now three more stations in operation—one at Shigatse and the other two in western Tibet. A radio was necessary at Shigatse for political reasons, because it was the seat of the Panchen Lama. The other two were of little use from the point of view of defence, and it seemed absurd that of the six stations operating only one was in Kham.

What was even more galling was the knowledge that yet another portable station, with two operators trained by Fox, had come with Ngabö—and was to return to Lhasa with Lhalu.

Perhaps I was unreasonable in thinking that Lhalu ought to have waived his right to the station and operators and left them in Kham. After all, he was a Cabinet Minister, and it had evidently been decided that when such a high official made the journey between Chamdo and Lhasa a radio station should be included in his caravan. But Lhalu knew how great the need was for stations at Dengko and Riwoche, and it was galling to think that a station and operators were kept idle in the Residency throughout the critical month of September.

I felt sure it was the critical month. There was little doubt that the Chinese were now in some strength on the Upper Yangtze and in Jyekundo as well. An attack might come at any moment. Reinforcements of men and materials were still arriving in Chamdo, and more Khamba levies were recruited and sent out; but most of the officials, including Dimön Depön, were preoccupied with the changing-over receptions and ceremonies at the Residency.

I spoke again to Tashi and Lobsang about sending their wives back to Lhasa.

"They could go with Lhalu Shapé's caravan," I said. I was sending most of my personal belongings with it.

But none of the other officials were sending their wives back, and Ngabö's wife and children were actually leaving Lhasa to join him in Chamdo. I was wasting my breath. The status of women in Tibet was high for an Asian country, although still low by European standards; and there was no equivalent phrase in the Tibetan language for 'the weaker sex.' Even now the troops still had their families at the frontier posts, including Dengko. I could not imagine what would happen to them in the event of a fight or a retreat.

I saw little of Lhalu after Ngabö had arrived, and knew less of what was going on. I paid official calls on Ngabö from time to time, but no confidences were exchanged. He did not consult me about defence preparations or ask for my advice. I felt more or less isolated in the radio station, and frustrated because there was so little I could do. When I was not working I spent most of my time trying to relax with Tharchi Tsendron.

I could never think of Tharchi as a monk. This was partly because he did not dress like one. Outside Lhasa all monk officials wore the same bright silks as lay officials, and could be distinguished only by their shaven heads and lack of earrings. When I first arrived in Chamdo I could hardly tell who was a monk and who was not; for, to make it still more confusing, the Khamba lay officials were all dressed like monks. The reason for this was that when they had been allowed to wear what they liked the richer Khambas dressed more splendidly than junior Lhasa officials, like Tashi and Lobsang; this was considered to lower the dignity of the Lhasa Government, so it was decided to put them in a uniform. The monk's robe was chosen because it made the regulation easy to enforce. Many Khambas had short hair and wore no earrings, so to me they looked just like monks.

Another unmonkish thing about Tharchi was that he liked bathing. Most monks never even washed. Saturday was a holiday in Tibet, and in the summer Tharchi and I used to go down to the river for a bathe, or rather a bath. I had a collapsible bath in my quarters, but it was more pleasant in the river, and I followed the local custom and took a bar of soap.

I also took shampoo, and this impressed Tharchi so much that once he asked me to shampoo his half-inch stubble. I had hardly begun when he suddenly jumped into the water and rinsed the shampoo off.

"What's the matter, Tharchi?" I asked him when he came back. "Didn't it feel good?"

"It felt all right," he said, "but I don't want my hair to go fair like yours."

I assured him my hair had always been fair, and was not due to the shampoo, but he was not convinced. Even when I had been in Chamdo nearly a year people sometimes stared at my strange features and colouring as if they could not really believe I had been born like that.

I taught Tharchi to swim. Tibetans are poor swimmers, and their only stroke is a kind of dog-paddle; being human, I showed off a bit. I also impressed them with my diving, for this was completely unknown to them. I never managed to persuade Tharchi to dive, but he learnt to swim quite well.

He also joined in the football I played with the Indians. I had brought a ball with me from India, and can fairly claim it was the first that was ever kicked at Chamdo. Other Britons had brought the game to Lhasa long before, and it had become so popular that at one time there was an organized league. But the Church had disapproved—it was said the monks wasted their time watching when they could have been praying—and when a hailstorm occurred during a match the game was doomed. Hailstorms in Tibet can be very powerful and cause immense damage to crops, and farmers used to employ special magicians to ward them off. Football could not be allowed to nullify magic that was vital to the country's economy, so in Lhasa the game was now forbidden.

For this reason I did not try to introduce it into Chamdo. We just kicked the ball about among ourselves in the compound, and occasionally other officials and the servants joined in. Horkhang Sé sometimes played, and once was nearly knocked out when the ball hit the charm-box on the crown of his head. Only Sonam Puntso and I ever headed the ball by design, and then there were roars of laughter as it was assumed it was an accident and we had not been able to get out of the way.

Tharchi was interested in the outside world, and asked me many questions about England. I amazed him most when I told him we had no yaks.

"How can a country live without yaks?" he asked.

It was beyond his imagination that life could be possible without this shaggy, bison-like animal that supplied most of Tibet's needs. In a land without machinery it was vital for transport and on the farms. Its hair was used for making tents, blankets, and very strong ropes. Its hide was used not only for boots and saddle-bags, but also for coracles, Tibet's only boats. Its horns were used as snuff-boxes, and its tail for making fly-whisks and Santa Claus beards (for export only). Its dung was used occasionally as manure but almost universally as fuel, for no coal was mined and much of the country lies above the tree-line. And the yak was the Tibetans' staple diet in the form of milk, butter, and meat. The butter was also used for lighting, making images, and polishing floors.

"How can you live without yaks?" Tharchi asked again, and I began to wonder how we did.

He helped me to improve my Tibetan, and translated the Khamba dialect into the Lhasa form for my benefit. In return I taught him a few words of English. Childlike, he would store a word in his memory and then produce it with a grin when an opportunity arose.

"What is the English for *nyingdu*?" he asked me one day.

"Sweetheart," I told him.

The next time I was at his house he pointed to one of his servants, a young boy, and said proudly, "I sweetheart."

I told him his English was improving.

There was nothing unmonkish about having a catamite. On the contrary: in this Tharchi was typical. Homosexuality was not illegal in Tibet, and among the monks it was encouraged on the grounds that it helped them to remain celibate. It also helped to leaven the ruling class with peasant class.

In Tibetan families of all classes it was the custom to put at least one child into the Church. Sons of nobles were eagerly sought after by individual monasteries, as they brought some of the family wealth; and of course many of the monk Government officials were of noble birth. But it was possible for a peasant's boy to achieve high rank as a monk, and Tharchi was an example. He had risen in the same way as his boy servant was likely to rise.

He had been a monk from the age of four, and he was still only a boy when he became the servant of a monk official. He was chosen for his good looks, and he had these to thank for his present rank of *tsendron*. It was the easiest way for a peasant's son to rise in the world.

In Delhi the Tibetan delegation was having talks with the newly arrived Chinese Ambassador, General Yuan. In Korea the tide had turned at last, and United Nations forces were pushing the Communists back. On the Upper Yangtse all was still quiet.

I reminded Ngabö of the portable radio station he had brought me by telling him for the second time that it was ready to be sent out.

"Thank you, Phodo," he said. "Please keep it in readiness. At any time we might need to send it out."

I could not tell him that the time was now—that, in fact, it ought to have been sent out long ago. Not to Dengko, which was no longer so important, but to Riwoche. According to the reports I heard there were now many Chinese troops in Chinghai.

Yet he seemed to have everything under control. Of a less volatile temperament than Lhalu, he gave me the impression of being cool and efficient and quietly confident.

Lhalu had spoken to him about my position in the event of a Tibetan surrender, and he gave me a similar assurance to warn me in advance. It was no longer much of a safeguard, now that the southern route to Assam had gone, but Ngabö promised that he would help me to get away through Lhasa.

"But you do not need to worry," he said. "We shall not give the Chinese permission to send troops into Tibet. If they enter by force we shall resist. If necessary, of course, we shall evacuate Chamdo and retreat on Lhasa. There will be no local surrender as long as I am in Chamdo."

Reinforcements were still arriving from Lhasa, and I felt reasonably reassured. I still had not received my new contract, but that was of little importance now.

Rimshi Trokao told me he was going back to Lhasa with Lhalu.

"But no relief has come for you," I said.

"One will be sent later," he said.

This worried me. Relieving Lhalu was bad enough, but to recall his right-hand man without sending a relief seemed madness at a time like this. Rimshi Trokao had more local knowledge than any other official, and if we had to leave Chamdo he was the man who would requisition the transport.

"I am sorry you are going," I said.

"It is unavoidable, Phodo Kusho. The State Oracle has said it would be inauspicious for me to stay."

From what I knew of the State Oracle it was unlikely that he had

said anything of the kind. I had seen him perform in public, gesti-
culating, gyrating, and beating his breast, hissing, groaning, and
gnashing his teeth, foaming at the mouth like an epileptic. I had
heard the unintelligible mouthings which his secretary repeated as
answers to the questions put to him by the Cabinet; and these
answers were usually ambiguous. But I could not believe the State
Oracle would have been consulted about Rimshi Trokao. He might
have been asked about the appointment or relief of a Governor-
General, but mostly the questions were on matters of major religious
or political importance, like the meaning of an earthquake or
whether to fight or give in to the Chinese. The whole function of
the State Oracle was to relieve the Cabinet of the responsibility of
making decisions that might turn out to be wrong. When this happened the Oracle was dismissed and a new one appointed, and there
were no set-backs to anyone's political career.

The obvious explanation was that Ngabö did not want Rimshi
Trokao to stay. The nature of Tibetan political intrigues made that
understandable, but I thought Ngabö might have kept him until a
relief could arrive.

Every one was going. By the end of September Fox had reached
India, and I heard from friends in Lhasa that the Indian doctor had
said it was doubtful if he would ever be well enough to return. Mr
Richardson handed over to an Indian officer and left the Mission.
Bull and I were the only Britons left in Tibet. We had never met,
and I thought, with uncanny foresight, that we were not likely to
now unless it was in a Chinese gaol.

It was worse for Bull, who was in greater danger and completely
cut off from the outside world. His only contact was by correspondence with me. At least I had my radio. And with even a low-power
transmitter like mine, a radio 'ham' need never be lonely wherever
he is.

I kept in radio contact with Fox in India. Every Wednesday evening I was in touch with Jefferies, and through him with my parents.
And long after Chamdo was in bed I sat by my radio talking to
friends I had made all over the world. The freemasonry of radio
'hams'—short for amateurs—is unique, and even pierces curtains
of iron and bamboo. Language is no problem, for all operators use
not only the international Q code but also the abbreviated English
peculiar to 'hams.' It was quite normal for a Russian to conclude
a conversation with "TKS FB QSO OM" ("Thanks for fine
business contact, old man"). Russians also confirmed contacts by

mail in the usual way, and I had quite a collection of cards adorned with photographs of Lenin and Stalin and a bearded gentleman named Popov, the true (*Pravda* truth) inventor of radio.

But most of my contacts were with England, and they kept my spirits up. I was beginning to feel homesick.

Then I had a letter from George Tsarong in Lhasa.

"Delivery of the new hydro-electric equipment has been promised for October," he wrote. "If Fox is not back by then, do you think you will be able to come and help to instal the plant?"

My thoughts went back to the last day I had spent with Fox and George.

George Tsarong was the most sophisticated and progressive Tibetan I ever met.

He was the son of Tsarong Dzasa, Horkhang Sé's sometime step-father and reputedly the richest man in Tibet. Tsarong Dzasa was a rare phenomenon in Tibet, a self-made man. The son of an arrow-maker, he had saved the Thirteenth Dalai Lama from capture by the Chinese and risen to become a Cabinet Minister. He was for-ward-looking and yet had his roots deep in the past. He had built the only steel bridge in Tibet, and claimed to have seen ghosts. He employed monks to pray for him, and subscribed to the *National Geographic Magazine*.

George, who had acquired his name at school in Darjeeling, had been one of the first of Fox's original trainees at the British Mission. He had his own ciné-cameras and dark-room, and had built a radio receiver himself. When the supply of electricity in Lhasa gave out he imported a wind-driven generator and installed it beside the prayer-wheels and incense-burners on the roof of his house. He was a moving spirit in both radio communications and the new hydro-electric scheme, and closest of all the Tibetans to the handful of Europeans who lived and worked in Lhasa.

There had never been many, and with the departure of Fox and Mr Richardson only three were left: Harrer, Aufschnaiter, and Nedbailoff. They had all escaped from the internment camp at Dehra Dun and gone to Tibet to seek refuge from the British. Nedbailoff's was the strangest story of all.

He was a White Russian, and had escaped from the Communists via Siberia. In the course of many years he had walked right down through China to Calcutta, earning enough to eat by doing odd jobs, mostly mechanical, on the way. He had picked up enough knowledge to become an efficient electrical engineer. In Calcutta he worked for a German electrical firm, and was allowed to go on working after the Second World War broke out. But when Soviet Russia was brought in on our side he withdrew his undertaking not to do anything detrimental to the Allied cause, and was interned in Dehra Dun. At the end of the War he heard that he was going to be sent back to Russia, so he escaped. He was caught in Tibet and brought to Gangtok, where I interviewed him. Mr Hopkinson, the Political Officer, was sympathetic and gave him a job in Gangtok. George Tsarong heard about him, and invited him to go to Lhasa to work on the hydro-electric scheme.

We Europeans never formed a colony in Lhasa, and our chief bond was a common desire to help Tibet. We wanted to help to make the country materially richer and yet not poorer in any other way. We were all working for Tibet. Aufschnaiter had done all the spadework—literally—for the hydro-electric scheme, and Fox had designed the plant. Nedbailoff came to help him install it. Harrer, who had helped Aufschnaiter in other feats of hydraulic engineering, had new plans to develop Tibetan education. With Fox's help I was opening up radio communications.

We had something else in common. With the exception of Aufschnaiter, who was an agricultural engineer, none of us had any professional degrees or diplomas. We had all come to Tibet more or less by accident—two of us to serve Britain, the other three escaping from the British; and although we had kept our respective nationalities, although none of us even wanted to be naturalized, we had a common loyalty to the Tibetan Government and people. And we had the proud spirit of pioneers.

I had spent a day with Fox and George Tsarong shortly before I left Lhasa. We talked about the future. I did not expect to be in Chamdo for more than two years at the most, and Fox hoped to be able to give up radio work before then. He already had plans for building more hydro-electric stations with Nedbailoff. I would supervize an ever-growing network of radio stations all over the country. Aufschnaiter would modernize Tibetan agriculture, and Harrer would open schools and the first Tibetan university. George would become a Cabinet Minister. Tibetans would be trained in our various techniques, and eventually we Europeans would all work ourselves out of our jobs.

George smiled at that. It would not be done so quickly, he said; and if it was we should only go if we did not want to stay. Tibet had never been a British colony, had never been under European rule. It was different in India, where British technicians might be regarded with a mixture of gratitude and resentment, to be retained only until they could be replaced by Indians. In Tibet we were on an equal footing from the start.

No, not equal, said Fox. We were only in the fifth rank; George was already above us, and would be in the third rank before long. George laughed and reminded us that we had been told specifically that our ranks were not merely honorary, and that promotion was equally open to us. I said we were not rich enough to be Shapés, but perhaps I might become Minister of Radio Communications. Fox said I would have to share the job with a monk, and as our hopes and plans became touched with fantasy laughter stopped us from taking ourselves too seriously. But the feeling of exhilaration remained. It had lasted long enough to help to keep me in Tibet.

I wrote back to George saying I did not expect to be able to leave Chamdo yet. Then I went to say good-bye to Lhalu. I took the customary white scarf and presents, and Lhalu received me formally. Then tea was brought, and he told his servants he did not want to be disturbed.

He thanked me for everything, and I thanked him; and then we both relaxed and talked as friends. We were closer than ever before, and when we finally shook hands emotion dried us up. I think we both had a premonition that we should never meet again.

"Phodo," said Lhalu, "I hope I shall see you in Lhasa soon."

"I hope so, too."

"At least the danger here is less now," he added. "The Chinese cannot hope to reach Lhasa this year. They will not try before the spring."

"No," I agreed. "It's too late for them to attack now."

A week later the Chinese attacked.

9

The Battle for Kham

SEE you same time next week," I tapped out. "Good night, Mum. Thanks, Jeff."

"Good night, Robert." My mother's voice was clear. "Look after yourself."

It was 11 P.M., Tibetan time, on Wednesday, October 11.

I switched off the radio and went to the window. All Chamdo was asleep. The huddle of mud houses looked beautiful in the moonlight, with the surrounding mountains silhouetted against the starry sky. It was a clear, frosty night, and the silence was broken only by the barking of dogs. I was turning to go to bed when I heard a faint tinkle of bells coming from the east.

As the bells grew louder I heard another sound, the clip-clop of a horse's hoofs. It was being ridden at a fast amble, and I went out on to my veranda to see it approach. It was coming down by the East River, and it passed my house on its way into the town. I saw the rider's fur hat and the silhouette of the barrel of his rifle sticking up above his shoulder, and knew him for an Army messenger. He rode on in the direction of the Residency. With a feeling of uneasiness, I went to bed.

I rose at seven the next morning, and was still dressing when Tashi burst in.

"Phodo Kusho, the Chinese are coming!"

"What have you heard?"

"They've crossed the river and killed all the troops."

"Where?"

"At Gangto Druga."

"How do you know?"

"The messenger told me. He's from Rangsum—no one at Gangto Druga got away."

Both places were on the normal trade-route from Kangting to Chamdo. The ferry across the Upper Yangtze was at Gangto Druga, a small village and frontier post. Rangsum, one day's march farther west, was a garrison town astride the trade-route. It was five days' march from Chamdo.

Tashi went out to see if he could glean any more news. At eight o'clock I had my first schedule with Lhasa, and I had just begun operating when Lobsang brought in a very long Government message. When we finished the schedule I told the Lhasa operator to come on the air again at ten in case there was further urgent official traffic. Then I went to see Ngabö.

We were going through the town when I heard bells from behind, and another Army messenger overtook us in great haste.

"He's one of Muja Depön's men," Tenné told me.

We rode on to the Residency, where several ponies were already quartered in the courtyard. On my way in I met Dimön Depön.

"What is the news?" he asked me automatically.

"It's my turn to ask you that," I said.

"The Chinese have attacked. We are throwing them back. We shall beat them," he said confidently. "Excuse me—I have to see my wife."

I had to wait ten minutes before Ngabö received me. He looked as cool and unruffled as ever.

"I expect you have heard the news," he said.

"I've heard that the Chinese have taken Gangto Druga."

"Yes," said Ngabö. "They also tried to take our forces at Rangsum, but Khatang Depön succeeded in withdrawing them in time. He will hold the Chinese at the next pass to the west."

"When did they start the invasion?" I asked.

"On Saturday."

So the war had been going on for nearly five days before Eastern Command Headquarters learnt that it had begun. If there had been a radio at Gangto Druga——

"The Chinese also tried to cross the river at Dengko," said Ngabö. "They were thrown back with heavy losses."

Good old Muja! With a few more officers like him the Tibetans could put up a good fight.

"What about north of Riwoche?" I asked.

"All is quiet on the northern front. As you know, the Chinese have troops in Jyekundo, but there are no reports of any movement southward."

If the reports were true the news was not wholly bad.

"I am placing a day-and-night guard on the radio station," Ngabö went on. "Please suspend all commercial traffic until further notice. When is your next schedule with Lhasa?"

"I've arranged to have an extra one at ten."

"Good. Can you work two-hourly schedules through the day?"

"Yes, of course."

"Then please arrange it."

Ngabö stopped talking and made me aware that the interview was over.

"Your Excellency," I said, "can I help in any other way? Apart from radio, I mean. If there is anything else I can do——"

"No, thank you, Phodo. Not at present. Everything is being attended to. If there is anything I shall let you know."

There was still something I had to say.

"Your Excellency, the spare portable radio is ready to go out at the shortest notice."

"Good. Please keep the batteries charged."

"They are always fully charged. Either or both of the Indian operators are also in constant readiness to go out."

"Very good. We may need to send the station out at any time." Ngabö stopped again, but still I did not go. Then he smiled. "Would you like me to send the radio to Riwoche now, Phodo?"

"Yes, Your Excellency."

"You are afraid we shall be cut off in Chamdo?"

"It seems possible that the Chinese will try to cut the Lhasa route."

Ngabö nodded.

"I know the possibility. That is why Riwoche has been reinforced. It is now very strongly held, and there is no sign of Chinese activity in that area. I want to keep the spare radio station here in case anything should go wrong with the other one. I must be in communication with the Government in Lhasa. Do not worry, Phodo. We shall win. The gods are on our side."

If they were not it could hardly be for lack of being asked. By the time I returned to the radio station a thin plume of smoke was already rising from the incense-burner on the roof of the monastery, and spiritual activity was being intensified everywhere. People left their work to go round the Holy Walk, turning prayer-wheels and counting beads. More prayer-services were held, monks muttered more rapidly, and the water-carriers quickened their step as they went up the hill. Two men and a woman decided suddenly to make a pilgrimage to Lhasa by prostrations, and set out the same day. Even old Smiler turned a prayer-wheel in one hand and manipulated a rosary in the other, and yet still managed to put his thumbs up when I passed.

"The gods are on our side," said Tashi, announcing the latest news he had picked up in the town.

"What are you going to do about your wife and children?" I asked bluntly. "And you, Lobsang? We may all have to withdraw from Chamdo. What then?"

"They will come with us."

"Have you got transport for them?"

"We have a pony each for ourselves. For them we can hire——"

"There'll be nothing to hire. I'll go and see Tharchi Tsendron and find out if he can do anything."

Since Rimshi Trokao had left Tharchi Tsendron had taken over as Transport Officer in addition to his other duties. I went to his house.

"Shiwala Rimpoche is to be asked if the Chinese will reach Chamdo," he told me.

"What's going to happen to my clerks' wives and children if they do, Tharchi?" I asked.

"They will have to look after themselves, like all the other officials' wives."

"Most of the other officials have got several ponies. Tashi and Lobsang have only one each. I've got four, but Tenné and Do-Tseten will need two, and I want Tsering to have the other. I'll need one each for the Indians from you——"

"You will need them, and I hope you will have them," said Tharchi Tsendron.

"I must have them."

"Yes, I know you must. But I do not know the position about transport yet. It is being requisitioned by the Residency. Ngabö Shapé has not given me any instructions yet."

"But we might have to leave at any time."

"We might not have to leave at all. Let us see what Shiwala Rimpoche says."

Just then one of Dimön Depön's servants came in haste and asked if I would go to see his master. I went at once, hoping I might get the chance to be of some help now. But Dimön wanted only medical assistance.

"My wife is ill," he said.

No close examination was needed to diagnose her complaint. "She's going to have a baby," I said.

"Yes, of course." Dimön Depön tried not to sound impatient. "But she isn't well."

I saw his point. A Tibetan woman did not expect a little matter like child-bearing to make her ill. Once at a friend's house a servant waited at table at midday very obviously pregnant, and was of normal shape when she served the afternoon meal: she had had her baby in between.

They had not taught me midwifery in the Boy Scouts, and I did not know what to make of Dimön's wife. But she evidently had a fever, so I promised to send Dimön some medicine for that. Then I had to hurry back for my ten o'clock schedule.

Tashi and Lobsang were not there. I hoped they had gone to try to get ponies for their wives. "They've gone to help cast out the devils," Dronyer told me.

Out of the window I saw about twenty monks carrying brush-wood down the hill. It was unusual to see them carrying anything heavier than a rosary, but they had not far to go. A clearing had been made by the river, and here the monks piled up the brush-wood in the shape of a pyramid.

Then the procession came down from the monastery, and I heard the first shots fired since the war began. There were about a hundred monks, including the abbot, in the procession. They came down chanting, while a monk band in the procession played independently: wailing clarinets, clashing cymbals and booming drums, and the piercing high notes of the conch shells, which were believed to be especially effective in scaring off devils. Every now and then Khambas flanking the procession drowned the other noises by firing their rifles.

They were old muzzle-loaders, such as I had seen in the Imperial War Museum. When they were fired flames and smoke shot out of the muzzles, and the recoil spun the Khambas round like prayer-wheels. They made a deep booming sound, which echoed round the mountains for several seconds.

The procession reached the bottom of the hill. Some of the monks were burning incense, and others carried fearsome-looking images made of coloured butter. These were the devils. They walked to the open space by the river, and already a crowd had come to watch. I saw Lobsang and Tashi there, together with some of the other

Lhasa officials. There was a brief silence as the abbot invoked the gods, and then the bonfire was lighted: more chanting, more music, more gunfire—and then the whole lot together, with every one shouting and yelling at the tops of their voices, as the images were thrown on the burning wood. The noise was deafening as the flames leapt up and burnt the cast-out devils.

Lobsang and Tashi came back excited and full of glee.

"Tharchi Tsendron will not be able to provide any transport for your wives and children if we have to leave Chamdo," I said.

I do not think they even heard.

"Shiwala Rimpoche says the Chinese will not come," they said.

No doubt Shiwala Rimpoche's statement was good for morale, but it seemed to me that something more Churchillian was needed. Again I felt isolated by my lack of faith in their gods. But there was nothing I could do except carry on with my work and get everything ready for evacuation. Dronyer and Wangda were less gullible —superstitious—devout (I do not know which is the right word) than the others, and shared my view that it was advisable to prepare for the worst in spite of what Shiwala Rimpoche had said. There was not a great deal of work to do, as I had long since gone into the question of what to take and what to leave, and I still could not make final decisions until I knew how much pack-transport I would have. We got all our personal belongings ready to pack.

I felt better when I saw Dimön's *rupöns* sending the troops up the river to man the Bren guns behind the stone barricades on the other side of the hill and to guard the bridges leading to the east. I saw that they still had no dynamite. Dimön did not appear, but Khenchi Dawala rode down to encourage the Khamba levies. He was still recruiting them, and about three hundred were available for the defence of Chamdo alone. Others had already been sent to Rangsum, Dengko, Riwoche, and Markham Gartok.

After my midday meal I went to see Khenchi Dawala.

"What is the news?" he asked.

"Nothing from Peking or Delhi." Lhasa did not broadcast till later in the day. "I didn't expect the Chinese to say anything yet."

"You heard about Gangto Druga?"

"Yes. Ngabö Shapé told me this morning."

"It seems that Khatang Depön has withdrawn from Rangsum," he said. "He is a very good officer. There is a high pass not far to the west of Rangsum, and I expect he will make a stand there.

H

There are several passes like that between Rangsum and Chamdo."
Khenchi Dawala paused. "Will Britain come to our help? Or
America? The United Nations?"

"I don't know," I said.

"But what do you think?"

There was no point in not telling Khenchi Dawala the truth.

"I think it is unlikely."

"Do you think Tibet alone can beat the Chinese? No, you need
not answer that. Of course we cannot. But we can keep His Holiness
out of their hands. We are not fighting only for our land, Phodo.
That is why we must fight."

Rather strangely, Khenchi Dawala cheered me up. He was not
only brave and determined to resist: he was also a realist.

I was not so happy about Ngabö. He seemed a shade too cool and
confident, and I did not like what Tharchi Tsendron had told me
about the transport. I was still less pleased about the spare radio
station being kept idle. I wished Lhalu was back, with Rimshi
Trokao as his right-hand man. They had shown they were realists
after the fall of Dengko. Things did not look so well organized now.

I was in radio contact with Lhalu's caravan, which had now
passed the danger-point on the track to Lhasa. They would certainly
reach Lho Dzong long before the Chinese could cut the route.

Between schedules I listened to news bulletins from all over the
world, but there was still nothing about the attack on Tibet. Then
Radio Lhasa went on the air.

While Fox was away there was no news in English, but I continued to relay the news in Tibetan and Chinese. Horkhang Sé and
several other Lhasa officials came to listen that day.

Not a word was said about the invasion.

"I don't understand," I said when it was over. "The Chinese
have attacked Tibet. Tibet wants help. Peking is silent for obvious
reasons. What on earth can Lhasa gain by pretending the war does
not exist?"

No one answered.

I decided to take my news summary personally to Ngabö.

"Radio Lhasa has not mentioned the invasion," I said pointedly.

"The Government only heard of it this morning," said Ngabö.
"It cannot be announced until it has been decided what we shall
say. I will tell you confidentially, Phodo," he added, "that the
National Assembly is meeting in Lhasa now."

The National Assembly was evidently having a long session, for

Radio Lhasa had no more to say the next day, or the day after that; and the first news I heard of the war was a report broadcast from Delhi on the Sunday to the effect that the Tibetan delegation in India had denied rumours of a Chinese attack!

I had not heard the rumours, which had begun in the political gossip-factory of Kalimpong. It seemed that on the Wednesday, even before the first messenger from Rangsum reached Chamdo, a correspondent of the *Statesman* filed a report that the Chinese had invaded Tibet from Chinghai and reached the pass of Dongma, just north of Riwoche.

The story was obviously false, and All-India Radio quoted the leader of the Tibetan delegation as saying that it was simply "a belated account brought by traders of a minor incident that occurred four months ago." Probably it was: it could have taken as long as that for news of the Dengko incident to reach Kalimpong, and the geographical error was normal. But for the Tibetan delegation to deny that there had been Chinese aggression several days after the news of the invasion had reached Lhasa could only mean either that the delegation had not been informed or that it had been told to keep quiet.

The actions of the Lhasa Government would have been easier to understand if it had intended to offer only a token resistance to the Chinese and then sue for peace, but it was not doing anything of the kind. The resistance was real, and Tibet's subsequent appeal to the United Nations showed that there was never any question of surrender. I could only think it was a matter of habit. The Lhasa Government was so used to the policy of saying nothing that might offend or provoke the Chinese that it kept it on after provocation had become irrelevant. It was still trying to avert a war that had already broken out.

What depressed me most was that no one outside Tibet was likely to understand this. When the news came out the obvious interpretation would be that Tibet had no real will to resist.

By Sunday the position in Chamdo had not changed much. Religious fervour was undiminished, and military activity also continued. Some more troops and supplies arrived from Lhasa, and Khenchi Dawala recruited more Khambas. Tharchi Tsendron was still vague about transport. The second portable radio station remained in my charge. Dimön Depön's wife recovered from her fever but was still waiting for her baby. The outside world continued to be unaware that a new war had broken out, and it was not for me to tell them on amateur radio.

The news from the frontiers was mixed. It was confirmed that Muja had prevented the Chinese from crossing at Dengko. There was no fresh news from Riwoche or Rangsum. From Markham Gartok came a report that the Chinese had crossed the river in force and Derge Sé had surrendered. This was the least important sector of the front, and presumably had not been greatly reinforced; even so, it was a great blow. I had corresponded with Derge Sé ever since I had been at Chamdo, and had come to regard him as one of the best of the Tibetan leaders. There was also the depressing thought that Bull would almost certainly have been captured.

This bad news was confirmed by a report from a detachment of Khamba levies south of Chamdo who had shown their resolution in an unorthodox way. Apparently some of Derge Sé's troops had escaped and fled northward—and had been stopped by the Khambas, who were disgusted by their cowardice and had sent them back to fight.

Markham Gartok was seven days' march from Chamdo, so the Chinese could not be expected from that direction for a little while. But it was evident that Chamdo could not be held much longer, and evacuation became certain on Monday, when we heard the news that Khatang Depön had been routed at Rangsum.

He had not merely lost a battle. He had lost his troops. They had ceased to exist as a united force—and there was nothing else to stop the Chinese on their march to Chamdo.

There was now nearly a panic. Lhasa officials and rich Khambas began to send their valuables up to the monastery, and hired ponies and yaks came in from the surrounding villages. Most of the officials found they were short of transport, and Horkhang Sé, who had a wife and four small children, decided he would not be able to take them to Lhasa and arranged to send them to an outlying village. I suggested to Tashi and Lobsang that they should do the same. Instead they went to see the local fortune-teller.

She was a very old woman, and reputed to have great powers of prophecy. I had also heard rumours that she dabbled in witchcraft, but nothing had ever been proved. The people went to her now because they had begun to doubt Shiwala Rimpoche's assurance that the Chinese would not reach Chamdo, and soon after we heard the news from Rangsum a queue began to form outside her door.

"She says the Chinese will either come within four days or not at all," Tashi told me when he and Lobsang came back.

"Then expect them to come, and send your wives and children out of the town," I advised them.

Pangda Rapga had gone. I had not seen him since the first news of the invasion had come in, but I heard that he had been seeing Ngabö every day. Now he had left with his servants, and gone to the east. He had no chance of getting back to Po without Chinese consent, and it was generally believed that he was trying to parley with the enemy to hold them up long enough for us to withdraw.

I tried to see Tharchi Tsendron about transport, but he was with Ngabö at the Residency. I called on Khenchi Dawala again to see what he had to say.

"You will be leaving Chamdo now," he said.

"I have not been told anything yet."

"You will have to leave, or you will be cut off."

"Will you come, too?"

He shook his head.

"I am a Khamba, and my place is here. I have lived under the Chinese before, and I shall not be unhappy so long as the fight goes on. Things are not as bad as they look. The Chinese attacked at the wrong time of the year, and cannot reach Lhasa before the spring. By then, perhaps, we shall receive help from other countries."

I said nothing.

"We have shown them that we are defending ourselves."

There was still nothing for me to say.

"Haven't we?" he insisted.

"Radio Lhasa has not even mentioned that the Chinese have attacked," I said at last. "The Tibetan delegation has just denied that there has been any fighting."

"It could not have heard yet," said Khenchi Dawala. "It takes time for news to travel."

"Not by radio," I said. "The news was received in Lhasa at eight o'clock on Thursday morning. By nine o'clock it could have reached London, Washington, and every other capital in the world. Now it is Monday, and still nothing has been said. Tibet has not admitted that she is defending herself."

Khenchi Dawala suddenly looked an old man.

Ngabö sent for me the same afternoon.

"We shall have to leave Chamdo," he said. "The Chinese have begun to attack from Chinghai."

"When shall we go, Your Excellency?"

"The day after to-morrow. The route will still be safe then. I am arranging for the transport now."

"I have told Tharchi Tsendron what riding animals I shall need," I said. "I shall also need three ponies to take one of the portable radio stations. For the rest of the equipment——"

Ngabö shook his head.

"You will have to destroy that," he said. "I doubt if we shall have enough pack-transport even for all our arms and ammunition, and they must come first. There will not be a yak to spare."

I made a last plea for my clerks' wives and children, but Ngabö waved it aside.

"I cannot spare any Government transport for officials' families," he said. "All the requisitioned riding animals will be needed for the troops."

"What will happen to their wives?" I asked.

"They must make their own arrangements. Most of them are only temporary wives, and the soldiers would not want to take them home."

I rode back to the radio station and told the Indians and the clerks the news. Tashi and Lobsang did not complain.

"We shall take our wives out to a village to-morrow," said Lobsang.

I felt sorry for them, although they had only themselves to blame. As Government officials they were bound to go with Ngabö, leaving their wives and children to the mercy of the Chinese. But most of the other officials were in the same position, and it was impossible to hire or buy a pony now.

Tsering would come with us on one of my ponies. Wangda asked what belongings she could bring.

"Nothing more than she can put in the saddle-bags," I said. "And she will need them for food. None of us will be able to take any personal luggage."

I had little sleep that night. I now had hourly schedules with Lhasa, and traffic was so heavy that sometimes one schedule ran on into the next. I was at the radio until very late, and arranged to call again early the next morning. In the meantime I charged the batteries, and then went over the radio equipment that I would have to leave behind. I was not going to destroy any of it until I knew for certain what transport I would get, but it had to be ready for quick destruction in case we had to move in a hurry. Finally I checked my personal belongings, getting them into some sort of priority in case I should be able to take some.

The next day the news that we were leaving was all over Chamdo.

When I reached the Residency I found Khenchi Dawala explaining to a group of monk-robed local officials why we had to leave.

"It is not a question of running away," he was saying. "The troops must retreat in order to continue the fight. If they stay here they will be cut off. The Khamba soldiers must go with them—all able-bodied men must go to carry on the struggle against the invaders."

"And what shall we do?" asked one of the local officials.

"We shall stay here. The Chinese will come, but we shall not encourage them to stay. They will be far from their base, and we shall help the Army by interrupting their supplies. We Khambas can hinder and even cripple their power to attack. Great damage can be done to them by small bands both here and across the river."

It sounded good, and could have been so if there had been anyone to organize the Khambas into mobile detachments of guerrillas and if the Pangda brothers had still been in the fight. But I knew—as Khenchi Dawala knew—that there was no effective resistance movement in Sikang now, and on our side of the river the Khambas who remained would be leaderless and unorganized. I think the local officials knew, too, but Khenchi Dawala was irresistibly inspiring. He alone persuaded Chamdo that we were not deserting the town.

Ngabö confirmed that we would leave the next day. He still seemed cool and confident, although he was evidently worried about transport. Yaks were already being brought in from the villages when I rode back through the town, but there were not many. Army messengers were coming in from the north, east, and south, and an undercurrent of excitement and fear ran through the town. The queue outside the fortune-teller's was twice as long as the day before.

I spent the whole day at the radio station, most of the time on the key. Neither Dronyer nor Wangda was quick enough to be able to help me with the volume of traffic. Tashi and Lobsang took their wives and children to a village, and then came back to their posts. Two hundred monks came down the hill to cast out more devils, and plumes of incense-smoke rose from the surrounding hills. No one believed Shiwala Rimpoche's assurance any longer, but the gods were still implored for help.

Late in the afternoon Khenchi Dawala came to see me. He had come to say good-bye.

"Will you leave Tibet now?" he asked.

"Not as long as you go on fighting."

"Go now, and tell the world that we are fighting. You are the only one who knows. Tell them we are not Chinese but an independent nation, and want to remain independent and free. Am I asking you to tell more than the truth?"

"No," I said. "I know all this is true. Yes, I shall tell the world."

"We may lose this war," said Khenchi Dawala slowly. "I know we are not likely to get help now, or even in the spring. I know that without help we are bound to lose in the end. The Chinese are clever and strong. If they could cross the Upper Yangtze they can cross the Salween. If they could beat Khatang Depön on the way to Chamdo they can also fight their way to Lhasa. They may occupy the whole of our land. But even if they do our struggle will not have been in vain. This is a war worth fighting to win and even worth fighting and losing; for defeat is not final when the fighting stops."

His voice was low when he spoke of defeat, but now he spoke more strongly.

"We lost against the Chinese in 1910, and they occupied the whole land then," he said. "I was young, and the future looked hopeless; and all round me there were men who said Tibet would never be free again. It would need a miracle. A year later we had that miracle, in the Chinese Revolution. We seized our chance and threw the Chinese out, and for the next forty years we were free. Now the Chinese have had another revolution, and have attacked us again. Why should we think they have had their last civil war? Chiang Kai-shek may attack them from Formosa—he is no friend of ours, but if we also fight these Communists he will want our friendship.

"We should not have become free in 1911 if we had not fought in 1910. If we did not fight now it would be the end of Tibet. We may have to wait longer than last time. For most of the country it was only a year—although in Chamdo we had to wait eight. Next time it may be ten, or fifteen, twenty, fifty, or more; but so long as we remember that they came by force, our will to be free will survive. We shall become free again because the gods are on our side. But tell the world, Phodo Kusho, that we did not run away."

I promised I would. I did not have the chance then, but I am trying to keep that promise now.

10

The Way to Lhasa

AGAIN I was transmitting messages until late at night. I sent the last at eleven, and then arranged to call again every hour from 4 A.M. The operator at Lhasa was clearly puzzled. Of course we could not talk freely, but from his brief remarks I realized that he did not even know that the Chinese had attacked. The people of Lhasa had still not been told that the war had begun.

I went to bed, and lay listening to the jingle of messengers' bells. Then I heard a pony stop outside the house, and Tenné came and told me the Governor-General wanted to see me.

There were pressure-lamps in the courtyard of the Residency, and several other ponies were tethered there. Many, like mine, carried a single tassel that showed the rider was a Lhasa official of the fifth rank or below. Ngabö's steward came and showed me into an anteroom, where several officials were standing in groups.

I saw Tharchi Tsendron and went over to him.

"What time are we going?" I asked.

"In the morning, I think."

"What about the transport?"

"I don't know. His Excellency——"

His Excellency called me into his private room.

"We leave in the morning," he said. "You must bring one radio station but nothing else. What transport do you need?"

I repeated my requirements. When I spoke of ponies for the Indians he frowned.

"You will have the transport for the radio," he said. "For the Indians I cannot promise."

"But they must have transport, Your Excellency."

"The soldiers are more important."

"Both the Indians can shoot," I said. I was appalled at the idea of leaving them behind. "If anything happens to me they are the only ones who can operate the radio."

"All right. I shall do my best." Ngabö nodded to a secretary, who was making notes. "But there is not enough transport for every one. The animals are not coming in from the villages. Everything is going wrong."

The mask was off now. Instead of the cool, self-assured Cabinet Minister I saw only a frightened man. His confidence had been a pose. He had lost control.

In that moment I compared him with Lhalu after the fall of Dengko, and I also felt afraid.

"What time shall we leave?" I asked.

"As early as possible. Wait at the radio station until your transport arrives."

I went back into the anteroom, and saw fear written in the faces there too. There is nothing inscrutable about the Oriental in times of stress. I looked for Tharchi, but he had gone. Army messengers were still coming in, and I picked up fragments of news. It was all bad. In the east the Chinese were only one day's march away. In the north they were advancing on Riwoche. They had succeeded in crossing the river near Dengko: Muja had been forced back, but at least he had fallen back in good order. He was retreating on Chamdo, fighting a rearguard action to give us time to get out. But even that news was little comfort now.

I saw Khenchi Dawala, and even he looked agitated. He was talking to Dimön Depön, and raised his voice.

"But you must take the Khamba soldiers," he was saying. "You may have to fight to get through."

"It does not rest with me," said Dimön. "Ngabö Shapé says there will not be enough transport for all the troops. My own troops must come first——"

"The Khambas cannot be left," said Khenchi Dawala. "You do not understand what it would mean. They would feel betrayed, and would stop resisting the Chinese. At least some of them must go."

"I shall do what I can," said Dimön. He looked frightened and worried.

Khenchi Dawala left him and went to see Ngabö. Tharchi Tsendron had still not returned. I rode back to the radio station, and sent my servants for the Indians and the clerks. In my own mind I decided that if the worst came to the worst I would give Dronyer and Wangda my ponies and leave Tenné and Do-Tseten behind. Then everything was packed up, saddle-bags were filled, batteries recharged, and all the spare equipment stacked up ready for destruction. I burnt all the official records and documents and also my private letters and diaries. At three o'clock I went to bed.

At four o'clock I kept my schedule with Lhasa, but there were no messages to send or receive. I continued to call every hour. Then, at half-past seven, Tashi and Lobsang burst in.

"Ngabö Shapé has gone!" they shouted. "Every one has gone!"

They could hardly talk coherently, but the gist of their story was that Ngabö and all the other Lhasa officials had left or were leaving Chamdo.

I told them to send for the Indians and to wait at the radio station. Then I removed the crystals from the transmitters, so that they could not be operated in my absence, and rode with Tenné to the Residency.

Already panic was breaking out in the town. People were running about in all directions, carrying or dragging their personal belongings. Monks were hurrying towards the monastery, gabbling their prayers. The stalls in the main street were deserted, and even old Smiler was not at his usual place. I passed Horkhang Sé's house, and it was shuttered and showed no sign of life. Then a small band of Khamba levies came running past, shouting angrily and looking murderous.

By the time we reached the bridge the civil evacuation of Chamdo had begun. Men, women, and children were leaving the town and climbing the hill to the monastery, taking what they could of their household goods. From behind them came the sound of rifle-shots.

As we crossed the bridge Tenné pointed up the track that led eventually to Lhasa, and I saw the backs of people walking to the north. Farther in the distance I could make out a few riders going in the same direction.

We rode over the plain at a fast amble, and straight into the courtyard of the Residency. There was no guard at the gate. No servants came to help me dismount. No steward appeared to greet me. I went in by myself, and ran upstairs. The place was deserted. I shouted, and there was no reply.

I ran down to the courtyard again. Tenné had tethered the ponies and was pointing to an out-building. It was one of the stores used by the Governor-General's bodyguard. An N.C.O. and two soldiers were just coming out.

The N.C.O. saw me and ran across and saluted.

"Where are your officers?" I asked.

"They have gone with the rest of the troops, Sé Kusho. We have been left to destroy the arms and ammunition."

"Has every one else left?"

"Every one."

Tenné and I mounted our ponies again and rode back across the plain. The trickle of people going up to the monastery had become a stream. Instinctively I looked up at the hills on the east, half expecting to see Chinese troops on the sky-line. Surely they must be very near. As we neared the bridge I heard more shots from the town, and a crackle that sounded like machine-gun fire. Had the Chinese Army arrived, or had infiltrating Communists got into the town? I was riding ahead of Tenné now, as fast as my pony could go. I had to try to destroy the radio equipment and petrol: more important, the Indians and the clerks were waiting for my instructions. At least I had to get Dronyer and Wangda out of this.

A man came riding from the town towards the bridge, and signed to me not to cross. It was one of Dimön's two *rupöns*.

"Ride away!" he shouted as he came up.

"I must go back to the radio station——"

"You cannot go back. They will kill you if you try!"

"Are the Chinese in the town?"

"Not the Chinese—the Khambas! Ride away, for your life!"

"What has happened?" I demanded.

"The Khambas were left without transport, and now they will kill any Lhasa official—even you. They nearly killed me."

He had stayed behind to destroy the arsenal. What sounded like machine-gun fire was the rifle-bullets going off. There were also the dull booms of exploding shells, and smoke was rising from where the arms and ammunition had been stored.

"Where are your troops?" I asked.

He pointed to the Lhasa track.

"All have gone," he said. "All the officials too. The Khambas are looting now. Listen!" I heard more shots fired in the town. "Come, let us ride away after the others."

"I must go and tell the Indians——"

"If you go back you will never come out again."

"I will go, Phodo Kusho," said Tenné. "They will not hurt me."

"It will be safer," said the *rupön*. "But do not go through the town. Go along the river. They will not harm your servant," the *rupön* assured me. "Send him instead if you want to help the Indians."

There was no time for argument.

"All right," I said. "Tenné, tell Dronyer and Wangda to take my two ponies, and come back round the back of the monastery to the next bridge up the river. I shall wait for you there. Tell them or the clerks to destroy all the equipment they can."

Tenné was off. When he crossed the bridge and turned right I wanted to call him back and go myself. I had never felt so unheroic in my life.

"Come on quickly," said the *rupön*. "Look—the Khambas are coming!"

They were running out of the town, about a dozen of them, making for the bridge. They shouted as they ran and fired shots in the air. We rode off up the Lhasa track.

But they were not chasing us. When they crossed the bridge they made across the plain. "They are going to loot the Residency," said the *rupön*. Then we heard explosions from the Residency compound, and I knew the arms and ammunition stored there were being destroyed. I thought how they might have been used for guerrilla activities against the Chinese, but Khenchi Dawala's plan for Khamba resistance groups could never materialize now.

"Tell me what happened," I said when we were out of danger.

"The Governor-General left before dawn," the *rupön* told me. "He took his equerry and secretaries and household staff. The Lhasa officials in the town began to leave as soon as they heard he had gone. The troops left at the same time. There were ponies for some, but many had to go on foot. There was almost no pack-transport for the arms and ammunition. For the Khamba levies there was nothing."

"Nor for the radio station," I said grimly. I would have liked to say what I thought of Ngabö, but I managed to control my anger. Even now the *rupön* would have been embarrassed if I had criticized the Governor-General. "Do you know why they all left so suddenly?"

"A messenger brought in a report that the Chinese are nearly at Riwoche."

The message must have been over a day old, so Riwoche could have fallen by now. It looked as if we might have to fight our way out.

I stopped at the bridge where I had arranged to meet Tenné and the Indians. The *rupön* saluted and rode on. He wanted to catch his troops up. I saluted and watched a brave man ride away. He had stayed behind to destroy the arsenal at the risk of his life, after his Commander-in-Chief had fled.

I was out of sight of both the town and the Residency, and it all seemed a bad dream. The track was deserted now, and there was not a sign or sound of life anywhere around. I tethered my pony to the bridge and paced up and down. Then I saw a thin plume of smoke rising from the incense-burner on the roof of the monastery— the last despairing appeal to the gods to make Shiwala Rimpoche's prophecy come true. But there was nothing to save Chamdo from the Chinese now.

I waited half an hour. Then I saw two riders approaching the bridge.

Only two! What had happened now?

As they drew nearer I recognized Tenné in front. Then I saw that the other was Do-Tseten.

"The Indians refused to come," said Tenné. "They could not get a pony for Tsering, so Wangda could not come, and Dronyer decided to stay with him. They are going into a village outside Chamdo. Lobsang and Tashi have already gone."

"What about Puntso? There was another pony——"

"Puntso will take the pony. We left him shaving his head."

"Whatever for?"

"He is going to disguise himself as a monk."

We laughed for the first and last time that day. I never met a Tibetan less monkish than Puntso.

As we rode on Tenné told me that the Indians had already begun to destroy the radio equipment, so at least that would not fall into Chinese hands. Do-Tseten said that all the houses of the Lhasa officials in the town were being looted, but the Khambas had not gone to the radio station yet.

Soon we saw people ahead, going on foot. They were soldiers from the garrison, and some were accompanied by their wives and children. A few had yaks piled high with pots and pans and other household goods. Some of the women had babies strapped on their backs. Then we overtook a few officials, and I was delighted to find that one was Tharchi Tsendron.

He had been the last official to leave Chamdo before me. Apparently Ngabö had simply fled without even arranging the allocation of the little transport there was, and Tharchi had used it to get some of the troops away.

"I thought you had already left," he said.

"I did not know we were leaving." I told him how I had heard the news, and what had happened then.

"I am sorry." He could not say any more without criticizing the Governor-General. But he was very quiet.

We were still passing soldiers and their families, strewn out all along the route. They looked tired and dispirited, but they had not entirely disintegrated as a force. N.C.O.'s kept them together as far as possible, and some were even carrying Bren guns. They were not all from the Chamdo garrison: some belonged to Ngabö's body-guard—he had not even provided transport for them.

Tharchi told me that not all the Lhasa officials were going the same way as us. Horkhang Sé had joined his wife and children in a village outside Chamdo, having resigned himself to capture by the Chinese. The monk Finance Minister had followed his wealth into the monastery, and other officials, monk and lay, had also sought sanctuary there. Dimön Depön had got away with his wife, and they were riding ahead of us. She was still waiting for the baby to arrive.

At four in the afternoon we reached the village of Lamda. It was the last stage on the journey from Lhasa to Chamdo, and I had spent a night in the Government rest-house when I came. This was the only building of any size in the village, and when we rode up to it the courtyard was full of ponies. I had been in the saddle for eight hours without food or drink, and went with Tharchi to join the other officials for tea.

I hardly recognized Ngabö. Instead of his usual silks he was wearing the serge robe that normally only junior officials wore, and he looked frightened and miserable. But he still sat on a higher cushion than anyone else, and we had to go through the formality of paying our respects. He could not have expected to see me again, but he was not quite beaten yet.

"Have you brought the radio?" he asked.

I fought down a sudden upsurge of anger.

"No, Your Excellency," I said. "The transport you ordered for it did not arrive."

Even as I said it I began to feel sorry for him. Only six weeks before he had ridden into Chamdo with all the pomp of an Emperor, in brilliant-coloured silks and brocades: now he was a fugitive, fearful and wretched, in a drab robe of dark-grey serge.

I did not know then—I did not learn it until five years later—that one of the messages I had transmitted to Lhasa the day before had been a request from Ngabö for permission to surrender to the Chinese, and that permission had been refused.

Tenné brought biscuits from my saddle-bag, and I ate them with the tea. There was little conversation. Tharchi Tsendron told me we should have only a short rest, and then ride on over the high pass west of the village.

Then a servant announced that a messenger had arrived.

He came in, bowed to Ngabö, and presented a letter. Ngabö opened it nervously, read it, and then let it fall from his trembling fingers. There was complete silence, and all eyes were on him, as he said:

"The Chinese have attacked Riwoche."

The attack had begun the previous night. The messenger had been sent off immediately. I calculated that if the Chinese took Riwoche at once they could, by forced marches, cut the Lhasa route, just before we got through. They had farther to travel than we had, but we had to climb a 15,000-foot pass. If they were held up for a few hours at Riwoche we could probably beat them to it. In any case, they could not reach the track in strength in time to stop us if our troops fought.

I told Tharchi the results of my calculations as we left the rest-house and mounted our ponies again. Ngabö went at the head, and the villagers bowed and stuck out their tongues as his pony, with two tassels to show his high rank, went past. We followed close behind. At the western entrance to the village the track divided to allow travellers to pass on either side of a low wall—a *mani* wall, inlaid with flat stones carved with sacred texts of which the commonest was the eternal *Om Mani Padme Hum*, from which the wall took its name. Villagers were walking round it, turning prayer-wheels and telling beads, always going in a clockwise direction to keep the wall on their right; for in Tibet also the left is sinister, and when we rode past we automatically took heed of the popular warning to "beware of the devils on the left-hand side." It was hardly appropriate, for the Chinese were on our right.

It was about six o'clock when we reached the foot of the pass, and dusk was falling. That meant it would soon be dark, for night comes quickly in Tibet. We were about to begin climbing when a messenger came down over the pass. He did not carry a written despatch, but had an oral message for Ngabö.

"Riwoche has fallen!" he said.

Apparently the garrison had been outflanked, and Changra Depön had been taken by surprise. This meant that we could hardly hope to get through without a fight. I looked back, and saw that our troops were some way behind. As most of them were on foot, they were already very tired. But the *rupöns* still maintained discipline, and all was not lost yet.

The messenger was still being questioned about the fall of Riwoche.

"The Chinese had Khambas with them," he said.

So it was true that the Chinese had recruited Khambas, in Sikang or Chinghai. Ngabö looked greatly alarmed. The news of his betrayal of the Khambas in Chamdo could not have reached Riwoche, but all Khambas were famous for their sword-play and dislike of taking prisoners, whatever side they were on.

Ngabö hesitated a little longer, and then led the way up the pass.

It was considered a hard climb in daylight, and I doubt if it had ever been attempted by night before. The track was winding and narrow, and soon we had to go in single file. Slippery rocks made the going dangerous in the rapidly fading light, and sudden rocky outcrops threatened to knock us off our saddles. The ponies were tired and could not share the sense of urgency and excitement that overcame our own fatigue. Every hundred yards they had to stop for breath. Progress was painfully slow, and all the time I was thinking of the Chinese riding fast down from Riwoche, gaining on us in their race to cut the track.

But when the light finally failed the goal became survival rather than escape. Tharchi Tsendron, who was riding in front of me, faded to a dim shadowy outline and then merged into the dark. Now I could not even see the track. It was like walking blindfolded on the edge of the precipice, except that the pony did the walking. We were travelling without bells, for better security, and the only sounds were the ponies' hooves on rock. I sat tensed in the saddle, alert for a fall. Twice my pony stumbled and nearly went down: another false step could mean a broken bone, and that would probably mean death.

I had started the ascent with Tenné and Do-Tseten close behind, but I had no idea how far away they were now. Even if I could have seen them I did not dare to look back, to make any movement in the saddle that might affect the balance of my exhausted pony as it felt its way up the narrow, winding, slippery track.

I

At last I could make out the shape of Tharchi again. The moon was coming up, and a faint light was getting through the overcast sky. Then there was a clatter, and Tharchi disappeared, and I nearly fell as my pony pulled up short. An out-jutting shelf of rock had caught Tharchi's shoulder, and he was down.

I shouted a warning to Tenné and Do-Tseten, and dismounted and helped Tharchi up. He was only winded, and with a great effort he mounted again and rode on. This time I waited till he was farther ahead. A rider from behind caught me up, but it was not Tenné.

"Did you pass my servants?" I whispered.

"Yes. One of them had to stop to look after his saddle-bags. They are all right."

My pony was reluctant to go on, and seemed to have lost its nerve. Then it pawed gingerly forward again, and we continued the ascent. Gradually the light improved, but it was still no more than a slight lifting of the darkness; and it even added to my fears. Now that I could see a little of the track ahead I kept imagining obstacles, especially rocky outcrops, and was continually fighting the desire to rein my pony in. A wave of fatigue overwhelmed me, and I wanted to stop and lie down and sleep.

The wind kept me awake. It was getting steadily colder now. Luckily I was wearing an old R.A.F. wind-cheater under my Tibetan robe, but there was no cheating this wind. I felt frozen in the saddle. Now I had to stop every fifty yards, for my pony was panting for breath. I had been riding almost without rest for nearly sixteen hours, and it was beginning to suffer from lack of oxygen as well as fatigue. We had come up nearly four thousand feet.

Then at last the track broadened, and I was riding on to a level open space. It was the top of the pass.

I dismounted, and joined the other officials and servants, who were standing together in a group.

"Are you all right, Tharchi?"

"Yes, thanks. But cold."

"So am I."

Ngabö's equerry passed me a flask. It was Scotch whisky, and felt like liquid fire. I whispered my thanks; we were all whispering, and that made it more unreal. Much noise is needed at the top of a pass to scare away the demons that haunt the mountains. But we had other demons to worry about.

I looked at the luminous dial of my watch. The ascent had taken us four hours: it was just ten o'clock. Four-thirty P.M. G.M.T.—tea-time in England on a Wednesday afternoon, the time for my weekly schedule with Jefferies. At that very moment I knew he would be searching the twenty-metre band for AC 4 RF, which had gone off the air for ever. Probably my mother or father would be in the room with him, getting more worried and only half believing him when he spun a yarn about bad radio conditions to try to allay their fears. Perhaps by now they had heard of the war. Lhasa and Peking could not maintain this strange conspiracy of silence indefinitely. Then I remembered that I still had my crystals—not only the ones for the frequencies I used for communication with Lhasa, but also the twenty-metre crystals I used for amateur radio. If we caught Lhalu up I could use them in his transmitter, and put AC 4 RF on the air again. . . .

"It will take us three hours to get down," said Tharchi Tsendron. "By then the Chinese will have cut the road. Probably they have done so already."

"They won't be there in force," I said. They also would have had to ride by night, and the track south from Riwoche was not as easy as that. "Our troops are not far behind. We can still fight our way through." I felt my revolver, and it gave me more confidence.

More officials joined us from behind.

"The gods have conquered, the devils are defeated," one of them muttered without much conviction. It was the conventional thing to say at the top of a pass, but it should have been shouted out and accompanied by a piercing yell of triumph.

A servant picked up a boulder, and was about to throw it on a cairn of stones when his master stopped him. I noticed the usual cairn and the prayer-flags for the first time. They were placed on the top of every pass, and normally no traveller crossed without adding to the pile of stones. Now even religious observances gave way to the need for silence.

Tenné and Do-Tseten had still not arrived when Ngabö led the way down. There was no point in waiting for them, so I followed Tharchi again. "It is not a pony if it will not carry you up a hill," the Tibetan proverb ran, "and you are not a man if you will not walk down the other side." Our mounts had indeed proved themselves ponies, and it would have been suicide for man and beast to try to ride down that steep, slippery track in the dark. Even leading our ponies we often slipped and sometimes fell. My ankles and calves were aching now, and the pain increased with every jolt.

About half-way down we heard another caravan coming up.

Ngabö's servants went out to reconnoitre, and found they were reinforcements from Lhasa. There were about thirty men, with mountain artillery and cases of rifles and ammunition. They had not heard of the fall of Riwoche, and were travelling by night to try to reach us before the Chinese attacked. Ngabö told them to throw the loads of arms and ammunition over the side of the mountain and to join our caravan. At least we had more troops with us now.

The descent took three hours, as Tharchi had said it would. When we reached the bottom we mounted again, and rode to the next stage on the Lhasa route. There we had to rest our ponies, and we had tea and biscuits and dried meat. It was only another eight miles to where the track from Riwoche joined the route. With luck we could still get through.

Then a messenger rode in from the next village to the west.

"The road is cut!" he shouted.

He did not know the strength of the enemy, but they had arrived only a few hours before. Ngabö had the choice between trying to break through on our own or waiting until more troops arrived.

He chose neither.

"Are they Chinese or Khambas?" he asked.

"Khambas!" replied the messenger.

I caught the shiver of fear that ran through the other officials.

Ngabö talked in whispers to his equerry and secretaries. Then he turned to the rest of us.

"I am going to seek refuge," he said. "There is a monastery near here. The Khambas will not shed blood there."

"Your Excellency," I said with an effort, "is there not still a chance of escape? Their force may be very small."

He looked at me coldly.

"You have my permission to do what you like. Escape if you can. The other officials will come with me."

"You had better come with us if you want to escape," said Tharchi Tsendron.

"Why?"

"You cannot go along the route by yourself—you are bound to be caught. The monastery is to the south, and you may be able to find a way through the mountains to the Salween. There is also a track from the monastery to Chamdo if you want to try for Assam."

"I am afraid that route is hopeless since the earthquake. The Chinese have probably reached Chamdo by now, anyway, and they're bound to be well to the west of Markham Gartok. Getting across the Salween is my only hope." I hesitated. "I suppose you couldn't come, Tharchi?"

"Of course not. I must do what the Governor-General tells me."

We rode back along the route a little way and then turned off to the right. Tharchi was right, of course: I had to get off the track, and it would have been foolish to wander about in the dark on my own. Unfortunately I did not know the country at all, as I had come to Chamdo by the northern route, via Nagchu and Riwoche. I had no maps, either—although they would not have helped much, as they showed little detail off the main routes. I knew that the monastery we were going to had not been marked.

In the dark we missed the way, and rode round aimlessly until dawn, when we came on a camp of herdsmen. They were semi-nomadic, and lived in heavy black yak-hair tents with sod walls. They gave us tea and put on a show of humility when they learnt Ngabö's rank, although I doubt if a Cabinet Minister had ever been treated with less respect. Then they pointed out the way to the monastery.

We had to ride for another few hours, and now I really felt my lack of sleep. I had been in the saddle almost continuously for over twenty-four hours, and several times I dozed and nearly fell off. My pony was equally exhausted, and rode on with drooping head and stumbled frequently.

At last we reached the monastery, standing at the top of a beautiful wooded valley that I never had time to appreciate. The monks came out and made a tremendous fuss of Ngabö, and looked terrified when they learnt why he had come. It was all very well for him to say the Khambas would not shed blood there, but according to past experience monasteries were first choice for blood-shedding by the Chinese.

I unsaddled my pony, and I was shocked by its appearance, I had never seen an animal lose fat so quickly. I gave it a feed and then took my saddle-bags into the monastery and ate some biscuits myself. That was all I wanted, for I was beyond hunger now. I was almost beyond trying to escape, and I had to fight off the overwhelming desire to lie down and sleep. I paid a monk to go and look for Tenné and Do-Tseten, and then made a quick survey of the lie of the land.

I could see the track to Chamdo, and Tharchi Tsendron told me that if I followed it I could by-pass the town on the west. But he shared my view that the country would be impassable where the earthquake had been, and agreed it would be better to make for the west. At least there were no Chinese there yet.

It was useless to make for Lho Dzong, for the Chinese were bound to reach the bridge before I could. My only hope was to cross the river lower down, and if I could not get on to the route to Lhasa to try to cross the Himalayas into Bhutan. The most important thing was to keep well clear of the Chinese, for my features and colouring made it impossible for me to pass as a Tibetan.

There was no track to the west, and none of the other officials had any knowledge of the country round the monastery. I tried to get information from the monks, but they were all muttering prayers at a tremendous speed and would not stop to talk to me. The whole monastery was in a religious fervour as the monks implored the gods to protect them from the dreaded Chinese. The prayer-hall was filled with the sounds of bells and drums and human droning, and the stench of rancid butter, incense, unwashed bodies, and fear.

I went out into the fresh air and looked at my pony. It would be impossible to ride it again until it had rested properly. All the other ponies were in the same condition or worse. I would have to walk my pony away, and one or two others if I could take them, and lie up somewhere until the Chinese had come and gone. There was the danger that they would be looking for me, but I might find a hide-out in the hills. The question was how long I could wait before I set out. I thought I could risk an hour or two, and I ought to have a little rest first.

Then Muja appeared, coming in on the track that led to Chamdo. He was riding at the head of about seventy soldiers, a swash-buckling figure with a big Khamba sword on his saddle and a Mauser pistol in his belt.

I hurried to meet him before he reported to Ngabö.

"How many men have you brought?" I asked.

"All my men. Another four hundred are coming up just behind. What are you doing here?"

I told him briefly, and outlined my own plan to escape.

"It is impossible," he said. "I know the country here. You will never get through."

"I'm not going to sit here and wait for them to come."

"Of course not. There is no need. The Chinese cannot have reached the road in strength, and my troops can easily break through to Lho Dzong. Wait here till I have seen Ngabö Shapé."

He told his troops to feed themselves and their animals but not to make camp. Then he went into the monastery to see Ngabö.

I felt a surge of new hope. Muja's men had brought two Bren guns, and although they were tired they looked fit and full of fight. I went to the *rupön* in charge and asked him what had happened.

"We had to retreat from Dengko," he said. "The Chinese crossed the river farther north, and were coming down our flank. We fought them off as we fell back towards Chamdo. Then Muja Depön sent most of the men to cover Lamda and keep the Lhasa route open, and rode with the rest to Chamdo."

"When did you get there?"

"Yesterday morning—soon after you left. Muja Depön went to the radio station in case you were still there. There was no one there. Your equipment had been destroyed, but the house had not been looted. It was the only one of the Lhasa officials' houses that the Khambas had not wrecked."

The *rupön* went on to say that the appearance of Muja's troops at once restored order in the town, but no doubt anarchy had broken out again when he left. Then I told the *rupön* what had happened at Lamda and afterwards.

"Of course we can reach Lho Dzong," he said. "The Chinese are not unbeatable. We have held them off without many casualties, and unless we are greatly outnumbered we can beat them in a fight. Ah, here come the rest of our troops."

Then I realized how remarkable Muja's orderly withdrawal had been, for the soldiers' wives and children had come too. The Tibetan Army was not designed for retreat. When troops went to the front line they took their families with them; and with Muja's men now came as many women and children, with all their household goods and personal belongings piled up on yaks and mules. There were tents, pots and pans, carpets, butter-churns, bundles of clothes, and babies in bundles on their mothers' backs. It was a fantastic sight. What made it more remarkable was the absence of panic or even anxiety. The women began to unpack at once, lit fires, and brewed tea. They would pack up again when their husbands moved on.

Then Tenné and Do-Tseten appeared. They had missed the track coming over the pass, and when they regained it they almost ran into the Communist troops.

"They are coming after us now," said Tenné.

"How many are there?"

"About a hundred."

"Are they Chinese or Khambas?" another official asked.

"Chinese."

There were groans of alarm from the monks, and the praying rose to fever pitch. Then some of Dimön's troops arrived, also with reports that the Chinese were not far behind. They looked much more weary than Muja's men, but they increased our potential force. I felt sure that the Chinese were only a small mobile unit.

Then Dimön appeared, smiling for the first time for a week.

"It's a boy," he said.

At last Muja came out of the monastery. His face was set and grim.

"Make camp," he told his troops.

I picked up my saddle-bags.

"We're not going to fight, then?"

"No. We are going to surrender. I am sorry if I have delayed you. Escape if you can."

But it was too late. Even as I was about to say good-bye to Muja I saw them in the valley. I turned and looked at the track to Chamdo, and they were there too.

The monastery was surrounded.

11

Return to Chamdo

THEY were Chinese, without a doubt. There was nothing of the Khamba about their khaki cotton-padded uniforms, peaked caps with Red Star badges, and purposeful-looking Russian-style tommy-guns.

I had time to give my revolver to Muja and my cameras to Tenné and Do-Tseten while they put up light mountain artillery to make sure we did not break out. Then they came in.

They had a few Khambas with them after all, but they were only guides. They brought two of them to the monastery to act as interpreters. One accompanied a party of about a dozen that went inside to dictate the surrender terms to Ngabö. The other was with a smaller party that came to arrest me.

"Ni Foo-te ma?"

"Are you Ford?" the Khamba translated.

"Yes."

I picked up my saddle-bags and was marched out to an open space.

"Sit down." I heard the bolt of a rifle behind me, and half looked round. "Keep still." I stiffened, expecting to be shot in the back. Nothing happened, and after a few minutes I relaxed. Then I was searched.

Ngabö was brought out of the monastery, looking less frightened than I had seen him since we left Chamdo. He summoned Dimön and Muja, and gave them some orders, which they passed on to the *rupöns*. Then all the Tibetan troops began handing over their arms to the Chinese.

I was taken to a lean-to below the monastery, and one of the Chinese and a Khamba came to question me. Probably the Chinese was an officer, although as they wore no badges of rank it was impossible to tell.

"Where is your radio?" he asked.

"I haven't got one."

"When did you have one last?"

"In Chamdo."

"Where are the other foreigners?"

"There aren't any."

"What about the two Indians who were with you?"

"I don't know where they are."

"When did you see them last?"

"In Chamdo."

In the evening I was given a meal of boiled rice and meat, and then I lay down in the lean-to and tried to sleep. Two guards stayed inside the shelter, and others patrolled outside. From time to time a torch was shone in my face, doubtless for curiosity rather than security. I was cold and frightened and utterly dejected, but at last fatigue overwhelmed me and I slept.

It was still dark when they woke me, and I had more rice for breakfast. Then I was taken back to the front of the monastery, where more Chinese troops were coming in from the Chamdo track. This was part of the force that had defeated the Tibetans at Rangsum. A newsreel camera was set up, and the Tibetan troops were given back the rifles that had been taken off them the previous day. The camera whirred as they came forward and laid down their arms for the second time. Then they all sat down and were given cigarettes and told to smile, and another film was taken. The Chinese then turned the camera on me, standing between two soldiers armed with tommy-guns. Other films showed the monks welcoming the Chinese and Ngabö signing the surrender of all forces in Kham.

Then one of the Chinese addressed the Tibetan troops. I learnt later that he was the Political Committee Member attached to the Army unit, and combined the duties of chaplain and political security officer. His normal job was to preach Communist sermons and investigate cases of suspected heresy. Now he told the Tibetans why the Chinese had come. One of the Khamba guides interpreted as he went along.

"We bring you peace," he said, and that caused much surprise. "We have come to liberate you from the foreign devils. The Chinese and Tibetans are brothers—one people, one race, one nation." This lost its point as he could not say it in their language. "We have been separated by the foreigners, who have sat on your necks and kept you apart from the motherland. You can tell these foreigners by their long noses and round blue eyes and light skins." He looked significantly at me. "The People's Liberation Army has come to throw them out and set you free."

He paused, and there was a buzz of conversation among the Tibetans. They were completely bewildered, for I was the only foreign devil most of them had ever seen. They could not imagine where all the other foreigners were that needed such a large army to turn them out.

The speaker went on in the same strain. Then he said the Chinese would respect the Tibetan religion and customs and, by implication, her medieval feudal system. There was no appeal to the workers of the world to unite. The masses were not invited to throw off their chains. Ngabö and company were evidently going to keep their jobs so long as they played ball with the Chinese. The only people who would lose by the liberation were the long-nosed, fair-skinned foreigners like me.

At least I was learning what it feels like to be on the wrong side of a colour bar.

The Communists were clever. They had learnt from the mistakes of previous Chinese invaders of Tibet.

There was no sacking of monasteries this time. On the contrary, the Chinese took care not to cause offence through ignorance. They soon had the monks thanking the gods for their deliverance. The Chinese had made it clear that they had no quarrel with the Tibetan religion.

Nor with the Tibetan people, who were treated correctly. In spite of the tremendous supply-problem, the advanced units of the Chinese Army did not live off the country. Each man carried a week's emergency rations in the form of a sausage-like bandolier of meat and rice. And the soldiers had strict orders to respect both the persons and property of civilians and to make friends with them by all possible means. The old contemptuous word *man-tze*, meaning 'barbarian,' was forbidden. Brotherhood was the keynote, and no Chinese troops in Tibet had ever behaved so well before.

Cleverest of all was the way the Chinese solved their prisoner-of-war problem. They simply had the Tibetan troops lined up and gave them all safe-conduct passes and money and told them to go back to Lhasa with their wives and children. Another newsreel film was made of this, and the soldiers did not have to be told to smile.

Nor would they need to be told to spread the news of what friendly people the Chinese were.

About midday we left the monastery to ride back to Chamdo. We stopped the night at a village, and I slept in a kitchen with a guard of six Chinese soldiers. I was the only member of the party who was closely guarded, and probably the only one who ever thought of escape. But it was not worth thinking about at present. I had the depressing feeling that I had lost my only chance.

During the evening the commander of the Chinese force from Rangsum came into the kitchen. "Englishman, cigarette?" he said. Nothing about foreign devils now, so perhaps they were going to be friendly even to me. But I was over-optimistic.

We left early next morning, and rode into Chamdo. A small crowd turned out to watch us come. Ngabö rode in front, and the people bowed and stuck out their tongues. He looked uncomfortable, and pretended that these demonstrations of servility had nothing to do with him. I received similar marks of respect and heard murmurs of sympathy. "Poor Phodo Kusho," one woman said. "The Chinese are going to cut off his head."

There were tents and bivouacs in the compound of the Residency, which the Chinese had made their Field Headquarters. The huge prayer-flags were still there, and apart from some broken windows the building looked unchanged. Standing outside, waiting for us, was an officer wearing a well-cut serge tunic and riding breeches and an impressive hat. This was General Wang, the Commander of the Second Field Army.

I was still kept apart from the other officials, who lined up in order of rank. The General shook hands with each in turn, beginning with Ngabö, and a newsreel camera recorded the scene. He did not shake hands with me, but I was told to follow the others into the Residency. We went up to the Governor-General's best entertaining room, where Wang sat down at the head of a long table. The Tibetan officials sat along one side, again in order of rank. Horkhang Sé was there, and so was the monk Finance Minister. I was put at the foot of the table. Chinese tea was served, and Wang made a speech. As usual, a Khamba from Sikang acted as interpreter.

The substance of the speech was much the same as at the monastery, but the wording was different. The oppressors of Tibet were no longer foreign devils but American and British imperialists.

"You know," said Wang, "that Tibet has been kept apart from the motherland by these imperialists. We have come to free you from them."

There was the same promise of respect for the Tibetan religion and customs.

"There has been friction over these matters in the past," he said, "but that was because China herself was ruled by a corrupt reactionary clique." I imagine that was his phrase, although the interpreter had to translate very freely to find a near-equivalent in the limited Tibetan political vocabulary. "Now China is ruled by the people, and her army is a People's Army that will respect the Tibetan people's rights. There will be no looting, and any complaints about the behaviour of our troops should be made to me at once."

He went on to speak of the great new benefits the Chinese people would bring to Tibet. They would help the Tibetans to build hospitals and schools and roads, and to develop their agriculture and industries. He spoke with enthusiasm of Russian wheat-farming in the Arctic. All would benefit, he said. "Tibet's resources are great, and her standard of living has been kept down artificially by the unscrupulous American and British imperialists." He nodded in my direction. "Not all the Tibetan people are aware of this," he went on, "and we rely on you to teach them and explain our policy to them. You are their leaders, and they look up to you. We shall help you to use your prestige and influence for the people's good."

There it was. Not a word about land reform or the rights of the peasants and the working class. The Chinese were backing the officials.

When he had finished Wang asked Ngabö if he had anything to say.

"We shall do as you tell us," said Ngabö.

The others murmured their agreement, and then Wang asked me if I had anything to say.

"Only that there are no Americans and only one Briton in Tibet," I said. "And I am simply a servant of the Tibetan Government."

When my reply was being translated to Wang he interrupted curtly.

"We know who your masters are," he said.

Then we were dismissed, and put in outbuildings in the Residency compound. I was given one to myself, and was presently joined by an officer named Liu who spoke fluent English with an American accent. He stayed with me for the rest of that day and most of the next, questioning me all the time.

"You must tell the truth and not try to hide anything," he began. "We know all about you, so it is pointless to tell lies."

Then he began questioning me as if he knew nothing.

First he asked what frequencies I had used for radio transmissions. I told him the truth, for it could not help the Chinese, even if they had not monitored all my broadcasts. I knew the frequencies would have been changed as soon as Chamdo went off the air, just as they had been after the capture of the radio station at Dengko. It was a normal security measure.

Liu knew this, too, and asked me what frequencies were to be used if Chamdo fell. That was easy to answer, because I did not know. I was more vulnerable when he asked about operating procedure, for there were certain points that I ought not to reveal. I took refuge in technicalities, and as Liu was unwilling to admit he did not understand he began another line of questioning.

"Who supplied you with information in Chamdo?" he asked.

"What do you mean by information?"

"You know what I mean. Information of military or political value."

"No one supplied me with any information of that kind."

"How did you collect it, then?"

"I didn't."

"Where did you get the information that you transmitted by radio?"

"I did not transmit any."

Liu made an exclamation of impatience.

"What were you doing here with a radio, then?"

"Working for the Tibetan Government."

"Don't be silly. Who were your radio contacts?"

"I transmitted Government messages to Lhasa."

"To Fox?"

"He received them when he was there."

"Didn't these messages contain military and political information?"

"I don't know what they contained. They were in code."

"Didn't you and Fox code and decode them?"

"No."

"Who did?"

"Tibetan officials."

Liu paused in his note-taking.

"Why are all the radio officers and operators in Tibet foreigners?" he asked.

"Because there are no Tibetans with the necessary technical knowledge."

"Did the Indians you were training have any technical knowledge before they came to Tibet?"

"No, but they went to school in India."

"Why couldn't Tibetans be trained?"

"Because they have no proper educational system."

"And yet," said Liu, "you ask me to believe that Tibetans can do highly technical and expert work like coding and decoding?"

"Some of the officials are educated, but they would not do radio work."

"And who made the code?"

"I suppose they made it themselves. It would not have to be very subtle—a simple schoolboy code would do. It could only be broken by a code expert who knew Tibetan, and I doubt if there are any in the world."

"Surely there were code experts who knew Tibetan at the British Mission?"

"There were no code experts there at all. Anyway," I said, "you can find all this out from Ngabö and the other officials in your hands. They will tell you I had no access to their codes."

Then he asked me about the other messages I had transmitted, and I explained the commercial code.

"How did you communicate privately with Fox?"

"By radio telephone."

"Is that how you sent him information?"

"I did not send him information. You would have heard it if I had. All my transmissions were monitored."

"Did you have contacts outside Tibet?"

"Only by amateur radio."

Liu had never heard of amateur radio. He listened with obvious disbelief as I tried to explain. He could not comprehend that I should sit up late at night talking to some one in England just for fun.

Then I remembered that I had not destroyed my amateur logs or the confirmation cards.

"You will find them all in the radio station," I told Liu. "They will show you it was quite innocent—there are even cards with pictures of Popov."

"Who is Popov?"

"The Russians say he invented radio."

"The Soviet Union would not say that unless he did," said Liu reprovingly. "Which British Government Department sent you to Tibet?"

"I was not sent by any Department."

"Then why did you come?"

I told him the whole story from the beginning. He went on making notes.

"It's not even a good cover story," he said when I had finished. "Every one knows that the British Mission in Lhasa is the centre of a spy-ring."

"I did not know that. And there has been no British Mission in Lhasa for over three years."

"It only changed its name. What were your relations with Richardson?"

"I met Mr Richardson socially once or twice."

"I don't mean socially."

"We had no other relations. He was working for the Indian Government. I was a Tibetan Government official."

"You were both working for the British."

Liu asked me about my work at the British Mission in 1945, my relations with Fox, the other foreigners I knew in Lhasa, my relations with Tibetan officials there, and the start and development of the radio communications scheme. I was not greatly disturbed by the way the interrogation was going. His suspicions were natural; if a British expeditionary force had found a Russian radio officer sitting near the frontier in a country like Tibet I dare say we would have been equally suspicious. But I knew that when they had investigated thoroughly, as they were bound to, they would discover that I was speaking the truth. What they would do then was a different matter.

It was not so easy to answer Liu's questions about my activities in Chamdo, for I had to consider others who were in, or might fall into, Chinese hands. I had nothing to hide about Lhalu, for he had never taken me into his political confidence. Liu asked me little about the Indians or my clerks, and I gathered they were already captured. I denied knowledge of any other Briton in Kham or Sikang. Liu did not mention Bull's name, and as he did not press these questions I concluded that he also had been taken prisoner.

"You are not telling the truth about this," Liu said, but he did not make an issue of it as he assumed that my whole story was a pack of lies.

I lied again to conceal facts about certain Lhasa officials and Khambas which I must still keep to myself. But I was able to tell the truth about Geda Lama, for Liu's questions were astonishingly naïve.

"How many times did he come to the radio station?"

"Only once."

"Why did he come?"

"To listen to Radio Peking."

"Who came with him?"

"Horkhang Sé."

"Did you give him a meal?"

"No."

"Nothing to eat or drink?"

"Only the usual tea and biscuits."

"Who served it?"

"My servant."

"What was his name?"

"Tenné."

"Where is he now?"

"I don't know."

Then he asked me when Geda moved into the quarters below the radio station, and how often I saw him while he was there. I told him I had not seen him at all, and he had died after a few days.

"What did he die of?"

"I don't know."

"Did you know he was ill?"

"I was told that he was."

"Did you go and see him?"

"No."

"Why not?"

"I wasn't asked."

"But you had medical supplies, and you were the only person in Chamdo with any medical knowledge."

"I haven't had any medical training."

"Didn't you ever give medical treatment?"

"Only when I was asked and thought I could help."

K

"Yet you let Geda Lama die in your house——"

"It wasn't my house."

"—without even offering to help. Wasn't that inhuman?"

"He was an incarnate lama."

"What has that to do with it?"

"There are medical monks. And if I had treated him and then he had died I might have been blamed for his death."

"So you preferred to let him die rather than risk your reputation?"

Liu continued to question me about every detail of my relations with Geda Lama. He asked whether I had had anything to do with his being moved to the quarters under the radio station, and then went over his visit to the station again.

"I didn't put arsenic in his tea, you know," I said sarcastically.

"Had you any arsenic?"

I had to smile.

"No," I said, "and anyway, he died about two weeks after he drank my tea."

Liu did not smile. He just wrote that down with the rest.

Altogether Liu questioned me for about sixteen hours. There were breaks for meals, and I had a good night's sleep; and if I was tired at the end of the questioning I have no doubt Liu was too. He never used unfair pressure or threats. Only once did he raise his voice in anger. That was when he asked me about the foreigners I had met in Lhasa, and I mentioned some Chinese.

"We are not foreigners!" he shouted. "The Chinese and Tibetans are one people. You are the foreigners, and you have kept us apart."

He was not putting on an act. This intelligent, well-educated man believed it was true. That was why he thought I was a spy.

I wondered how long it would take the Chinese to discover the truth. I did not doubt that they would have to admit it eventually—at least, admit it to themselves. What they were going to do with me depended on other factors, and my replies to Liu's questions were unlikely to affect these. All I could do was to continue to tell the truth, except when it might compromise others or help the Chinese in their war against Tibet, and hope for the best.

When the interrogation was over I was taken to the radio station, and a newsreel camera took shots of me standing outside. They also took photographs of the radio equipment—which the Indians had smashed up very thoroughly—with close-ups of "Made in U.S.A."

It was rather childish. They might just as well have photographed their own radio equipment, much of which they had captured from Chiang Kai-shek's troops and which had been made in the same place.

The town had not changed much, except that there were Chinese troops everywhere. There were also telephone wires, for the first time in the history of Chamdo, and posters showing a map of Greater China with the five-star Red Flag firmly planted in Tibet. This aroused much interest as hardly any of the population had ever seen a map before. Leaflets were being handed out, explaining the liberation in both Tibetan and Chinese. They were presented "with the compliments of the Second Field Army," along with photographs of Mao Tse-tung and Chu Teh, then Commander-in-Chief of the Chinese People's Army. The most interesting thing about these leaflets was the date at the bottom. It was simply "195 "—with the space for the last digit left blank.

As they took me back through the town I again heard people expressing regret that I was going to lose my head. Generally life was going on as before. Prayer-flags were still waving, prayer-wheels still turning, and old Smiler on the corner put out his tongue and stuck up his thumbs. There was again a queue outside the door of the fortune-teller, who had been right after all. Most people had returned from the monastery, and the water-carriers were still trudging up the hill.

I had now learnt that the Indians and the clerks were definitely prisoners, and when I returned to the Residency I asked Liu if I could see them. He went to ask General Wang, and then came back and took me to the old barracks, where they were kept.

"Just tell the Chinese the truth," I told them. "You have nothing to hide."

They told me they had all got safely out of Chamdo after I left, although Lobsang's pony had been stolen.

"I saw a man riding a white pony that looked just like mine," he said. "I pointed it out to Tashi, and he thought so too. Then I went for my own pony, and it had gone."

"What did you do then?"

"I went to the fortune-teller, and she told me where to look."

"Did you find it?"

"No, but I found another pony. She is a very wise woman."

My captors did not ill-treat me, although they warned me that the guards had orders to shoot at once if I tried to escape. They gave me two meals a day, always of rice with dried meat. They awakened me every morning at half-past four (they were still using Peking time), and then left me alone.

On the fourth day I was allowed to go into the next out-building to talk to the officials who were held there. My neighbours turned out to be the four *depöns*—Muja, Dimön, Changra, and Khatang. Muja was bright and cheerful, Dimön quite happy, and Changra frightened and nervous. Khatang, the only one I had not met before, looked dejected but not afraid. I noticed that he was wearing a pair of Khamba boots.

"I left my own on the battlefield," he explained. He did not speak very clearly, as he had left his false teeth in the same place. He told me about the disaster in the east. "They crossed the river and took Gangto Druga by surprise," he said. "We knew nothing until they attacked us at Rangsum. We held them off and withdrew, and camped on a plain. We were going back to the pass the next day, but they fell on us during the night."

It had been a fierce battle, but in the end the Tibetans were routed. Khatang Depön had left everything on the battlefield. "My boots, my teeth, my charm-box, and my wife," he said disconsolately. Then he suddenly tensed and his eyes flashed as a burly Khamba swaggered past. "The Vulture!" Muja had to hold him back to stop him from running past the guard and attacking the man.

I had heard of Chago Tobden, "the Vulture," a notorious bandit chief. Many years earlier he had plotted a revolt against the Lhasa Government, and had only just escaped with his life. He was a confederate of Pangda Topgye, and it had been hoped he would help in the resistance against the Chinese in Sikang. Instead he had gone over to them with his private army, and had provided them with Khamba guides. Now he was strutting up to the Residency as if he owned the place, with Liu and other Chinese officers bowing and smiling and Khatang Depön spluttering toothless threats.

Muja and Khatang fought over their battles again and explained to each other why the Tibetans ought to have won.

"If we had had one of your radios, and there had been another at Gangto Druga, they could not have caught us like that," said Khatang.

"If there had been a radio at Riwoche I should not be here now," I said.

On my way back to my quarters a woman came up and gave me a basket of food. She had just taken tea and cakes to Khenchi Dawala, and had brought this for me. It was the mother of the baby that had been scalded after the earthquake. I offered her money, but she refused.

I saw Khenchi Dawala for a few moments the next day.

"Tell the world we fought," he whispered fiercely, "and that we'll fight again."

I wondered if I would ever have the chance to tell the world anything, although I did not think they were going to shoot me now. I had to admit that their behaviour so far, to me as well as to the Tibetans, was very correct. The only offensive Chinese I had met so far was the Army medical officer. I saw him several times, as I acted as interpreter when he treated the Tibetan officials.

One day old Khenchung Samdo, the monk head of the Executive Council, reported sick. He had recurrent trouble with his eyes, which I had previously treated, with temporary success, with penicillin ointment. He was reluctant to go to this godless Chinese, and sat miserably telling his beads and saying his prayers.

"Ask him if he's married," said the medical officer.

"But he's a monk."

"Then ask him if he's been with a woman."

"But——"

"Ask him."

I asked him, and the old man nearly dropped his beads in horror and began praying faster than ever.

"What does he say?"

"He says he hasn't."

"Ask him if his parents had V.D."

I asked, and Khenchung Samdo looked blank.

"How would I know?" he said.

I explained the Tibetan attitude to venereal disease to the doctor, who said this was typical of the British policy of keeping subject peoples in ignorance, and jabbed Khenchung Samdo with a needle as if he was sticking a pig. That did not hurt the old man as much as the suggestion that he had broken his oath of celibacy.

Then another Army security officer came to see me, and he was really unpleasant. His name was Hsu, and he had been born in Shanghai.

"Have you been to Shanghai?" he asked. "No? A pity. You should have gone to the racecourse. You could have gone into the enclosure. I couldn't. There was a notice outside: do you know what it said? 'Dogs and Chinese not admitted.' Wasn't that nice?"

His English was poorer than Liu's, but he was much more aggressive.

"You think we're inferior, don't you?" he said. "You British are the lords of the earth. But it's not like that in the New China. It's no good asking your Consul to help you now. Your Foreign Secretary won't send a gunboat. You haven't any more extra-territorial rights. This is our own country now. You have to deal with the Chinese people, and they are strong."

He asked me some questions, going over the same ground as Liu. When he received the same answers he became impatient.

"Lies, all lies," he said. "You will suffer if you go on like this."

Then Liu told me that I was to leave Chamdo the next day.

I went to General Wang for a final interview.

"You have not been very helpful," he said. "You are being sent away for further questioning."

"Am I a prisoner-of-war?" I asked.

"Of course not. There is no war. You are being detained for further investigation of your crimes."

"By what right?"

"By the right of the Chinese people."

"May I know where I am going?"

"To Kantze, in Sikang. What happens to you after that depends on you."

Later I learnt that Dronyer and Wangda were going with me. We were to be under the charge of Hsu.

I said good-bye to the *depöns* before I left. Muja shook hands and thanked me for what I had done for Tibet. Then he gave me the traditional but now ironical Tibetan send-off to anyone beginning a journey:

"Please go peacefully on your way."

12

Journey to the East

WANGDA and Dronyer were waiting at the old barracks, and Tsering was there too.

"I am going with my husband," she told Hsu.

He did not speak Tibetan, so I interpreted this for him.

"Tell her she cannot come," he said. "Tell her we are taking her husband to Kantze."

"I've been to Kantze," she replied irrelevantly. "If he goes there I go too."

Some soldiers' wives had gathered round to listen, and there were murmurs of sympathy. Hsu was furious, but he had his orders not to offend the Tibetan people.

"Ask her if she has a pony," he told me.

"Of course I haven't a pony," she replied. "Nor has my husband, but you've got one for him. You must give me one, too."

There were more murmurs of sympathy, and after a moment's hesitation Hsu stamped off. First round to Tsering.

While we were waiting I walked across to a group of junior Tibetan officials who were sitting on the ground near by. They were being harangued by a Political Committee Member, and a Khamba guide translated his speech. He was evidently giving them a history lesson. "Labour created the world," they were told. The Communists were not wasting any time.

I spotted Tashi and Lobsang in this indoctrination class, looking as bemused as the rest. When they saw me I went to say good-bye, but a soldier with a tommy-gun drove me off. At least we exchanged final looks.

Hsu came back with a pony for Tsering, and then she said she wanted another one for her box. He could hardly control his temper.

"Tell her she can come without her box or stay behind," he said. "We haven't asked her to come."

"My husband hasn't asked to go," she replied. "Why don't you leave him alone? He's done nothing wrong. He's not going alone, and I'm not going without my box."

She had the crowd on her side, but Hsu said there were no more ponies available. At length he agreed to try to hire one at the next stage, and the Indians and I decided Tsering's box could be put on one of our ponies while we took it in turn to walk. As they all had wooden pack-saddles this turned out to be quite a relief.

The wives of Tashi and Lobsang came to see us off, and gave us presents of cake and other foods. They also wanted to give us a tin of cigarettes, but with an effort we refused. While their husbands were learning history they would probably need them to sell for food.

Before we set out Hsu warned us that if we tried to escape we would be shot.

"If we are attacked by bandits you must remain perfectly still," he said. "Your escort will protect you."

Our escort consisted of a hundred armed soldiers. Only a private army would attack such a force, and if it did I was determined to try to join it. Later I found out that Dronyer, Wangda, and Tsering all had the same idea. From what I knew of Tsering she would bring her box too.

Our first halt was at a small village a few miles from Chamdo, where a girl brought us butter from the farm where she lived. She was Do-Tseten's sweetheart, and she told me my former cook was safe. Then she asked if I had Chinese money, and I said I had not. She went back to the farm, and returned with her brother, who gave me twenty Chinese silver dollars in exchange for Tibetan money. He also wanted to give me a saddle for my pony, but they were too poor for me to accept it as a gift, and I could not afford to offer a reasonable price. Later I made some yak-hide stirrups for myself.

Hsu hired an extra pony for Tsering's box, and she thanked him in Chinese, which she spoke fluently. He spoke sharply in the same language, and I gathered he was asking her why she had not used it in speaking to him before.

"Because we are not in China," she replied in Tibetan. It would take more than Communism to conquer her wild Khamba spirit.

We crossed the East River by a cantilever bridge, and rode along the track to Kantze. No European had made this journey since

Teichman in 1918. I had read his account of it, and in different circumstances I would have been thrilled by the chance to travel through this wild and exciting country. I was still determined to enjoy it as much as I could.

We climbed slowly up to the Tamar La (14,000 feet). There were the usual prayer-flags and cairn of stones at the top of the pass.

"The gods have conquered, the devils are defeated!" Tsering was the first to let out the traditional shout, and we all yelled with her to let off steam, adding our stones to the pile.

Hsu, who was some way behind, evidently feared we were being rescued by bandits, and hurried up the pass.

"What was all that noise for?" he asked.

I explained.

"But you aren't a Buddhist," said Hsu accusingly.

"No," I agreed, "but I believe in observing the customs of the country I am in." Tsering's example was making me bold.

But my heart was heavy as I looked back on Chamdo for the last time. It was the best view I had had of the town, and it looked almost picturesque. Then I turned to the east again, and began to walk down the pass, into country more rugged than any I had seen.

We spent the night at the village of Reya, at the foot of the pass, in the kitchen of a private house. We ate Army rations of rice with a few tiny pieces of dried meat, buying fuel and *tsampa* (barley-meal) from the people in the house. We also asked for milk and meat, but they said they had none. When Hsu was out of the room they whispered that they had sent their yaks into the hills to keep them from the Chinese, and milked them up there.

We were still following Peking time, and set off again the next morning at dawn. We climbed over rock to the top of another pass, the Japé La, nearly 16,000 feet high. There was snow on the top, and the wind was fierce and keen. The devils seemed to have got the better of the gods up there. On the way down the valley contracted at one point to a narrow gorge, completely hemmed in by sheer cliffs of rock several hundreds of feet high. I recognized this as the first of several places mentioned by Teichman where the Tibetans had put up a few stone barricades and held up a Chinese Army with only a handful of riflemen.

With Bren guns the pass could have been defended even more strongly, but from Rangsum to Chamdo there had been no one to resist the Communists. With better tactics on the Tibetans' part, and guerrilla forces operating behind their lines, the Chinese could not have reached Chamdo before winter set in.

We went on through this deep gorge country for another week. It was incredibly rugged and desolate, with only a few farms and houses in the valleys between the gaunt mountain ranges. We did not meet any trade caravans, but daily we passed reinforcements moving up with supplies for the Chinese troops in Tibet. At night we usually camped in a tent improvised out of groundsheets, Hsu sharing it with us. We collected some bracken and made a fire, and after our meal we sat round it for warmth. It was now the beginning of November, and bitterly cold. The journey was becoming unpleasant.

But it was harder for the Chinese troops. They were not used to high altitudes, and their clothing gave them less protection than ours, although they had fur-lined overcoats to sleep in at night. We rode, and they had to walk all the way. They had only their army rations, while we supplemented our diet with food bought on the way. Yet they did not seem to grumble, as any non-Communist Army would have done, nor did I see any signs of discontent.

We watched them sitting round their camp-fires in the evenings. Sometimes they held discussion groups. These meetings began with a speech by the Political Committee Member, and then developed into general discussion in which every man was required to take part. Mostly they were about current affairs, but they bore no resemblance to the A.B.C.A. discussion groups held in the British Army in the Second World War. The soldiers did not give their opinions on current events, for there was only one line—the Party line—and that was given by the Political Committee Member in his opening speech. But it was not enough for the soldiers to repeat this in different words. They had to relate it to what they were doing themselves. If, for example, the subject was the Korean War, the soldiers had to do more than just praise the valour of their comrades. They had to identify themselves with the struggle by comparing it with their own part in the fight for world freedom and peace, which was the liberation of Tibet.

These meetings, which Hsu explained to me, usually ended with popular songs. The music was European martial, not Chinese traditional, and the lyrics were about Western war-mongers and moribund capitalism, the glorious Communist Party and the great Chairman Mao Tse-tung. These are literal translations of the actual words they sang. I could not imagine how anyone could sing them without blushing, but I had that lesson to come.

At other times the groups held criticism and self-criticism meetings, which are normal features of everyday life in a Communist society. Each man in turn stood up and criticized himself for all the "errors" he had committed since the last meeting: in the case of soldiers these were mostly lack of zeal and perhaps minor breaches of Army regulations. Having confessed his sins, the self-critic had to analyse his motives in order to relate them to the people's struggle. When he had finished his comrades added their criticisms —not to score off him, but to help him to mend his ways. Some would mention additional errors they had seen him commit; others would point out that his analysis had not gone deep enough, and would bring out the ideological reasons for his shortcomings.

Every man criticized himself and his comrades. Failing to find fault with either would have been a matter for criticism. At the end of the meeting there were the usual songs about the glorious Party and the great Chairman.

We also had our camp-fire life. We told stories, and during the course of the journey I heard a whole treasury of Tibetan folk-tales. They are very ancient, yet none of them has ever appeared in print. Most are unprintable. But I think they have a certain charm, so I shall try to retell one of the less bawdy ones about a legendary character called Uncle Tobden, the hero of Tibet's *Decameron*.

Once upon a time Uncle Tobden dressed himself as a nun and entered a large convent. After some months several of the nuns were found to be pregnant, and the Abbess was greatly worried. She knew they could not have been with any man outside the convent, and, although they refused to say anything, she soon guessed the truth.

But there were a thousand nuns in the convent, and it was not easy to discover a man with a hairless face in a shapeless gown in a community where all the women shaved their heads. The Abbess therefore decided to hold a sports day, and ordered all the nuns to enter for the long jump.

Now in Tibet long-jumpers always run slightly uphill and then take off from the end of a ramp. As they sail through the air their robes billow up, and nuns do not wear underclothes.

The Abbess put the long jump last in the order of events, and she sat by the ramp herself to act as judge. As the nuns ran up she encouraged them to jump higher and higher, and watched them closely as they passed almost over her head. But she was a little short-sighted, and the light was beginning to fade at the end of the jump, and Uncle Tobden was a very ingenious man. So the Abbess counted a thousand nuns; but the next day there were nine hundred and ninety-nine.

Hsu asked me what we were laughing about, so I repeated the story in English. He listened with a completely straight face.

"Such crimes are inevitable in a corrupt reactionary society," he said finally. "All priests of the bourgeois Churches indulge in immoral practices of this kind. Whereabouts in Tibet is Uncle Tobden now?" he asked alertly.

"He does not exist. He never did," I said sadly. "It is only a tale."

Hsu made an exclamation of disgust.

"It is a pity you are wasting your time on immoral nonsense when you have such serious problems to solve," he said. "Here is something to help you with your studies." He gave me a pamphlet in English entitled *On Democratic Dictatorship*, by Mao Tse-tung.

I had always thought that Communism encouraged free love, and I was surprised to discover a great streak of Puritanism running through this godless faith. I learnt that asceticism and even celibacy were high social virtues, and young persons were encouraged to spend their passions on the Cause instead of wasting their time in making love. Even a mild flirtation was regarded as decadent and bourgeois, and the sexual morality of the People's Liberation Army was astoundingly high.

Hsu himself was fanatically high-principled, and had the zeal of a typical convert.

"I was a reactionary once," he told me. "I fought in the Kuomintang Army against the Japanese. After the War I went to Nanking University, and I was there when the town was liberated. Then I saw the error of my ways, and went over to the people. But I still had reactionary ways of thought, although I did not realize it at first, and I failed to disclose that I had been in the Kuomintang Army. As I progressed I saw that this also was an error, and I made a clean breast of it. The people did not hold it against me, but helped me to clear up my problem completely. The people can help you in the same way."

"But I am one of the people myself," I said.

"Of course you are not! By your crimes you have forfeited your status of people, and that is why we are detaining you now. You are not fit to be let loose on society until you have solved your problems."

"I have not committed any crimes."

"You say that out of a mistaken loyalty to your masters and your friends. Your masters do not care about you, and those whom you consider your friends are really your enemies. You must turn your back on them if you want to join the people. When I became progressive," he went on, "I wrote to my father in Shanghai, and asked him to support the Party and give up his lands. But he was stubborn and selfish, and so I have not written to him again. I never shall unless he reforms."

All the countryside was frozen hard now, and for water we had to melt snow or crack the ice over streams. It was bitterly cold at night, and washing was painful except when we came upon the hot springs that are common in this part of Tibet.

We came down to a plain, and there was a man lying behind an earthwork as if taking aim at us—but his rifle had gone, and he was no longer a man but a corpse, a frozen corpse. There were about a dozen of them, all round the plain where Khatang Depön had left his boots, teeth, charm-box, and wife. None of these relics was visible now. There were only the corpses, terribly lifelike, and about twenty graves of Chinese soldiers that showed that the Tibetans had fought. I could imagine the night battle, with all the women and children encamped on the plain, for when the troops had retreated from Rangsum their wives and children had gone with them. I heard that Khatang Depön's wife was safe in a near-by village, and managed to send her a message saying that her husband was alive and well in Chamdo.

The next afternoon we reached Rangsum. The barracks were occupied by some Chinese troops and a few Khambas, and we slept in a hut that was infested with starving dogs and rats. We were getting breakfast next morning when a Chinese soldier looked in and said, "Are you all right?"

"Yes, thanks," I said without thinking—and then suddenly realized we had been talking English.

I went after the soldier, who turned out to be a woman, and met her husband, who looked like another ordinary soldier. The People's Liberation Army still had no badges of rank, although colonels and above could be distinguished by the fact that they wore serge. There was one of these standing beside this man.

"I suppose you're Ford," the man said. "I'm Professor Li An-che." He held out his hand. "I went to London last year at the invitation of the British Council. I was very hospitably received."

"This is my first visit to China," I said. "So far the hospitality has been disappointing."

"I am sorry to meet you in these circumstances." He made me feel a boor. "I suppose you were only serving your country."

"The point is that I wasn't," I said.

The General Staff officer did not seem to understand English but he was not looking pleased, and the conversation petered out. Later Hsu told me the professor was a famous Tibetan scholar on his way to help the people of Tibet.

The next day we reached Gangto Druga, on the Upper Yangtze. A Khamba survivor of the garrison of fifty told us how the invasion had begun.

"The Chinese crossed the river in coracles above and below the ferry during the night, joined up behind us, and attacked at dawn. They had more men than us, but it was a good fight."

"Where are the rest of the Tibetan troops?"

"Dead, mostly. The others were set free. They are strange people, these Chinese," he added. "I cut off eight of their heads with my sword, and they just let me go."

We were put into small yak-hide coracles—the current was too strong for big ones—and were spun round like tops as we were rowed across. Above the ferry the Chinese were taking food and supplies across on a huge pontoon hauled by rope. Only twenty-five of the escort troops crossed with us, for there was little chance of escaping on the other side.

So I left Tibet and entered the province of Sikang, or Chinese Kham.

We had not been able to buy food for several days, and we were all beginning to suffer from the unvaried diet of rice. Hsu had a small allowance for extra food for his prisoners, and when we met a Khamba with some sheep we asked him to sell one. After much haggling the Khamba reduced his price to twelve dollars, but Hsu said he could not pay more than eight. The Indians and I put up another two dollars, and the Khamba agreed to take ten if he kept the head, skin, feet, and entrails of the sheep.

"All right," said Hsu. "Tell him to kill the sheep."

I could not tell him that. The slaughterers in Tibet were almost an untouchable caste, and no ordinary Buddhist would dream of taking the life of an animal. When I explained this to Hsu he called to some soldiers to slit its throat, and the shepherd averted his eyes and prayed for the happier rebirth of the departing soul.

"Come on, skin it," Hsu told him.

It was probably only a post-mortal reflex action, but when he began to skin it the sheep seemed to come back to life. The Khamba dropped his knife in terror and prayed furiously for his own soul. At last Hsu had to finish the sheep off.

"These Tibetans are very superstitious," he said, forgetting that we were now in China.

Actually we were in the Kingdom of Derge, which the Chinese had always left alone. It was famous for its metal-workers and gold-smiths, and made some use of its mineral wealth. Sometimes we passed a group of Khambas by the side of a stream, hand-pumping up water and letting it run down a series of wooden steps, leaving a deposit of fine gold-dust behind.

Two days after crossing the Upper Yangtze we reached Derge Gönchen, the capital of the Kingdom. It looked bigger and cleaner than Chamdo, and the houses were better built. We were put into a kind of storeroom and kept there for three days. We were allowed to walk in the courtyard, and from there we could see a little of the town.

It looked entirely Tibetan, with a large proportion of monks; but there were also Chinese troops, including many walking wounded cases brought back from the Tibetan front. Slogans in large Chinese characters had been painted on some of the walls of the houses, while prayer-flags still fluttered above. I learnt that Derge Sé's mother was still Queen, and when we bought food we were given change in locally minted silver coins of the Derge Kingdom.

Tsering knew Derge Gönchen, and some of her old friends brought tea and cakes. Most of them handed over their gifts sur-reptitiously. Tsering asked for permission to go to the monastery for a blessing, but Hsu said he could not give her an escort as the monastery was out of bounds to troops.

"Why do I need an escort?" she asked.

"Because you have placed yourself in custody."

We spent most of our time picking lice out of one another's hair and killing them with our fingers. Once we were allowed to go down to the river to wash our clothes. Then we were taken out of this famous Tibetan centre of culture and rode east again. It was still deep gorge country, and we crossed some of the passes in driving snow. We passed the junction of the east-west trade route with the track to Dengko and Jyekundo, went over another pass, and saw a long line of tents and four jeeps. The long pony ride was over.

The Kuomintang Government had begun to build a motor road from Kangting to Jyekundo before the Sino-Japanese War, and this was as far as they had got. The Communists had improved the road and were starting to extend it.

The jeeps were the first wheeled vehicles I had seen for over two years. I was not sorry to get off the pack-saddle and into a ten-ton Russian truck. Tsering had never been in a motor vehicle before, and as soon as it started she was sick. It was snowing when we left, but later it cleared and we had a wonderful view from the back of the snow-covered mountains bathed in moonlight.

We reached Kantze at about eleven. We had to get out of the truck to walk across the suspension bridge over the Yalung river, and then American jeeps drove us through the town. We were put in a room in a two-storied building, and for the first time for three weeks Tsering had the benefit of a screen. Before we went to bed Hsu came in and told us that Chinese "volunteers" had entered the Korean War. This made me virtually an enemy alien.

The next day I was taken before an intelligence officer for further interrogation.

He was young and quite friendly, and began by offering me a cigarette. He asked me how I had been treated on the journey, and I said I had no complaints.

"I expect you were surprised, after the terrible stories you must have heard about Communists," he said. "But now you see that those stories are all false. We do not use brutal methods with prisoners, as your troops do in Korea. We don't want to force things out of you. We want to help you to see your mistakes and admit them freely, and to come over to the side of the people. Now tell me the truth about your activities in Chamdo."

I told him the truth, and he thought I was lying, and we spent hours going over the same ground again: information and contacts, Fox and Mr Richardson, amateur radio, Geda Lama, and all the rest. Day after day it went on, pointless and seemingly endless; but surely in the end they were bound to discover the truth.

Otherwise life in Kantze was not bad. We no longer had to forage and cook, but were given three good meals a day with meat and

The Author wearing Tibetan dress, after being captured by the Communists

One of the radio sets captured in Changtu.

A photograph from *People's China*: "All of them bear the mark: 'U.S. Army.'"

"Jeff" at Radio G5 JF

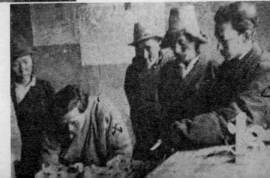

Chamdo Radio Station

On the left: Lobsang.
Second from left: Wangda.
Second from right: Tashi.
On the right: Dronyer.

Tibetan military band

Tibetan troops setting out from Lhasa
By courtesy of Heinrich Harrer

Tibetan soldiers off duty
By courtesy of Heinrich Harrer

vegetables as well as rice. We were allowed to wash our clothes in the courtyard, and we could look down on one of the streets in the town. It was completely Tibetan, but sometimes the prayer-flags were obscured by banners and huge pictures of Mao Tse-tung and Chu Teh when a procession went along.

Tsering asked Hsu if she could go out to do some shopping.

"It would not be safe for you," he said. "The people of Kantze are very angry with all of you. Geda Lama came from the monastery here."

I asked for something to read, and Hsu brought me copies of the magazines *People's China* and the Moscow *New Times*. They were two or three months old, and I read that the people of Tibet were eagerly awaiting liberation from the American and British imperialists. Hsu told me more recent news: the great Bernard Shaw had died, and Chinese volunteers were throwing the imperialist aggressors out of North Korea. He gave me no news of Tibet, so I knew the fight was still on.

One day a Chinese soldier came to me when I was alone and said in halting English:

"I am a Christian. Very sorry about you. Hope you be all right."

Only when I had been through the full course of thought-reform did I realize what the strength of his faith must have been.

Tsering saw an aeroplane for the first time in her life, and called us out into the courtyard to look. It was bringing up supplies for the troops. We watched it make a circuit of the town and then fly towards a plain on the other side of the river. It dropped rice, packed in yak-loads with double skins, without parachutes.

After we had been in Kantze ten days my interrogator told me we were to be taken farther east.

"You have not been helpful to us or to yourself," he said. "You are young and should think of your future. Your loyalty to your masters is misplaced. Surely you realize you will have to tell the truth in the end?"

I thought I detected a note of grudging respect in his voice, as if he admired me for holding out. Clearly I had not sown a seed of doubt in his certainty of my guilt.

The next morning we left Kantze by truck, and I saw the multi-coloured buildings and gilded roofs of the great monastery, the largest in Sikang. Tsering was sick again. The road was icy, and progress was slow. We stopped for the night in a village, now a normal convoy halting-place, and I saw trucks full of troops on their way to Tibet.

We drove on, along a rough-surfaced road with innumerable hair-pin bends. Then we went down what seemed like a precipice into Kangting, the old provincial capital of Sikang. It was already dark, and I saw street-lighting for the first time since I had left Gangtok in 1948.

Now that we had almost reached the eastern limit of Sikang I had my first indication that we were in China, and not just Tibetan territory ruled by the Chinese. I saw Chinese houses, with Chinese lettering on the doorposts, and men carrying pails of water suspended from bamboo poles in the Chinese way. But there were also Tibetans, prayer-wheels and prayer-flags, and there was a monastery on the outskirts of the town. I also saw a cross on top of the Roman Catholic Church.

The town was packed with troops, and we saw them marching in procession with the usual banners and huge portraits of Mao and Chu. They sang and shouted slogans with the enthusiasm and precision of a football supporters' club chanting the letters of its team. Hsu translated them for me—they were beyond Tsering's vocabulary—and I learnt that they were composed of the clichés I was soon to know so well: "Down with the American war-mongers! Long live the peoples' democracies! Increase production and practise economy! Long live our great leader, Mao Tse-tung!" Similar slogans were pasted on the walls of the buildings, with crude cartoons showing a symbolical Chinese soldier preventing Uncle Sam and John Bull from grabbing Korea.

I was allowed to buy soap and cigarettes, and we were well fed before we got into another truck and drove down along the banks of the Tung Ho. Troops were blasting away the hillside in preparation for the building of a traffic bridge. We walked across the old chain-and-plank bridge, sixty feet above the water, into the town of Luting. This was really Chinese, and warm after the mountain air of Kangting. But the next morning we climbed again, up another six thousand feet, to the top of the famous Er Lang Shan pass. It was snowing hard, almost a blizzard, and I missed the view of the 25,000-feet peak of Minya Gonka, said to be one of the most beautiful sights in the world.

The drive down was hair-raising, and Tsering was too scared to be sick. We spent the night at a small village, and the next day we drove through tea plantations to the new provincial capital of Yaan. We had at last left the mountains for good.

Soon after Yaan we came to the frontier between the provinces of Sikang and Szechwan. The boundary was marked by Chinese characters painted on a rock by the side of the road. The next day we began to cross the Szechwan plains, green and fertile lowlands, intensely cultivated and, after the sparsely populated plateau of Tibet, teeming with people.

At Hsin Ching we were taken to an old temple, still full of idols, that was being used as the local Army Headquarters. The aide-de-camp of the Commanding General came to look at me, and told me that British representatives had arrived in Peking to negotiate for the establishment of diplomatic relations with the Chinese People's Government. At least we were not formally at war.

We drove on to Chengtu, the provincial capital of Szechwan and once the capital of China: a large, sprawling town with old temples and palaces, new factories and buses, and an airfield with Dakotas taking off to drop rice at Kantze. This was the beginning of the supply-line to Tibet. We passed open trucks with maps of Korea on the sides and soldiers with megaphones appealing for funds and volunteers.

We stayed the night on the outskirts of the town. The next day we saw men working on the railway that the Nationalists had begun to build. There were thousands of them carrying earth away, without any sign of mechanization to help them.

The following day—December 10, 1950—we entered Chungking.

13

Interrogation

WHEN you want to go to the latrines you must ask one of the guards to take you," said Hsu. "They are necessary for your own protection. The people are very angry with persons like you."

The people did not look angry when we were marched along the road to the public latrines. They did not even look curious. Evidently it was commonplace in Chungking for a man to be marched through the streets with a bayonet pointing at his back.

We had been put on the upper floor of what had once been a private house. Wangda and Tsering were given one room, and Hsu came into another with Dronyer and me. There was no furniture in our room except some long planks on trestles, which served as beds. We were well fed, with meat and vegetables and Chinese steamed bread, and water was brought for washing. The house was thick with guards, but we were allowed to walk freely on the upper floor, and could call on Wangda and Tsering.

We were left alone all the first day, but in the evening Hsu took Dronyer, Wangda, and me to another house, where we were marched into a large room. There were about twenty Army officers sitting at a long table, with the usual huge portraits of Mao and Chu behind. I was given a stool and offered nuts and sweets, and then a cigarette. Dronyer and Wangda were taken to a smaller table, where they were interrogated by two or three junior officers. My chief interrogator was a senior officer, in a serge uniform, who spoke English. The other members of the panel put in questions in Chinese, which were translated by an interpreter.

The first questions were almost social courtesies. Had I been treated properly on the journey? Was I getting enough to eat? What did I think of my quarters? Had I any complaints? I answered with equal civility, and mentioned the lack of sanitation in the house.

They said they would attend to that. Then they got down to business.

"I must explain to you," said the chief interrogator, "the policy of the People's Government towards criminals. It is a policy of leniency on the one hand; on the other hand, suppression. The choice lies with you. If you confess your crimes freely we shall try to help you to make yourself fit to re-enter society. If you remain stubborn you will be utterly suppressed."

He paused to let this sink in.

"You are not entirely to blame for your offences against the people," he went on, "and we take this into consideration. You are largely a victim of the society in which you were brought up, although you must bear part of the guilt yourself. You can only expiate this if you achieve a correct social outlook and, through re-education, eradicate the basic errors of thought that caused you to commit your crimes. Do you understand?"

"I think," I said, "that there has been a misunderstanding. I am not a criminal. I was employed by the Tibetan Government in a purely technical capacity. I have given a full account of my activities in Tibet, and when you have all the facts you will find that I have told the whole truth."

"We already have the facts," said the chief interrogator without purely technical capacity. I have given a full account of my activities have been. You have not told the truth. You have told a tissue of lies. Fortunately we are patient even with persons like you, and now you have another chance."

Mostly the questions were the same as before, and I gave the same answers. I had not been sent to Tibet by the British Government. I had not collected or transmitted military or political intelligence. I was not a secret agent or spy.

"What did you think of the liberation of Tibet?"

"I thought the Tibetans did not want to be liberated."

"Did you advise them to resist?"

"They did not ask my advice."

"Answer yes or no."

"No."

"Did you help them to resist?"

"I continued my technical duties as a Tibetan Government official."

There was no pause between the questions, but the use of an interpreter reduced the speed of the bombardment. Notes were taken all the time. They did not ask me about Geda Lama, so I thought that probably they had already discovered the facts about his death.

The interrogation lasted about two and a half hours. The last question I was asked was my opinion of the war in Korea.

"I have not been in Korea," I said carefully, "but I believe there are two versions. The Communist Powers say that South Korea attacked North Korea. The Western Powers say that North Korea attacked South Korea."

"Which do you believe?"

"I believe the West."

It was not just bravado, certainly not heroics; nor an abstract love of truth. They knew what I thought, and I wanted to convince them that I was being truthful.

I was not surprised that they still suspected me of espionage. I thought that by now the Chinese in Chamdo would have learnt that most of their suspicions were unfounded, but their reports could not have reached Chungking yet. They were unlikely to send dossiers by radio, and written dispatches would take as long to travel as we had.

Nor was I so naïve as to think that once my innocence was established I would be set free. I was at least a useful political pawn, and my capture was the best they could produce in evidence to support their claim that they were liberating Tibet from American and British imperialism. No doubt they had already told the world that they had captured a British spy, and they were unlikely to let me loose to deny the charge merely because it was unfounded. But I thought that even Communists might be more lenient to the innocent than to the guilty.

And so far they had treated me better than I had expected. They could have shot me out of hand, or tortured me until I signed a false confession. Instead they seemed to be genuinely seeking the truth. I thought they were bound to find it before long, and that would not do me any harm even if it might not do me much good.

I still did not know much about Communists.

The next day I compared notes with Wangda and Dronyer. They had been asked similar questions about radio contacts, and had been questioned closely about their recruitment for Tibetan Government service by Fox. Then they had been asked about military installations in northern India.

"Also they asked us where the police in Darjeeling kept their arms," said Wangda.

"What did you tell them?"

"The truth—that in India the police do not need to be armed."

We had not yet forgotten how to laugh.

We were taken back to the big room again that evening, and this time the interrogators included some men in the blue uniform of the Security Police. Their questions covered the same ground, and I gave the same answers.

"You still do not seem to understand the gravity of your problem," the chief interrogator said at the end. "Our patience is not inexhaustible."

The next morning Hsu and another officer brought a map of northern India and asked us to point out airfields and military installations. We feigned ignorance, and they seemed to believe our lies. I wished they were as credulous when I told them the truth.

After three more days, without any interrogation, Hsu told me that as a result of my complaint we were moving to another building with proper sanitation. This was a disused hospital, now occupied mainly by troops. All four of us were put together in an upstairs room about twenty feet square with plank beds and a table and bench. This time Hsu did not come in with us. He occupied another room with three other interrogators who had been assigned to our case.

The senior interrogator was a hard-faced man of about thirty-five named Yang, who obviously enjoyed his work. He did not speak English, and Hsu interpreted when he called us in for an interview.

"If you continue to be stubborn you are going to suffer," he told me. "The people will not tolerate your lies much longer. You have been given the choice—leniency if you confess, otherwise unmitigated suppression!" My heart fell, for I could see that this man was a sadist.

But after the first interrogations, which were very unpleasant, he handed us over to his juniors. Hsu and a man named Li took the Indians, while a mild, neatly dressed man named Chen took charge of me. He spoke perfect English and had been a colonel in the Kuomintang Army before he saw the light. He was smooth.

"You have nothing to worry about," he said. "You are in good hands here. You have only to tell the truth and realize your mistakes, and you can become a new man—as I have done myself. Like you, I was brought up in a bourgeois society and committed many crimes against the people. Now I have cleared up my problem and begun a new life, and I want to help you do the same. You mustn't think of us as your enemies—we want to win you over." He paused. "But first I must know how you got into this terrible condition. Write out the story of your life from the age of eight."

At least it was something to do, and I amused myself writing at length of my experiences in the village school at Rolleston-on-Dove and other matters that I thought could not possibly help my captors. Here I was wrong. This was the first preparation for thought reform.

Chen went over my autobiography, asking questions and making notes. At last he came to 1945.

"Why do you think you were chosen to go to the British Mission?" he asked.

"I was not chosen," I said. "The job was going, and I volunteered."

There had been three of us in the orderly room at No. 3 Radio School, R.A.F., when the Chief Instructor waved a signal-form like a Cup Final ticket and asked which of us wanted to go to Tibet. I had jumped in before the other two had a chance to make up their minds.

"Why did you volunteer?" asked Chen.

I had applied for a posting because I was tired of the job of instructing and of the dull routine of a base station. I had asked for an operational unit, but Tibet sounded exciting. I vaguely recalled reading about yak-dung fires and icy mountains, the Roof of the World, the God-King called the Dalai Lama, and Lhasa the capital, the Forbidden City that no foreigner was allowed to enter. It appealed to my spirit of adventure.

I had always sought excitement. I nearly blew myself up with a home-made motor-bike when I was a boy. I had always wanted to travel, and I joined the R.A.F. to see the world. A safe white-collar job seemed the fate of most grammar-school boys in 1939, but I hated the idea of spending the rest of my life in a bank or office in Burton-on-Trent. I was an easy victim for the recruiting posters, and I enlisted as an apprentice when I left school at the age of sixteen. A week later the War broke out.

I was posted to India in 1943, and disillusionment soon began. Like all Service units abroad, the Radio School was a self-contained British island, with a Sergeants' Mess like an English pub and everything laid on to make us feel at home. Even in Secunderabad, the nearest town, with its out-of-bounds notices and patrolling Service Police, I felt it was the world that was seeing me, not I seeing the world. The uniform was the insulator—and this job in Lhasa carried a temporary release from the R.A.F.

I tried to explain something of this to Chen, but he did not understand.

"But what was your political reason?" he asked. "Why did you want to join the British Secret Service?"

I was not joining the Secret Service. I went to Lhasa to do a purely technical job.

"But surely you knew that the Mission was the centre of the British spy-ring in Tibet? Why did you think the British were in Tibet at all? Why did they go there in the first place?"

The British went into Tibet partly to open up trade but mainly to protect two thousand miles of the northern frontier of India. These were the purposes of the Younghusband Expedition of 1904.

"Were the British invited to enter Tibet?"

No; they entered by force, and fought their way to Lhasa. They routed the Tibetan Army, and the Dalai Lama fled to Mongolia.

"Was this not imperialist aggression?"

A difficult question, like asking if Drake was a pirate. It would have been now, but imperialism was regarded differently in 1904. And the British did not try to annex the country but supported Tibetan independence. Sixteen years later the same Dalai Lama wrote to the Viceroy of India saying that "the Britons and Tibetans have become one family," and I never met a Tibetan who bore us any resentment or ill-will. Whatever harm we may have done was later effaced from the Tibetan memory by our subsequent conduct.

"Why do you think the British Mission went to Lhasa in 1936?" asked Chen.

Because China had sent a Mission in 1934 and was trying to bring Tibet back under Chinese control.

"Why did it take a radio station?"

Because there was a radio station in the Chinese Mission, and the British policy was to counter every Chinese move.

"Did the British have permission to take a radio station?"

No; nor had the Chinese. When the British Mission arrived the Chinese asked the Tibetan Government to confiscate their radio. The Tibetans replied that if they did that they would have to con-fiscate the Chinese radio too.

The Tibetans always played off the Chinese and British against each other. It was their obvious policy if they were to keep their independence, and that was their only aim. They had the misfortune to be sandwiched between two Powers that regarded each other with mistrust and fear. China's Tibetan policy was governed by similar motives to Britain's: she wanted to keep her trade monopoly; and especially she wanted to secure her south-west frontier from British imperialism, of which she already had bitter experience. The difference was that China wanted control over Tibet, while Britain sought only an autonomous buffer-state. Britain could thus champion Tibetan independence; but, as Sir Charles Bell pointed out, it was difficult to answer the Chinese when they asked why we thought home rule a good thing for Tibet but not for India.

But all this was history now, and British interest in Tibet had ended with the Transfer of Power.

Chen did not think so.

"Power has not been transferred to the Indian people," he said. "Nehru is a running dog of Whitehall and a lackey of Wall Street." It sounded a graphic way of putting it, but he was only repeating clichés. "Your masters are still trying to separate Tibet from the rest of China and to use it as a back-door for further aggression."

Anyone who believed this—and all China seemed to believe it except Mao and a few cronies at the top—was bound to think I was a spy.

The case against me was becoming clearer. For half a century Britain had sought to prevent Chinese domination of Tibet, and since 1936 the centre of political activity had been the Mission in Lhasa. Now, according to the Chinese, the British had sent me to Chamdo in order to extend their influence farther east. The Tibetan radio communications scheme was a purely Anglo-American enterprise. The Americans had provided the equipment, and almost all the staff were from the British Commonwealth, with the two key men—both Britons, and trained in the Mission—at Lhasa and Chamdo. And I had sent two men to Dengko, right on the Chinese border.

The case against me began to look stronger than I had thought.

"Why didn't you return to the R.A.F. when you left Lhasa in 1945?" Chen asked.

"Because there was a vacancy for a radio officer in Gangtok."

"Who gave you your orders while you were there?"

"Mr Hopkinson, the Political Officer."

"Did the Mission at Lhasa come under him, too?"

"Yes."

"Who interviewed the first lot of Indians that applied for service on the Tibetan radio?"

"I tested them in Gangtok to save them the long journey to Lhasa."

"You stayed in Gangtok for nearly two years, in daily communication with Fox. Then you say you applied for service with the Tibetan Government. Did Hopkinson know this?"

"Yes, of course; I told him."

"Before you applied?"

"Naturally I asked his advice."

"And what advice did he give?"

"He thought it was a good thing. He was very fond of the Tibetan people, and wanted them to have all the help they could."

Chen smiled.

"And did you return to Tibet to help the people?"

"It was one of my reasons."

"If you had wanted to help the people," he said, "you would have lived with them and worked with them. But you didn't. You became an official, and had servants running round waiting on you. You were not helping the people—you were sitting on their necks. Now," he went on, "did Hopkinson recommend you to the Tibetan Government?"

"I don't know."

"Do you think he might have done?"

"I suppose it's possible." I knew very well that he had.

"Before returning to Lhasa," continued Chen, "you went back to England. What training in espionage did you receive there?"

"None. I was never trained in espionage—anywhere."

"What Government Departments did you go to?"

"None."

"Then why did you go back?"

"To get my release from the R.A.F."

"How much longer did you have to serve?"

"Six years."

"Then why did the R.A.F. release you?"

That was a difficult question to answer. The true answer was that Mr Hopkinson had recommended them to, both for my sake and to enable me to help a nation with which Britain wanted to remain friendly. I could hardly say this.

"They released me," I said, with perfect accuracy, "on the grounds that my services were no longer required."

"Really," said Chen, "you must think we are very simple. But you spent six months in England. Why did you stay so long?"

"I was waiting for my contract from the Tibetan Government."

"And when you returned to Lhasa Fox was still at the British Mission?"

"It was the Indian Mission by then. Yes, he was still there."

"Why did he go into Tibetan Government service?"

"Because he expected to be replaced by an Indian."

"Who recruited all the Indians for radio work in Tibet?"

"The Tibetan Government advertised for them."

"Who interviewed the applicants?"

"Fox and I."

"Do you still say you were not working for the British Government."

"I was not."

I could not blame him for not believing me. I felt that with every answer to Chen's questions I was knocking another nail into my own coffin. The evidence sounded damning. My only comfort was that there was no evidence that I had carried out any espionage in Chamdo.

But Chen soon disillusioned me about this too.

"Did you take any photographs?"

"Yes, of course."

"What did you do with them?"

"I sent some home."

"To the British Government?"

"No, to my parents."

"You cannot expect us to believe that. When you spoke to Fox on the radio telephone what did you talk about?"

"Oh, nothing in particular."

"You must have said something."

"General things. The weather."

"You gave him meteorological information, then. You know that is of military importance."

"I wasn't giving him information. All Britons talk about the weather."

"What meteorological equipment did you have in Chamdo?"

They were bound to find out that I had maximum and minimum thermometers and a rain-gauge, although they had been destroyed with the radio equipment. Every one in Chamdo had seen them and asked what they were for.

"Do all Britons carry thermometers and rain-gauges?"

"They were obvious things to take to an unknown place like Chamdo. Of course I wanted to get geographical information. For the same reason I went to the Natural History Department of the British Museum while I was in England and learnt how to collect specimens of plants."

Chen came on to what he called my anti-Communist activities in Chamdo. At first I denied spreading anti-Communist progaganda, but he made short work of my defence.

"Did you listen to the news on the radio?" he asked.

"Yes, of course."

"From what stations?"

"All over the world. Peking, Delhi, London, Moscow."

"Did Tibetans ask you what the news was?"

"Sometimes."

"Did you tell them?"

"Yes."

"You told them what you heard from London and Delhi, therefore you were spreading anti-Communist propaganda."

"I also told them what I heard from Peking and Moscow."

"That does not lessen your crime."

Then he came to my amateur radio activities. He asked me what I talked about to my contacts.

"Radio conditions, mostly," I said. "Technical matters."

"More military information. What else?"

"Nothing much. We just exchanged greetings, and told each other where we were."

"Where did you say you were?"

"In Chamdo, of course."

"What else did you say?"

"That's all."

"Did you ever broadcast separatist propaganda?"

"No."

"What did you say about Chamdo?"

This was typical of their indirect methods of questioning. They would never reveal how much they knew themselves, and would go round in circles rather than give away information in a question. This time I could guess what Chen was after, but hedging would only have prolonged the interrogation. I had evidently been monitored when I told American and British contacts that Chamdo was in Tibet.

"I said Chamdo was in Tibet."

"Why did you say that?"

"Because I was asked." I explained about the "Worked All Zones" certificate.

"Where did your contacts think Chamdo was?"

"They weren't sure."

"You are not being frank," Chen reproved me. "You cannot expect us to believe anything you say when we know you are concealing the truth. You must think more about this."

That was a typical ending to a period of interrogation. Chen knew from the monitor's reports what my contacts had said, but everything had to come from me. He came back to this at a later session, and I admitted that they had said they thought Chamdo was in China.

"Why did they think this?"

"Because it was marked in China on some of their atlases."

"On English and American atlases?"

"Yes."

Chen shook his head sorrowfully.

"All Tibet is part of China, and Chamdo is not even in Tibet," he said. "Even your own maps admit that. Surely you see that you were broadcasting separatist propaganda? Your problem is very grave."

I was beginning to think so, too. I could no longer hope to prove my innocence of all the charges that might be made against me. Under their laws it was a crime to spread anti-Communist propaganda, and repeating news-bulletins broadcast by non-Communist countries came under that heading: therefore I was a criminal. According to them Tibet was a part of China, and by saying Chamdo was not in China I had been guilty of propagating separatism, which was another crime under their laws. And even by entering Tibet I had committed a criminal offence, as Hsu pointed out when he took my passport from me.

"You entered China illegally," he said after looking at the visas.

"I did not come here of my own free will," I said thoughtlessly.

"Do you mean your Government sent you by force?"

"My Government did not send me anywhere. The Tibetan Government——"

"Tibet is a part of China, and you had no right to enter the country without a Chinese visa."

That was not even a Communist innovation. The Kuomintang Ambassador in Washington had described the members of the Tibetan Trade Mission as Chinese subjects with false passports and had formally protested against their admission to the United States.

Serious as these matters were, they did not compare with the accusation that I was a British Government spy. I still hoped to convince them that I was not. I realized now that their grounds for suspicion were even stronger than I had thought, but when they had finished their investigations at Chamdo they seemed bound to discover the truth. Meanwhile I had to try to persuade them I was telling the truth and had nothing to hide, and this meant admitting everything about myself that they could find out from other sources. As Chen often reminded me, all the Tibetan officials I had mixed with, except Lhalu and Rimshi Trokao, were now in their hands, and they would soon have stronger evidence of my anti-Communist and separatist propaganda than the dissemination of B.B.C. news-bulletins. I therefore anticipated this by admitting the substance of what I had said about Tibetan independence, Communism, and the possibility of invasion by the Chinese.

Apart from the interrogations our conditions of imprisonment were not too bad. We were given facilities for washing our clothes, a daily cigarette issue, and relatively good food. On Christmas Day we were given duck for dinner. Our normal rations were better than Hsu's, as he continually reminded us.

In the field the Communist Army had a single ration scale for all ranks, but in base areas there were three different scales. The first was for colonels and above, the officers who wore serge; the second was for all other officers down to the rank of captain; the third was for all other ranks. Yang, Chen, and Li were all on the second scale, but Hsü was graded only a subaltern and had to mess with the troops. The Indians and I were given second-scale rations because we were used to more protein and had suffered on the journey from a surfeit of rice.

Hsu was an unpleasant man with a chip on his shoulder. On the journey he had sometimes been almost human, but now he was invariably harsh and bitter. Apparently he had suffered some humiliation from the British in Shanghai, and he was getting his revenge on me. He was malicious.

Yang was worse. Sometimes he interrogated me himself, and there was no mistaking his pleasure in causing pain. It was always mental pain—there was never any physical violence—but it was calculated and refined.

I saw little of Li, the fourth interrogator, although sometimes he paid me what were almost social visits. He talked about English literature, and said how sorry he was about the death of Shaw. He asked me who the coming authors in England were, and I said I liked Nevil Shute. "Is he progressive?" he asked. I said I thought he was. "Have you read Howard Fast?" I said I had not, but would like to read any books he could let me have. He said he would see what he could do.

Instead of books I received copies of the magazines *People's China* and *Soviet Union*. I looked for news of Tibet, and learnt that the Chinese had reached Lho Dzong; at least it had been admitted that the war was on. There was nothing about Chamdo, but some pieces of the magazines had been cut out. I found the magazines dreary reading, but Li explained that they were not meant to be read for fun. "They aren't like your pornographic film-star magazines," he said, "but are food for the mind. Study them carefully, and they will help you to solve your own problem." Re-education had begun. It was carried a step further by a visiting officer who gave us a lecture on the Korean War.

Dronyer and Wangda were undergoing similar interrogations to me. When we were alone we compared notes, but we did not have to try to concoct stories or even to agree on what not to reveal. They did not know the pieces of information I had to withhold in order not to compromise others or help the Chinese in the invasion. They were in good spirits, but Tsering was beginning to pine.

We had all been searched, and I had had to surrender my money and valuables, which included a watch and a ring. Tsering was searched by a woman soldier in a separate room, and was deprived of her earrings and other jewellery including her charm-box, which the Chinese thought was only an ornament. This upset her, and she protested that she was not a prisoner but had come to Chungking of her own free will to be with her husband. She was told she had placed herself in custody.

In January we were separated. I was put in a separate room and forbidden to communicate with the others. My period of loneliness had begun.

At first it was not too bad. Chen often had his meals with me, and

Review of Communist troops after the occupation of Lhasa

The Communist army moves into Eastern Tibet

The Tibetans are introduced to political processions

First attempts at political indoctrination: Tibetan nomads listen to Communis

sometimes we had almost normal conversations. He told me his experiences in India during the War, when he had been liaison officer for Allied troops going into Burma. In different circumstances I might have come to like him, for he was certainly the most human of the four interrogators.

He was a bit too human for his own good. One day he shut up like a clam, and for nearly a week we ate our meals in silence. Later I learnt that he had had a bad time at the interrogators' criticism and self-criticism meeting, when he had been accused of fraternizing with an imperialist agent. This was a serious matter for Chen, as his own conversion was comparatively recent. His accuser was Hsu, who had come over to the people before Chen and resented being junior to him. He also resented seeing Chen and me eating second-scale rations together.

My dossier was still growing. I had had to go through the whole business of amateur radio again, and sometimes Chen was irritating.

"Who was your main contact in England?" he asked.

"A man named Jefferies."

"What Department is he in?"

"He's not in any Department."

"Then what is his job?"

"He's a tailor."

"A tailor?" Chen made an exclamation of impatience. "Why should an English tailor waste his time talking by radio with a man in China?"

Then he wanted to know which Government Departments I visited to get my passport, and was incredulous when I said I simply got it through the local Labour Exchange. If a Chinese wanted to go abroad he had to go to a dozen or so different Government offices to get his passport and all the other documents, and Chen could not believe we did not have to do the same.

Sometimes I had to write essays on set subjects, such as my relations with Mr Hopkinson or Fox. Once he told me to write about my connexion with Mr Richardson.

"I hardly ever saw him," I said. "And all we talked about was Mr Richardson's garden at the Mission."

"But you and Richardson were the only two Britons in Lhasa for several months. Don't you think it's odd that you didn't see more of each other?"

It was odd. In fact I had deliberately stayed away from the Mission because I did not want to arouse the suspicions of the

M

Chinese (Kuomintang) officials in Lhasa. They also suspected that the hidden influence of Whitehall was behind my going to Chamdo.

Chen also questioned me about my correspondence with Bull and Derge Sé. I admitted that in my letters to Derge Sé I had sent a summary of the news I had heard on the radio, and that was interpreted as spreading more anti-Communist propaganda and trying to corrupt a Tibetan official.

Then the subject of Geda Lama reappeared. Chen told me to write down all I knew about him, and then questioned me about Geda's visit to the radio station and his illness and death. I had thought this matter had already been settled, at least as far as I was concerned. I was beginning to be disturbed by the absence of any sign that the results of the investigations in Chamdo had been received.

"I am only telling you the truth," I said. "You will realize this when you get your reports from Chamdo."

"You are talking nonsense," said Chen. "We have already received full accounts of the investigations into your case from Chamdo. That is why we know you are telling lies."

I hoped he was bluffing. Then it did not seem to matter if he was. For a few days later I had my biggest alarm since I heard the rifle-bolt behind me when I was sitting outside the monastery just after being captured.

It was in the second December (1950) issue of the fortnightly *People's China*. This is what I read:

> Full investigations are being made into the espionage activities of the Englishman R.W. Ford, who was arrested during the battle for Changtu [Chamdo] and is being held for, among other charges, causing the death by poison of the Living Buddha Geda.

14

Fear

I FELT as if I had just read my sentence of death.

This was the end. There was no hope now. They were bound to kill me.

From the beginning I had feared that they might shoot me as a spy, but there had always been reason for hope. There are degrees of espionage, and even in Communist countries not all convicted spies are shot. Also I thought that the fact that I was not a spy might count in my favour.

But this was murder.

The fact that I had not killed Geda was irrelevant. They had told the world I had. And I knew that once the Communists had published a charge they would never withdraw it. Chen had virtually admitted this. "We do not make accusations unless we know they are true," he said.

I had known from the start that they suspected I might have had something to do with Geda's death, and that was reasonable enough. If the positions had been reversed, and a British peace emissary had been murdered in a house where a Communist was living, we should at least have wondered if it was just a coincidence. If we had thought the Communist was a spy we should have been highly suspicious. I had expected them to suspect me and to investigate the matter closely. I had not expected they would decide the case in advance.

When they had finished their inquiries they were bound to discover that I had nothing to do with Geda's death. Probably they had found out already. This magazine was published two months after my capture, and they should have learnt the truth by then. Presumably they had published the charges at the beginning, and they were bound to stick to them now.

The espionage charge seemed trivial by comparison. It no longer mattered whether I was convicted of spying when I had already been virtually pronounced guilty of a much worse crime—the most horrible crime of all. I was bound to be executed. Even in my own country the only statutory punishment for murder was hanging, and I thought we were more civilized in penal matters than Communist China.

I read the sentence again. It was followed by a brief obituary of Geda Lama that made the charge look worse than ever:

> Geda was a prominent Tibetan leader who helped the Chinese Red Army during the Long March in 1935. He supported the P.L.A. when Kangting was liberated early this year. He was poisoned while on his way to Lhasa to arrange for the peaceful unification of Tibet with the Motherland.

So I was not only branded as the murderer of an incarnate lama— I was made responsible for the war, too! There would have been no fighting if Geda had lived: all the blood that had been shed was on my hands! The enormity of the crime with which I was charged was appalling. They could not do other than kill me for this. I had no reason for the slightest hope.

But hope does not die easily, and it can survive without reasons, or it even makes its own. As I read the paragraph again and again I seized on the wording of the charge. They did not say I had murdered Geda. They said I had caused his death.

Did it make any difference? It only meant I had not necessarily administered the poison with my own hand. That would still make me a murderer under English law: I had no reason to think that constructive murder was regarded more lightly by the Chinese.

Yet I hoped.

Then I wondered whether I had been meant to read this paragraph. Had it been left in deliberately or by mistake? I gathered a prisoner was never told the charges against him until he was taken to court to be sentenced: by withholding the charges and claiming to know everything they drove him to confess to crimes they did not even suspect. But I thought perhaps they had now discovered my innocence and realized that I could not confess until I knew what I was supposed to have done.

I would soon find out. Chen was coming in now.

·   ·   ·   ·

"What have you been thinking about?" he asked.

It was a favourite opening to an interrogation, and I rarely knew what to reply. This time I did.

"This," I said, showing him the paragraph.

Without a word he snatched up the magazine and went out of the room. A few minutes later I heard Yang's voice raised in anger. Then Hsu came in and collected all the other magazines in the room. I heard Li, then Yang again, Chen, Hsu, and finally Yang shouting in anger with the others all quiet. Some one had blundered. I hoped it was Hsu.

Yang called me for interrogation. He began as if nothing had happened.

"I did not kill Geda Lama," I burst out. "I had nothing to do with his death. It's a lie!"

"What is a lie?"

"The piece I read in *People's China*."

"The people do not lie," said Yang. "The people's newspapers are not like your prostituted Press. We print only facts."

"Even the people could make a mistake."

Yang gave me one of his cruel smiles.

"This will not help you," he said. "You know what you did. So do we. All that remains is for you to confess and strive to reform. If you don't"—suddenly he stood up and barked the words out—"you will be suppressed!"

Chen remained smooth. When I did not respond he became eloquent.

"You do not have to despair," he said. "The People's Government is merciful, even to persons like you. No crime is too terrible to be forgiven, provided it is freely confessed. We don't want to have to suppress you. We want to save you! Admit the truth now, before it is too late. Confess your errors, repent, and come over to the welcoming arms of the people!"

"I did not kill Geda Lama," I said flatly. "I am not going to confess to something I have not done."

Chen stared at me in surprise.

"The people do not want to hear false confessions," he said. "Our only interest is in the truth. Now—tell me what happened with Geda."

What was he playing at? What was the purpose of this cat-and-mouse game? I could have understood if they had brought in a written confession and told me to sign, if they had stuck bamboo-shoots under my nails and forced me to sign. Did they think they could make me believe I had killed Geda Lama? Was he trying to mesmerize me?

No, there was no doubt about it. Chen thought I had done it.

Presumably so did Yang. So they hadn't found out yet—or the interrogators had not yet been told. Perhaps they never would be told. Perhaps some one high up had realized he had blundered and was suppressing the truth. What would happen then? Or perhaps—the most horrifying thought of all—they never would discover the truth.

I knew that innocent men had been convicted of murder even in Britain, where a man was presumed innocent until his guilt was proved. If that could happen in my own country, where there were so many safeguards, how much more easily it could happen here! They thought I was guilty, they wanted to find me guilty——

No, it could not happen. They were too thorough. And when they investigated they were bound to find that I could not have murdered Geda, either personally or by getting one of my servants or staff to administer the poison. There was only one way he could have been poisoned, and they were bound to find that out.

But they were not bound to find out who did it. That was going to be very difficult to discover. And they could still think I had persuaded the unknown murderer to commit the act, and even supplied the poison—although if a toxicologist examined my medicine chest he would find nothing there that could be administered in a lethal dose without the victim's knowledge.

Suppose the mystery was still unsolved. They would have found that I could not have poisoned Geda myself, but might still suspect I had plotted the crime. They would not tell the interrogators this, but would hope that under pressure I would disclose evidence against myself that they had not been able to find.

It seemed plausible. It still does.

Hope returned. I still thought they would discover that I was not a British Government spy. If the interrogators reported that I was generally truthful they would have to admit—to themselves, anyway —that there was no reason to believe I had been involved in the murder. Establishing my innocence might not make any difference to my fate, but at least it could do no harm. My immediate task was to persuade Chen that I was telling the truth. And that meant that I would have to tell it. The whole truth. Almost the whole truth, anyway.

·   ·   ·   ·   ·

First I had to cut out two segments of knowledge and try to banish them from my mind. One segment was facts that could compromise others. The other segment was facts that might help the Chinese in the war against Tibet.

They were both quite small segments, and in both cases my captors were very unlikely to discover the facts from other sources. I did not have to be noble; just careful. I could even conceal facts about persons who were still in Lhasa but might later fall into Communist hands. I did not even have to worry about what I knew of the murder of Geda, for I had learnt it all after his death and no one could be sure I knew anything at all.

Having made this decision, I told Chen everything else.

I told him what I had said to the other officials, including even Lhalu and Rimshi Trokao, in case they should fall into Communist hands. I told him what I had said about Communism and the threat of liberation, and of the part I had played in preparing for the defence of Chamdo. I even admitted I had advised Lhalu to put Bren guns on the hills.

I repeated exactly, as far as I could remember, all that I had said in my letters to Derge Sé and Bull. I poured out information, and kept Chen scratching away. I wondered what had happened to Bull. Then I looked out of the window and saw him.

I could not be sure it was Bull, but he was unmistakably a European—the first I had seen since Harrer said "Auf Wiedersehen!" on the outskirts of Lhasa eighteen months before.

I saw him get out of a lorry, wearing an Australian bush hat and a European raincoat. He was brought to the house under guard. A few days later I became sure it was Bull when I saw some washing hanging up that included a pair of Tibetan socks. They had put him on the ground floor, and it was a week later before I saw him face to face.

I was on my way back from the latrine, which was a trench in a hut outside, sheltered by bamboo and banana plants. Bull was coming the other way. My guard saw him and pushed me off the path, but Bull passed near enough for an exchange of winks. "I could see his spirit was unconquered," Bull wrote in his description of the encounter in his book *When Iron Gates Yield*. He would not have thought that a week or so earlier. Or a week later, when Hsu suddenly told me to pick up my things and had me marched down to a closed van. I wondered if this was the end.

I breathed more freely when Wangda and Dronyer were brought in. They had not been accused of killing any lamas, so the journey might not end with a firing squad. Then Hsu and the guards climbed in, and we were told not to speak. From the noise of the traffic I gathered we were being driven through the town.

The van stopped, and I relaxed when I saw that we had been taken to another house. It had three storeys, and I was put on the ground floor. The window was locked and pasted over with rice paper, and I was told not to open the door without first calling the guard.

Soon afterwards I heard another truck arrive, and some one was taken into the room next to mine. There was a grille at the top of the dividing wall, and I stood on the trestle bed to look through. It was Tsering. I heard a noise outside and got down quickly. A guard came in and pasted rice paper over the grille. Then I heard movements in the room above. Someone was pacing up and down in heavy boots. Bull had been wearing boots that could make this noise.

The guard brought me a meal. The food was still good. The sanitation was excellent: I used a water-closet for the first time since I left Calcutta in 1948. The interrogation was worse—much, much worse than anything I had had before.

Chen was off my case now. Yang had taken over, with Hsu as his interpreter and deputy. There was nothing smooth about them.

"The people's patience is nearly exhausted," said Yang. "This is your last chance. Confess now, or you will be"—pause, bark—"suppressed!"

"But I have nothing to confess," I said. "I have told you everything."

"You have told us nothing we did not already know, and only a fraction of what we know about you."

He totted up the score. It sounded formidable to me. I was guilty of entering China illegally; spreading anti-Communist and separatist propaganda; exploiting the Chinese people (by being a Tibetan Government official and having servants); taking photographs of military value and sending them to a country hostile to the People's Republic of China; transmitting meteorological information; assisting a separatist rebellion (by continuing to transmit Government messages during the invasion); and actively engaging in illegal military operations against the Chinese people (advising Lhalu to put Bren guns on the hills). I had admitted all these "crimes," although not in those words.

Yang flicked them aside.

"You have told us nothing about your activities as a British Government spy," he said. "You have not begun to tell the truth about the death of Geda. You will start now. Who were your contacts?"

"I had no contacts. I was not a spy."

"Stop lying. What organization did you work for?"

"I worked for the Tibetan Government."

"What organization did you work for? Who were your contacts? How did Geda die? . . ."

Hour after hour it went on. After a few days more interrogators came and joined in, one or two in serge and some in the blue uniform of the civilian Security Police. They all asked the same questions. The pressure became remorseless. After interrogations I flopped down on my bed and tried to let my mind go blank. It was impossible.

The heavy boots paced ceaselessly overhead. From the next room I heard Tsering crying. I pulled myself together and sang a Tibetan song. Tsering stopped crying and replied in the same way, as if I was a human being after all. Then more interrogations . . .

After two weeks the climax came. I was taken into another room and grilled by about fifteen interrogators for five hours. An officer in serge was nominally in charge, but he was continually prompted by a man dressed like an ordinary soldier. I returned to my room in a state of complete exhaustion.

The next day Hsu came in and urged me to confess. He was almost kind.

"You're playing with your life," he said. "You're testing the law with your body. Confess now, while you have the chance. You will confess in the end, for the guilty always do. You will bow your head in shame before the people—but quickly now, before it is too late."

Yang came in.

"We can't keep you here any longer," he said. "If you don't confess you will be taken away and put in a small dark room. And then——" He left the rest to my imagination.

At about six in the evening I was taken out again. This time I had only one interrogator: the soldier who had prompted the officer in serge the day before. Only now he was dressed in Security blue.

I never learnt his name, so I shall call him Kao. He was the most ruthless man I ever met in my life. He was not sadistic, like Yang, or malicious, like Hsu: he was completely unfeeling. He did not care whether I suffered or not. His only interest was to make me talk.

He did not speak English, and his questions were translated by an elderly officer in a peaked cap who had a horrifying knowledge of English slang. He made the interrogation like the sound-track of a gangster film. "If you don't come clean you'll be snuffed out," he said.

For the first time I was not given a stool or bench, but had to stand throughout the interrogation. It lasted about an hour. Every question was pointed, and I realized I was in the hands of an expert. Kao set one trap after another, and if I had been hiding anything I am sure he would have caught me out.

At last he gave it up.

"I'll give you one more chance," he said. "Tell me something you haven't said before—something to show you're prepared to see reason. It doesn't matter what it is, so long as it's something new."

I racked my brains for something to say. But I had said it all dozens of times.

"About Geda, for instance," Kao prompted. "What can you say about his death?"

"I had nothing to do with it. I——"

"Stop!" Kao banged his first on the table. "Don't you realize your position? You can't appeal to the British Consul for help—we've kicked him out. We can shoot you to-morrow if we like. Your Government can't send a gunboat—those days are over. We can crush you like an insect. Now! What have you got to say?"

I stood silent. I could think of nothing to say that would do me any good.

"All right," said Kao. "You've nothing to tell us. Well, I've something to tell you. Lhalu's here in Chungking. He says you killed Geda. What do you say to that?"

"I didn't——"

Kao shouted an order that was not translated, and I was taken back to my room. With a voice like an executioner Hsu told me to pick up my belongings. The guards took me out to a jeep. I was driven to a military prison and put in a small dark room. I took it for granted that I was in the condemned cell.

15

The Small Dark Room

It was ten feet by four, with an earth floor and a wooden platform that took up the whole space except a square in front of the door. It was under a staircase, and the ceiling sloped from eight feet at the door end to one foot at the other. It was lit by a single low-wattage bulb enclosed in a cage, which was kept burning day and night. The door was made of wooden bars, and through these I could see across the corridor into the cell opposite. The single small window also looked on to the corridor, and I could not tell day from night.

My first meal was rice with a little boiled cabbage. So was my second, and there were only two meals a day. Hsu was on a better ration scale than I was now, but I did not expect to see him again. When the warder jangled his keys and unlocked my door I thought my time had come. As the guard marched me along the corridor I wondered if I would be hanged, shot, or beheaded.

He opened another door, and there was Kao.

"Well," he greeted me, "how do you feel now?"

"What do you want me to say?" I asked.

"Only the truth."

"I've told you the truth."

"So you haven't changed. What do you think will happen to you now?"

"I don't know."

"What did the British do with German spies they caught in the War? What would they do if a Chinese spy went to Wales and did what you have done in Tibet?"

"I am not a spy."

Then the interrogation began again, and the questions were sharper this time. Kao had been through Chen's notes and picked out the weak points in my story, and he was a cleverer interrogator.

Why the R.A.F. released me from my regular engagement, why I spent so long in England, the part played by Mr Hopkinson in my entry into Tibetan Government service, how and why Fox joined me, why I saw so little of Mr Richardson in Lhasa—these were the points that he pounced on; and my answers sounded weaker than ever.

Then he came back to Geda Lama's visit to the radio station.

"Did you give him anything to eat and drink?"

"Only tea and cake."

"Who poured out the tea?"

"My cook, Do-Tseten."

"Why did you say before that your boy Tenné served it, and you gave him biscuits, not cake?"

"I don't remember saying that."

"Think harder, and you will."

I remembered. I had given this version to Liu during my very first interrogations at Chamdo. The questions had seemed trivial then. Usually I gave guests tea and biscuits, and Tenné served. It was only after I learnt that I had been charged with murder, and when I was questioned minutely about every detail of my relations with Geda, that I recalled that on this occasion Do-Tseten had just made a cake, and he had served the tea because Tenné was out on an errand.

I made another mistake about the date Geda had moved into the Summer Palace. I had given Liu the date by the Tibetan calendar and Chen the date by our own, and there was a difference of a day.

"You have made a lot of mistakes," said Kao when I explained. "How many more mistakes are you making in your answers now?"

He was trying to shake me, and he succeeded. The interview lasted about three hours, and I was exhausted when I was taken back to my cell.

The next day I was taken out again.

"Do you know what these are?" Kao asked. He threw a pair of chromium-plated handcuffs on the table. "And these?" A pair of fetters joined them. "Do you know what they're for? Do you know whom they're for? They're for you! And do you know who sent them? They're from your American friends—look, made in the U.S.A. They sent them to be put on young Chinese. They never thought they'd be saved for you. But you don't have to wear them. You don't have to stay here at all. Think it over."

On the way back to my cell I passed a prisoner in fetters, shuffling along the corridor with the chains clanking on the stone floor.

The next day Kao had a tommy-gun.

"You know what this is?" He took off the magazine. "You know what's in there? Yes, bullets. It needs only one—and there's one already up the spout." The interpreter was still the fiendishly colloquial old man in the peaked cap. "It's got your name on it. If you don't spill the beans you've had it. Now tell me about your radio contacts if you want to go on living."

Day after day I was taken before Kao for questioning, threats, and ultimatums. This technique was more effective than it sounds. When a man threatens to kill you, and you know he can, the fact that he has not carried out previous threats is not very reassuring.

And all the time Kao was questioning me remorselessly, probing for a weak spot in my defence.

He said nothing more about Lhalu being in Chungking. That had just been a ruse, and it was one of many. Kao was continually firing unexpected questions at me, trying to catch me off my guard so that I would give away something that I had been holding back.

That was the appalling thing about it all. He seemed still to believe that I was a British Government spy and had killed Geda.

Yet he had Liu's report on me from Chamdo, and Derge Sé's letters; and the rest of my dossier must have arrived too. They would have the results of their interrogations of all the other officials; some of them—including Ngabö—were undoubtedly collaborating with the Chinese. And even if these had not reached Kao —if, perhaps, they had been deliberately withheld from him—he had the results of the interrogations of Dronyer and Wangda, and these alone should have made it clear that I was telling the truth.

Then why did he think I was lying? Why did he go on questioning me in this senseless way?

It could not be that they were seeking an excuse to shoot me, for they needed none. According to what I had already admitted, I was guilty, under their laws, of illegal entry into China, spreading anti-Communist and separatist propaganda, and taking part in an armed insurrection; the last charge alone was certainly a capital offence. If they wanted to add espionage and murder, for propaganda purposes, their only course was to try to make me sign a false confession. But there was no question of that.

"Your hands are stained with the people's blood," Kao said one day. "You have been doing in China what Truman and Attlee are doing in Korea. You're a war criminal, like them."

"All right," I said. "If they're war criminals you can call me one as well." I was near breaking-point. "Is that what you want me to say?"

Kao sighed.

"When will you understand," he asked, "that we don't want you to say anything except the truth?"

"I've told you the truth. Now you're trying to make me confess to something I haven't done."

"This isn't the Spanish Inquisition," said Kao. "We have no use for false confessions."

"You're trying to make me say I was a spy."

"We know you were a spy. We want you to tell us how you spied, where you were trained, how you collected information, what organization you worked for, and who your contacts were. When you tell the truth you will have to prove it is true. Nothing less than that can save you."

Then I could never be saved, not even if I cooked up a story just to please them. If it was hard to prove my innocence it would be even harder to prove my guilt. I never thought such ironies could exist.

Suddenly Kao changed his tactics.

"I can't waste any more time on you," he said at the end of a long and fruitless interrogation. "I shan't send for you again. You can go back to your room and rot."

It was the right place to rot.

The whistle went at dawn, and that was the signal for me to sit on the platform that served as my bed. I had to remain sitting there until the whistle went again at ten o'clock at night.

Sixteen hours of sitting. I was not allowed to stand, or lie, or even lean back. If I rested my head on my pillow I was bellowed at by the guards, who patrolled the corridor with their tommy-guns day and night and passed my cell every few minutes.

Twice a day a bowl of rice with a little inferior cabbage was pushed through an aperture in the door. The only time I was allowed out of my cell was when I went to the noisome latrines. To enjoy this privilege I had to stand at attention, raise my clenched right fist over my head, and shout "*Bao Gao!*" (meaning "I want to report").

If I was lucky water was brought for me to wash in the morning. I had no soap. Again if I was lucky a sanitary bucket was put in my cell. More often than not one was placed outside and I was told to aim through the bars of the door.

The corridor was five feet wide, and I could see into the opposite cell. There were about a dozen prisoners there, all Chinese. One had gone mad and shouted and screamed during the night and made faces at me through the bars.

My own cell was infested with rats.

I had nothing to read, nothing to do but sit and stare at the wall; and think.

I had little hope now.

The best that could have happened was that they had discovered their mistake and called off the investigations as a waste of time. What would they do with me then? They still had enough against me for a capital conviction under their laws. I wondered if I had been wise in telling Chen so much about my activities in Chamdo. Was it foolish to tell him about advising Lhalu to put the Bren guns on the hills?

Of course not. All the other officials in Chamdo had known it was my idea, and some of them were bound to have told the Chinese. If I had kept back things like this I could never have hoped to convince them I was telling the truth.

Then why had I failed?

I went over their questions again, trying to discover what was in their minds. They seemed to have asked me about everything—no, not quite. They had asked hardly anything at all about Sonam Puntso and Sonam Dorje and the radio at Dengko.

Was this a clue? It seemed a strange omission. According to their views this was Britain's farthest east in Tibet, on the very back doorstep of China; and Dengko was the perfect place for collecting military information about the Chinese in Sikang and Chinghai. Yet none of the interrogators had shown any interest in it at all. Why not?

Sonam Puntso and Sonam Dorje had been in Chinese hands for over a year now. They were bound to have been interrogated closely, not only about what they were doing in Dengko, but also what I was doing in Chamdo. Their answers must have gone a long way towards establishing my innocence of espionage. Perhaps they had been withheld from the interrogators in Chungking.

But they had been prisoners for six months before the invasion, so according to this the Chinese ought to have known I was not a spy before I fell into their hands. Was the whole thing a trumped-up affair, then? But that would make nonsense of all the interrogations.

Eventually I concluded—rightly, I think—that at this stage they still had genuine suspicions that I was a British Government spy and that I had played a part in the murder of Geda Lama. They refused to believe that both Fox and I had ceased to have any connexion with what they still called the British Mission, or that Geda's death in the house where I was living was simply a coincidence. The evidence they had collected so far must have pointed to my innocence, but they thought I was still holding something back.

As if to confirm my theory, after I had been rotting for a week the interrogations were resumed.

If I had had anything to hide I think Kao would have got it out of me. He mixed his questions brilliantly, and tied me in knots even when I was telling the truth.

He asked me about everything and about every one I knew. He asked me about the officials I knew in Lhasa; about Harrer and Aufschnaiter, although he never suggested they were in the British spy-ring; about Lhalu, Rimshi Trokao, Tharchi Tsendron, Pangda Rapga, and every one else I knew in Chamdo. But he never asked the questions that would have put me in danger of compromising them. I did not have to worry about that even when he asked me about my conversations with Lhalu; for I had been his evil genius, not he mine.

"What were your relations with Muja?" he asked.

"I hardly knew him."

"What did you talk about with him and the other *depöns* when you were in custody in Chamdo?"

Yes, they were clever. They had left us alone deliberately, so that they could question each of us separately afterwards and compare our replies. This simple trick was a standard part of their technique. They had done the same with me and Dronyer and Wangda and Tsering, both on the journey through Sikang and during the first weeks of our capivity in Chungking. If there had been a conspiracy among us it could hardly have survived this.

Kao darted here and there, sometimes repeating an old question to try to make me contradict myself, then asking something quite irrelevant to make me relax my guard. But always it came back to Fox, contacts, information, and the death of Geda Lama.

The two segments of knowledge I had cut out from my mind at
the start remained intact, although they were not quite so easy to
exclude from my answers as I had expected. Kao came nearer than
anyone to asking the key questions about Geda Lama, and the fact
that no one shared my knowledge no longer guaranteed my silence.
I could, of course, have volunteered information to enable them to
solve the mystery and so clear me; but I cannot claim any credit
for not doing that. It would have shown them that I had been withholding information, and make them press all the harder for more;
and even if the Geda case was cleared up I should still have the
charge of espionage. I would not like to say what I would have done
if I had been offered my freedom in exchange for this information,
which would probably have cost another man his life. But the
question never arose, for it did not occur to any of the interrogators
that I might know the facts about Geda's death and yet not be
implicated myself.

Kao was cleverer than Yang at causing me mental anguish,
although I do not think he derived any pleasure from it. He hurt
and humiliated me for purely objective reasons. He played on all my
emotions in turn.

"Why are you so loyal to your Wall Street masters?" he asked,
trying to sting me. "You were just a lackey and you're no more use
to them now—they don't care two hoots what happens to you." It
was the old man with the peaked cap who was putting it into his
fiendish slang.

"How old are you?" Kao asked another time. "So young—such
a waste of a life. Where did you live in England—in a small village?
Did you like to walk in the country? Did you enjoy hearing the
birds singing, seeing the sky? Do you remember what the sky looks
like? And aren't you an only child? What do you think your parents
feel now? Do you want to see them again? You never will if you
go on like this. Never!"

Then he tried to shame me.

"Look at what you did in Tibet, lording it over the people. You
weren't brought up to be a parasite: you're a traitor to your own
class. Your own father would spit in your face!"

And always he played on my fear, especially my fear of being
shot.

Sometimes he interrogated me in a different room. It sounds a
little thing, but even the slightest change in prison routine aroused
alarm. The guard led me along the corridor—and then turned right

N

instead of left. Or he took me across a courtyard towards the sort of wall a firing squad might use. Once I was taken outside the prison and made to walk towards a wood. I cannot describe the fear I felt.

And he sent for me at different times. When I was called out of my cell I was never told it was for an interrogation, but at first there seemed to be more or less regular hours. Then I was called out late at night, another time at dawn . . .

Sometimes I was left for several days, alone with my thoughts. And they began to frighten me, too.

The first darts of Communism were pricking my skin.

It is impossible to explain in so many words how anyone, already opposed to Communism, can become less so instead of more so when he is suffering agonies in a Communist gaol. Of course I hated them; but one gets used to everything, including hate.

I tried to explain earlier why I went to Tibet, and why I stayed in Chamdo. My reasons were mixed: some selfish, and some, I thought, mildly altruistic. I had been infected by the enthusiasm of men like Sir Basil Gould and Mr Hopkinson to help the Tibetans.

I said so when I was interrogated on the subject, and they tore my reasons to shreds. I was deceiving myself: I had gone because the money was good and I could live as one of the ruling class. What was my future in the R.A.F.? How many servants had I at home? I had been sitting on the necks of the people, exploiting them for my own selfish benefit.

I had been asked about the radio equipment, and had admitted that I had sold my own portables at a profit. Where did I think the money came from? From the Tibetan people—the poor peasants who were already paying taxes to keep me in luxury. I could never have done this at home. I was taking advantage of their ignorance, selling my scanty knowledge at an exorbitant price.

I think that was the first Red dart that got under my skin. From that I was led to the exploitation of the working class in general, to the evils of capitalism and imperialism; and why had Younghusband gone into Tibet?

I had never been a diehard imperialist. As a boy I had acquired most of the contemporary nationalist prejudices, but in India I had got rid of most of my feeling of superiority for having a white skin. In Sikkim I had seen how much the people had benefited under British rule, but I applauded the Transfer of Power. I knew that many mistakes had been made in British imperialist history, but I thought that on balance we had done more good than harm. I thought we could look back without shame, and with some pride, now that it was time to go. So long as we went.

Kao changed some of my ideas.

It must be remembered that I was no longer able to think straight. Mentally I was battered and bewildered, my stable little world had been turned upside down. And I was ignorant. When he asked me what we had done with half a million of the Chinese in Malaya I could only say I had no idea there were so many there. The Opium Wars were only a vague memory. On economics I was in the infants' class.

I was fair game.

I had Kao for a month. Then he said he had finished with me.

"You've cooked your goose now," was the old interpreter's version of his words. "You'll never get out now. You can stay here till you die of old age."

Then Yang and Hsu took over again.

"Well," Yang greeted me unpleasantly, "how do you like it here? There are worse places than this, you know."

They were enjoying themselves—Yang because he liked to see people suffer, Hsu because he liked to humiliate a European. They would have enjoyed themselves more if they could have used physical violence, but at least I was spared this. Throughout the whole of my captivity none of my interrogators or guards ever laid hands on me or struck me a single blow. But in mental violence no punches were pulled, no holds barred.

It was now the spring of 1951, and the great purge of counter-revolutionaries had begun. This was the time when hundreds of so-called enemies of the people were executed before the eyes of fanatical mobs.

"Your turn will come if you go on like this," said Hsu after telling me about it. "Your white skin won't save you now." And every time the warder jangled his keys outside my cell I wondered if my time had come.

When they interrogated me they did not shine bright lights in my eyes, but I always had to stand, sometimes for two or three hours at a time. If I relaxed and moved my feet apart I was ordered to stand to attention. They did not deprive me of sleep, but sometimes I was questioned until far into the night. I was not starved, but often I was summoned just before the evening meal, when I could smell the rice coming up, so that when I went back it was cold and nauseating.

I thought I would go mad, like the man in the cell opposite, and when I was alone I tried to force my thoughts away from myself. I tried day-dreaming, and imagined I could smell the countryside at home; and that made it worse. I studied the spiders, and watched them catch flies, and thought of Bruce. Try, try again—that was what they were doing: they were the spiders and I was the fly.

I tried playing mental games, remembering dates in history, or multiplying two by two until I reached the ten thousands and then could not remember, and it became ridiculously important that I should. I stared at the wall, although I knew every crack. I imagined I saw a girl's head, a map of Africa, of Tibet—there was the Mekong, and there the Salween—Chamdo, Lhasa, the monastery where we had been captured . . .

Why hadn't I escaped? Why hadn't I tried then, when I had the chance? Or when we were going through Sikang—it would have been easy then. I fell into a purgatory of self-reproach. I blamed myself for staying in Chamdo, for ever coming to Tibet. All this had been inevitable; I should have seen it before.

For brief periods I succeeded in thinking of nothing, making my mind completely blank. Then I began to dream at night. I dreamt I had quarrels with my parents—something that had never happened—and woke up as if out of a nightmare; and every morning when I woke I wondered if this was the day when I would be shot.

Yang and Hsu were going through the papers that had been taken at the radio station—my logs and amateur contacts' confirmation cards.

"What does this mean?" asked Hsu. "SRI OM CONDK PR."

"'Sorry, old man, conditions poor.'"

"Nonsense! How do you spell 'sorry'?"

I actually laughed.

"Don't laugh in the face of the people!" shouted Yang.

It was the last time I laughed for four years.

I had to go through the whole story of amateur radio again, explaining about Jefferies being a tailor and early-closing day on Wednesday, and countering their suspicions by pointing to old Popov on the cards. Then they asked me about my medicine chest, and where I had learnt to administer drugs.

"I saw the doctor at the Indian Mission before I left Lhasa."

"Were some of these drugs poisons?"

"Well, technically I suppose they were, but——"

"Either they were or they weren't. So you went to the British Mission and learnt how to administer poisons. Where did the drugs come from?"

"I brought them from India."

"Ah! Did you receive any from anywhere else?"

They knew, of course.

"Bull sent me some bandages and iodine."

"Isn't iodine a poison?"

"You can't poison anyone by putting it in their tea," I said in desperation.

They asked me how I had ill-treated the people of Chamdo, and after they had gone round and round the subject a dozen times I realized they had found out about the yak that had strayed into my vegetable garden.

"Why didn't you confess this before?" they asked when I had told them the story. "How can you expect us to believe you have told us everything when fresh crimes come to light after all this time?"

They kept nagging away, until my life was dominated by a dread of the jangling of the warder's keys. If only the interrogations would stop, if only they would leave me alone, I could go on living in that small dark room. It wasn't bad—really it wasn't bad—I could live there indefinitely if I was left in peace.

For I still wanted to live. If they had given me the choice between painless execution and a life-sentence in that hovel I would have chosen to live. For life is hope, however hopeless it may seem. Even when it is not worth living there is the thought that it may be one day. There is no instinct so strong as the desire to go on living, no agony to match the fear of execution.

I had lost all sense of the passage of time. At first I had tried to keep a check on the date, but now I could not be sure what month it was. I knew it was summer, because the warmth brought me mosquitoes and the stench of the latrines. It made me stink worse, too. Hsu added a fresh humiliation by telling me not to stand so close. Even the guard made me walk a little farther in front. I offended the nostrils of every one except the rats.

They always came out when they smelt the rice, and if I dropped a few grains on the floor they gobbled them up. At night they ran over my legs and sniffed round my rice-bowl until I shooed them away. Then they went into their holes and stared at me, and I stared at them. I wondered what a rat would taste like. I was suffering increasingly from this diet of rice.

The madman in the cell opposite was violent now, and they had him in handcuffs and fetters. One night he ranted and raved and kept every one awake, and in the morning he was dead. I saw them carry him away on a plank with the handcuffs still on. Perhaps that was the only way out.

Three women went past with a little girl. I waited till the guards had passed, and then knelt on my platform so that I could look through the window to where the other prisoners washed. I saw them there, and the little girl saw me and smiled, and said "Good morning"—in English! I whispered the words back, and then got down before the guards came by again.

I had something to look forward to now. Every morning I watched the prisoners go by, and often the little girl turned her head to look into my cell, and sometimes she smiled. It was dangerous for me, but it was worth it. At other times she was talking to her mother, and forgot to look, and then I was depressed. When I had a morning interrogation I worried all the time if I would be back in my cell in time to see her. Then the women and the girl disappeared, and I was alone with the rats again.

It was the middle of June, I discovered later, when Yang and Hsu greeted me jubilantly with the announcement, "Lhasa is ours!"

So it was all over. With a feeling of guilt I realized I had almost ceased to care about the Tibetan war. But at least it had gone on long enough to make my part in it worth while.

"Every one has come over to the people," said Yang. "The Dalai Lama and all the officials. We have all the facts now."

"I hope you have," I said, so spiritedly that they looked surprised. "Now you will find that I have been telling the truth."

Had they got Fox? It was very unlikely. No doubt the Dalai Lama had left the capital while terms were being discussed, and all the Europeans would have gone too. It was impossible for the Chinese to have got round and cut them off. But it was uncertain whether Fox had ever gone back from India.

They were bound to find out now that the British spy-ring was pure fiction if they did not know already. Hope flared up again. The death of Tibet might mean life for me. And then Hsu said I

could have a bath. How auspicious! No doubt he could not stand
the smell any longer. I was given a small piece of soap and taken to
a washplace where there was a small wooden tub, and I stripped and
washed my body for the first time for five months. Then I washed
my stinking Tibetan robe.

A few days later I was called out at seven, and told to bring my
things. I was marched out to a jeep. Fear mingled with joy as I
looked at the sun and the sky, trees and grass, and the river below,
as I felt the breeze on my face and smelt the fresh air, and saw
people working and living like human beings.

The jeep drove off, and I had a bewildered impression of fields
and buildings and people, real people; and then we stopped.

I had been here before. It was the house from which I had come.

16

The Only Way Out

THEY took me to the first floor, to the room above the one I had been in before. They gave me a meal with meat and steamed bread, and soap to wash myself and my clothes. The room seemed wonderfully large. There was a criss-cross of stud-marks on the wooden floor, the impressions of Bull's ceaseless pacings from corner to corner. I trod in his footsteps, and revelled in the freedom of movement. My spirits revived wonderfully, for I felt I had achieved something.

Nothing heroic, of course. I was not the story-book hero who would have died rather than reveal the truth. Just the opposite. Nor could I boast that I had withstood any pressure to make me sign a false confession, for I had been specifically warned not to try anything of the kind. But I had not begged or whined, not compromised anyone else, not reviled the society from which I had come; and now, I thought, they realized I had been telling the truth.

Then Yang came in and told me that this was my last chance.

"You have until Sunday," he said. "That's in four days' time. If you haven't confessed by then you'll wish you were back in the small dark room."

Oh, God, why couldn't they have left me there, with the rats and stench and bad rice? My next meal nearly choked me. This was the worst torture of all.

Hsu came the next day.

"It's useless to hold out any longer," he said. "We've found out everything now—the Indians have told us all about your spying methods and contacts. Fox told them before they left Lhasa."

So they had not got Fox! Or was it a trap? No, that was too subtle for Hsu—if it had been Kao I would not have been sure. This was a slip. Fox would not have to go through this ordeal, which would surely have been lethal in his state of health.

But it was going to end fatally for me: I was sure of it now.

Yang came back on the Friday, and told me this was my last warning.

"You must confess to-day if you want to live," he said.

I made another useless effort to convince him of the truth, but he stamped out as soon as I began. I could not sleep that night. The next morning the good food tasted worse than ever. Condemned men don't eat hearty breakfasts. Then I heard the truck drive up.

I held my breath to listen. People were getting in—then it drove away. I relaxed—tensed again as another truck arrived.

Hsu came in.

"Pick up your things," he said.

I was shivering and sweating with fear as I went down with the guards. Into the truck—and there were Dronyer and Wangda.

Surely we weren't all going to be shot? Surely they wouldn't take them if I was going to be shot alone? Or was it to let them see, to frighten them into confessing?

We drove off. Yang and the guards were with us, so we could not talk. I managed to force a feeble smile, and it was returned. The truck was covered, so we did not know where we were going. The journey seemed to last for ever. Then we were made to alight on a piece of open ground. This was it, then.

We were kept standing for about five minutes. Then Hsu told us to walk towards a new brick building about two hundred yards away. I saw the small barred windows, but it was not until we were inside that I realized properly that I was in another prison.

It was the Prison for Counter-Revolutionaries, and it had only just been finished: indeed, this was opening day. I was simply being transferred, and my move had none of the significance I had read into it. Yang and Hsu had known all along that I was coming here, but had kept me in ignorance to play on my nerves.

We were received by the Governor, who told us how to report.

"Like this?" asked Wangda, raising his clenched fist above his head. So they had already been in prison, too.

Then we were separated, and I was put in solitary confinement again.

It was a larger cell, with two barred windows through which I could see the sky and the tree-covered hills. The walls were of brick, and there were no rats. I was given better food, with meat twice a week, and soap for washing. But I was still alone.

Then I heard footsteps in the cell above.

Hobnailed boots again, the same measured stride—it was the same man, the man I thought was Bull.

I heard him cough. I coughed back. The footsteps stopped for a moment, then went on.

I began to sing. Very softly at first—singing by a prisoner was a serious offence—then, as no one came, a little more loudly, as loudly as I dared, in the hope it could be heard in the cell above. I sang *Onward, Christian Soldiers*, because it seemed appropriate and was bound to be recognized by Bull.

I stopped, listened—and it came back!

We sang other hymns, sometimes separately, sometimes in unison. The man above had a bigger repertoire than I had, so he was probably a missionary. But he could have been an American, and I had to find out. I sang some English folk-songs—*The Lincolnshire Poacher, Love's Old Sweet Song, On Ilkley Moor Ba't 'At*. They were all returned, with some more—yes, it was Bull. I no longer felt quite alone.

It was dangerous to sing, for the door, which was solid instead of barred, was kept open in the day, and patrolling guards continually looked through an aperture in it at night. As in the other prison, the lights were kept on all the time. The routine was the same. So were the interrogations. But at least I had a new interrogator.

His name was Fan, and I learnt later that he was the chief interrogator at the prison. He was nearly as clever as Kao, and used a similarly varied technique. He could be as smooth as Chen and as rough as Yang and Hsu.

First I had to fill up a form of about twelve pages entitled "Registration of Aliens." It was a long series of questions about my personal history from the age of eight. I had answered them all before, and I answered them again. The last part of the form was headed "Thought Reform," and Fan told me to leave this blank.

"You have made no progress, so there is nothing for you to say," he told me. I was back at the beginning.

Then he produced an American magazine.

"Read that," he said.

It was an instalment from Lowell Thomas junior's book *Out of This World*.[1] I read, and was horrified. Fox was described as manager of internal communications, with radio stations at strategic points along the Chinese frontier. "His station in Lhasa is the nerve

[1] Macdonald, 1951.

centre of the whole system," Thomas had written. "The Tibetans must have some one they can trust on confidential government assignments. After all these years they have confidence in London-born Reggie Fox." Then came the really damning piece:

We also watched Reggie put in a call to Bob Ford. Ford, an ex-R.A.F. radio operator, arrived recently. Fox brought him over and stationed him, equipped with a portable radio outfit, at a particularly critical spot in north-eastern Tibet, when the lamas became uneasy about the onward sweep of the Chinese Reds. We talked back and forth with Bob after he had made a report to Reggie on border developments.

"Well?" said Fan. "This was not written by a Communist. It was written by a violently anti-Communist American. Compare it with your lies. You have told us that Fox had nothing to do with your coming to Tibet. You said you entered Tibetan Government service before he did. You said neither of you were in the confidence of the Government: you did not even know the code. You denied that Fox sent you to Chamdo. You denied that you ever gave Fox information about border developments. Well, what have you to say now?"

I could only repeat my denials.

"I expect Thomas assumed that Fox had brought me in because Fox had been in Lhasa so much longer than I had," I said. (It was an understandable error: Harrer made the same mistake in his book *Seven Years in Tibet*.) "Fox did not send me to Chamdo. It is true that I spoke to Thomas after I had sent Fox some coded Government messages, and they could well have been reports on border developments."

"How could Thomas know they were if they were in the Government code?"

"He couldn't. Presumably he guessed."

"Why should he do that?"

"Well," I said, floundering, "Thomas is a journalist, and he wanted a story. Putting it in that way made it sound more dramatic."

"Ah," said Fan, "I know what you mean. We are well aware that American and British journalists have no regard for the truth. But that doesn't explain it. Of course they lie about Korea for propaganda reasons, but Thomas had no reason to invent this story about you and Fox. He was not paid to reveal the depth of British penetration in Tibet—just the reverse."

I could not blame Lowell Thomas, for he did not know I was going to be captured when he wrote his book. It was published before the invasion; and as the Communists doubtless read it at that time, I could not blame them for thinking I was a spy. I could hardly blame Fan if he still held this opinion.

And yet, for the first time since I had been captured, I had the feeling that they might not be quite so sure.

Fan was the chief of the Interrogation Corps at the most important prison for counter-revolutionaries in the whole of South-west China, and it was hardly possible that he had not received reports of the investigations in my case from Tibet. I dare say he still thought I was a spy—it may have been inconceivable to him that I was not—but I think he was beginning to doubt whether I had committed all the offences of which I had been accused.

"You do not seem to realize the great harm you caused by spreading anti-Communist propaganda," he said once. "If you had done nothing else this would have made you responsible for Geda's death."

He did not suggest I might have done nothing else; but his remark was food for thought.

So was his new emphasis on the therapeutic side of my treatment.

"You must not regard us as your enemies," he said. "We want to help you. This is not a prison in the ordinary sense of the word. You must think of it rather as a hospital. You are sick, mentally and socially sick. We are your doctors; the warders are the nurses. We want to cure you of your wrong thinking and help you to see things from the standpoint of the people."

And always he came back to the absence of any alternative.

"This is a new prison," he said. "It will last for many years—longer than you can hope to live. We have plenty of rice. You can stay here until you die, if that's what you want. There is only one way out, and that is by confession and thought reform."

He gave me improving books, like the Stalin authorized *Short History of the Communist Party of the Soviet Union*, which I believe is now out of print. I had to write examination papers on what I had learnt. Then Fan gave me some history lessons, and he was appalled by my genuine ignorance of the history of British imperialism in the Far East. All this led back to my own problems, and when I still protested my innocence Fan changed his manner again.

"If you won't take advantage of the people's leniency you will have to be suppressed!" he snapped. "Go away and think it over. Change your attitude, or you will be sent back to the small dark room—and this time you'll have the handcuffs and fetters on!"

I did not want to go back to the small dark room, with its squalor and the poor food. I was already in a bad shape physically, and was suffering from bad pains in my toes. I did not connect this with my diet but put it down to lack of exercise, and practised running on the spot when no one was watching. But the pains became worse.

Fan left me alone for two weeks. It was now October, and I passed the first anniversary of my capture. I had been in solitary confinement for ten months.

Then three more prisoners were brought into my cell.

Their names were Tan, Huang, and Sun. Tan made a speech. Huang, who spoke English, translated for my benefit.

"We are all criminals," said Tan, "and we must strive to purge ourselves of our errors and return to the people. We must confess our crimes and reform our thoughts through study and labour. We must help one another to become new men."

Huang and Sun agreed, although Sun showed little enthusiasm. Apparently he had not made much progress, although a good deal more than me.

Tan had been appointed cell-leader, and he said we must address one another as *Tsung Hsioh*, meaning fellow-student. He told each of us where to sleep and allotted us cell duties. Huang translated the Prison Rules. Our personal relationships were made clear by Rule No. 18:

> Criminals have the mutual responsibility of watching over each other's actions and of reporting secretly to the Government authorities. Anything of an irregular nature should be immediately reported. Failure to report will lead to involvement in the guilt of the offence.

There was no need for stool-pigeons or telescreens. We were all Big Brothers watching one another.

To begin our studies the backward members of the cell had to be brought up to scratch. Tan got to work on Sun, and Huang started on me.

He had been a high-ranking officer in the Kuomintang Army, and he told me he had committed terrible crimes. From his glib fluency with the slogans and embarrassing self-abasement I thought he had been pretty thoroughly reformed, but he assured me that he still had much progress to make. He was genuinely astonished when I told him I had made no progress at all.

"Haven't you confessed?" he asked.

"I've nothing to confess. I didn't do the things I'm accused of." Huang stared at me.

"How lenient the people are," he said, "to let you begin your studies even before you have confessed. But you mustn't delay any longer. Every one has to confess in the end."

Then I was taken out again for interrogation, this time by a man named Ho. He had a deformed leg and walked with the aid of a crutch, and on his face was an expression of unparalleled fierceness. But his manner was mild.

"Tell me," he said, "how do you propose to get out of here?"

With a sickly feeling of excitement I thought the time had come for me to try a different line.

17

Confession

WHY did I confess to crimes that I had not committed?

Most people who ask me this expect me to say that I was physically tortured into making a false confession. I was not. It would even be inaccurate to say my confession was due to the mental torture I had to bear; for the purpose of that was to draw out what my captors believed to be the truth. This was a contributory factor to the extent that it made my ordeal worse and therefore increased my desire to get out, but that is all.

Other people expect me to say that it was a result of indoctrination: that I was persuaded to believe I had committed the crimes to which I confessed. There is no truth in that, either. It is true that eventually I was seduced part of the way to Communism, but at the time of my confession the degree of contamination was very slight.

I made a false confession simply because I thought it gave me the best chance of getting out: indeed, the only chance.

They told me many lies, made threats and delivered ultimatums never fulfilled; but one thing they said I was sure was true.

"No one is released until he has confessed," said Fan. "No one ever has been, and no one ever will be."

I had no doubt that the British Government was trying to obtain my release, as indeed it was. I was equally sure that the Chinese would not respond to such representations unless it became politically expedient. It was unlikely that it would. Therefore if I was to get out I had to do it under my own steam.

"Confess your crime and live! Hide it and die!" shouted one of the slogans pasted on the walls of the interrogation huts outside the prison where I was sometimes taken.

I had thought of making a false confession before, but the temptation had never been very strong. They had not defined the word 'leniency', but I had assumed rightly, as I learnt later—that it meant a harsher punishment than the comparable sentence under English law. If I had confessed to espionage and murder my sentence could hardly have been less than execution or imprisonment for life. I preferred to let them shoot me or keep me unconfessed. I was not going to offer them my life.

When I tried to persuade them of my innocence I doubtless underrated their ability to reject undesirable facts. To deceive oneself is human, and without self-deception a sincere and intelligent Communist could not keep his faith. He has to deceive himself afresh every time the Party line is changed. The People's Government said I was guilty—so I was. The devout had to believe: it could be doubted only by the cynical men at the top.

Fan was one of the men at the top, and his attitude gave me the first chink of hope. Some of his remarks seemed to suggest that he might be satisfied with a more limited confession than had been demanded before. Then there was the growing emphasis on re-education, and the ending of my solitary confinement. Huang's astonishment when I told him I had not confessed seemed genuine: evidently it was very unusual for a study-group to include a prisoner who had made no progress at all. Finally there was the fact that I had been handed over to Ho, a comparatively junior interrogator; and his opening words increased my hope.

The Chinese had been in Tibet over a year now, and in Lhasa for six months. They must have received all the information about my case they were likely to discover or admit to themselves. They would have found that after all their investigations not one fact had come to light that disproved any of my answers to their questions about my alleged espionage or the death of Geda Lama. I could not hope for anything more than this. I also had to bear in mind that they were unlikely to accept a confession that fell short of the charges against me which they had published to the world.

True to my British upbringing, I wondered if it was possible to reach a compromise.

Any false confession I made would have to satisfy four conditions.

Firstly, it must not compromise anyone else in Communist hands: assuming Fox was safe, and I was sure he was, I did not anticipate any difficulty here. Secondly, it had to be plausible: this was difficult, but not impossible if they would enter into the compromise;

and if they would not it was hopeless. Thirdly, my confession would
have to go far enough to support the published charges. Fourthly, it
would have to fall short of earning a sentence of death or imprisonment for life.

The main difficulty would be to reconcile the third and fourth
conditions; but I thought this was possible if they would co-operate
in the word-twisting, at which they were such artists.

I spent many days and nights thinking all this out, and considering
how far I could profitably go. Finally I had to ask my conscience
whether I should go at all. I left this till last because I did not want
to upset myself over moral problems until I was sure that expediency would throw them up. Now I had to face it. I was contemplat-
ing confessing to crimes that I had not committed merely in order
to save my own skin.

The fact that it was unheroic did not worry me. I never thought
I had the moral fibre of a martyr, and I had become painfully aware
of my instinct of self-preservation in the panicky flight from Chamdo. In any case, I had nothing to be heroic about. By refusing to
confess I could not save anyone's life, protect any secrets, or prevent
the Communists from gaining any sort of advantage anywhere.
There was no compelling positive reason why I should not confess.

Nevertheless—I know this sounds 'pi,' but I cannot express it in
any other way—I hated the idea of lying my way out of trouble.
What made it worse was that I would have to tell lies of a specially
degrading kind. It was not a matter of lying to conceal guilt, which
may be sinful but is not necessarily humiliating; I would have to
tell grovelling lies, accusing myself of fictitious crimes, and abase
myself in the way Huang was doing now. I would not only have to
confess sins that I had not committed; I would also have to pretend
to repent.

These qualms would have vanished if I had been lying for the
benefit of some one, or for some other unselfish purpose; in fact it
was just the reverse. By lying I would be letting the side down—not
just my country, but the whole non-Communist world.

But surely, I thought, I was exaggerating. I was not as important
as that. And what side had I been playing for, anyway? I had not
been a member of any team. I was in a very different position from
a Serviceman captured in Korea. He was linked with all the other
Servicemen in Korea who were carrying on the fight: I had no link
with any organized body at all. I had not been serving my country
in Tibet. I had not been serving the United Nations. I had been a

private individual employed by the Tibetan Government. My only loyalty was to Tibet—and Tibet had gone. It would have been different if the war had still been in progress, but it had ended six months ago.

So there was only the vague ideal of anti-Communism to demand my loyalty, and that was too abstract and nebulous. Had I confessed immediately after capture the Chinese could have used my confession to prove to the world—especially to the uncommitted Asian neutrals—that Tibet really had been liberated from British imperialism; but no one was likely to take much notice of a confession that had taken twelve months to extract.

So I satisfied my conscience, or at least quietened it down. No doubt I rationalized, just as parents may persuade themselves that what is most convenient for themselves happens also to be best for the children, or as a voter may convince himself that, by a happy coincidence, the political party that is most likely to help him personally is also the best for the nation. But I am rationalizing again. The fact is that I subordinated ideals to expediency, and it is still on my conscience to-day.

My mental turmoil lasted for some weeks. I was not going to plunge into a confession recklessly, and during the early interrogations by Ho I continued to give the old answers. But I was watching him warily, waiting for a chance to put out a feeler. At last, after a fresh series of interrogations on the photographs I had taken at Chamdo and the weather reports I had given to Fox, I took the first cautious step forward.

"Wasn't that spying?" asked Ho.

"I suppose," I said haltingly, "according to your way of thinking it was."

"You suppose? Don't you know?"

"All right," I said. "According to your way of thinking it was."

"What do you mean by our way of thinking? What other way is there? The imperialist way? Which do you think is the right way?"

I could not get the words out that time, but in the next interrogation I crossed the border.

Ho was ready for me.

"Were you or were you not a spy?" he asked.

"I was a spy."

"At last! It's taken you over a year to admit that." He was almost jovial. "Now let's have the truth. What organization were you working for?"

"I wasn't actually working for an organization," I said. "I was a free-lance."

"A what?"

I explained the term.

"I spread anti-Communist and separatist propaganda and collected and transmitted information on my own account," I said, reciting a prepared speech. "I did this to further British imperialism in the East. I was not ordered or paid to do it. I was merely acting according to my—er—mistaken loyalty to the West."

Ho was disappointed but not cross.

"You must think more about this," he said. "You are still not being frank. You have made a start at last, but you have a long, long way to go."

I had chosen to begin with this naïve free-lance idea because it gave me an easy line of retreat. I had not told Ho anything new, but merely used different words. I could still continue to deny being a British Government agent if events took an unhealthy turn.

I kept to this story for about a week. Ho was very patient, and at last I thought I could safely take a more decisive step.

I compromised Mr Hopkinson.

I still feel ashamed when I think of it, for no one deserved my gratitude more. I hated besmirching the integrity and honour of one of the kindest and finest men I ever met in my life and, I imagine, one of the best Political Officers this country ever had. But I knew Mr Hopkinson was beyond the reach of the Communists, and once I had committed myself to this course I had no option.

"Mr Hopkinson helped me into Tibetan Government service."

"How did he help you?"

"Through the British Mission in Lhasa."

"What did he do?"

"I don't know the details. He was a very senior officer, so I could not ask him questions." This was a line they always accepted, as it fitted their experience of their own system.

"What did he tell you to do in Tibet?"

"He told me to help the Tibetans."

"What else?"

"He told me to learn all I could about the country."

"And what did he tell you to do with your information? Who were your contacts when you were in Chamdo?"

Now I had to compromise Fox. I had racked my brains for some other story, but there was none. I could not have compromised Jefferies, who was safe in Burton-on-Trent, for I would never have been able to substantiate this. It was difficult enough with Fox.

By now they must have received confirmation, from Ngabö and perhaps even from Lhalu or Rimshi Trokao, that I did not know the Government code. I could not expect them to believe that I had sent Fox information in clear. Therefore I said we had used a simple private code.

This was one of the trickiest parts of my confession. Ho asked me for details about the code and the frequencies I used and my times of transmission; and I had to commit my lies to memory so that I could repeat them accurately during future interrogations. The code was easy—I adopted one of my old schoolboy codes—but with the operating details I was on dangerous ground. Whatever story I gave might well be exposed as false by the Chinese monitoring service. But that chance was inherent in my idea of a compromise with Fan.

Ho wrote it all down, and gradually my story grew. My evasive answers to his questions were given a more definite shape, and soon I had to admit that Mr Hopkinson had not merely helped me to get into Tibetan Government service but had got me the job. But I said I did not know how Fox passed information back to London, and I denied having had direct contact with Mr Richardson.

"He was very senior," I explained. "Fox was senior to me, and I worked entirely under him."

I had a bad time with my conscience while all this was going on. Sometimes I woke at night with the paralysing thought that they might have caught Fox in Lhasa after all. I told myself I had no right to assume they had not. Then I went over everything again, and convinced myself that Fox could not have been caught.

But he could have been.

Next Ho asked me about the Indians, and I was ready for him there. I said they were our ignorant dupes. They had no idea that we were spies, and we simply used them for our own ends.

"Then why did you send two to Dengko?" Ho asked. "How did they send you information from there?"

I was ready for this.

"I did not need direct information from them," I said. "It was enough for me that they transmitted Government messages to Chamdo. I did not know what was in them, but I knew I would hear about it before long. You see," I went on, "nothing was secret in Tibet. If one official told something to another official in confidence it would be all over the town in an hour." This was an exaggeration, but it contained some basic truth; and I was quite sure the Chinese knew it.

I used this to explain how I collected all my information.

"It came of its own accord," I said. "I only had to go to the others officials' houses, or invite them to mine, and listen to their conversation."

This enabled me to avoid compromising any Tibetan officials. Similarly when Ho asked about information from Sikang I did not have to incriminate Bull or Derge Sé.

"They had no radio transmitters, and could only have communicated by sending letters with traders," I said. "They would have been useless to me as contacts. I could learn much more about conditions in Sikang from the traders themselves."

"Which traders gave you this information?"

"Oh, I didn't know their names."

"But you must remember some of them. What did they look like? When did they come? Where did you meet them? What information did they provide?"

It was not so easy to avoid incriminating others; and I was going much further than I had meant in incriminating myself. Often I doubted the wisdom of confessing; sometimes I wished I could unsay it all; always I feared where it would lead. But there was no retreat now. I was slipping willy-nilly down a steep slope, dodging sharp rocks and other dangerous hazards but never able to check my descent, and always haunted by the fear of what lay at the bottom.

And it went on all the time now, not only during interrogations but also in the cell.

Huang was helping me to solve my problem: in plain English, he softened me up for Ho. After each interrogation he asked me what I had said and then suggested how I might carry my answers further the next time. He gave me ideas for developing my confession, and was genuinely helpful in teaching me how to translate ordinary words into the Communist language.

He was also my tutor. Besides Stalin's *Short History* I was given a number of other improving books, including translations of Mao's apostolic works. I had to read these with Huang and discuss them paragraph by paragraph. These study-discussions were not as easy as

they sound. It was no good just saying Stalin and Mao were right—
that would have been an impertinence. Nor was it enough merely to
paraphrase what they wrote. I had to apply their general wisdom to
my own particular problem, showing that I was now seeing my
crimes from the correct ideological standpoint. Here again Huang
was a great help.

Obviously he was a genuine convert, and that frightened me. He
was intelligent and well educated, and had held a high rank in the
Kuomintang Army. He was only in prison because he had failed to
get away to Formosa. He had lost everything in the Civil War
except his life: and I supposed that to keep that, and in the hope of
regaining his freedom, he had, like me, decided that the only
possible course was to confess and "come over to the people." At
first it may have been a calculated decision, like mine; but now he
believed. When I looked at him as he earnestly explained the
beauties of Communism I wondered if I was seeing a mirror of
myself in a few months' time. If it had happened to him might it
not happen to me?

Was it not beginning to happen already?

I had to pretend to believe. I could not just let the words flow over
me, but had to think in order to apply them to my own case. And
I did not know enough about economics or social and political history to be able to see the flaws in these apparently logical arguments.

The brain-washing had begun.

I was lucky it was Huang who spoke English, and not Tan. He
was vile. He nagged away mercilessly at Sun, a weedy-looking man
with spectacles, wretched and neurotic, who had been a junior
officer in the Kuomintang Army. Huang sometimes translated for
me. I gathered that Sun had confessed all the crimes he could think
of, and was pressed so remorselessly by Tan for more that he
invented obviously fictitious ones, for which he got into worse
trouble than ever.

"He will never solve his problem by telling lies," said Huang;
and I felt oppressed by an unbearably complicated feeling of guilt.

Once or twice Tan spoke to me in Tibetan.

Apparently he had been a junior official at the Chinese Mission in
Lhasa. He remembered me, and accused me of lying when I said I
did not remember him.

"You don't want to admit it, because you know I saw you sitting
on the necks of the people," he said. He reminded me of the party
given by the Chinese to celebrate VJ Day, when Tan and I had

apparently drunk each other's health and sworn eternal friendship.
I remembered that party.

I was politically innocent when I went to Lhasa in 1945, and I was
shocked at the mutual distrust and hostility between the British and
Chinese. Since Japan came into the War I had thought of the
Chinese as gallant allies, and I could hardly believe we had been
waging a cold war with them in Lhasa all the time.

Very little provocation was needed for a party to be given in
Tibet, and the VJ Day celebrations lasted over a week. Most of the
parties were lively and gay, but there were sinister undercurrents
when we went to the Chinese Mission. As a new arrival I was asked
many questions, mostly about my radio work at the British Mission;
and nowhere else in Lhasa did I feel such a need to guard my tongue
and not drink too much.

When I returned to Lhasa in 1948 as a Tibetan Government
official the Chinese were even more curious; for the Communists
were not the only ones who suspected I might be secretly working
for the British Government. It was for this reason that I went only
rarely to see Mr Richardson at the Indian Mission.

I gained a little more political maturity when I heard what
Tibetans thought of victory over Japan and the end of the Civil
War in China. They liked the Chinese to be kept occupied. The
Communist victory was the worst thing that could have happened,
but they did not want a total Communist defeat.

"The Chinese will seize Tibet if they can," Sir Charles Bell wrote
before the Civil War. In his conversion to Communism Tan was at
least spared the trouble of having to change his attitude to Tibet.

"Imperialism is the cause of all wars," said Huang.

"Yes," I agreed. "I helped to cause fighting in Tibet by spreading
separatist propaganda in order to further American and British
imperialism."

"You are beginning to make progress," said Huang.

I was also told that I was learning to live a communal life.

We passed resolutions about where to put the sanitary bucket at
night (although there was only one place where it could go) and
how we should share the various cell tasks. In fact Tan decided, but
there was no need for coercion. The way to reform was through
labour as well as study, and a prisoner was unlikely to graduate to
a labour camp until he had shown an enthusiastic desire for the

privilege of emptying the bucket or fetching the rice. In this as in other respects I was at first a bit slow off the mark, to the great annoyance of my fellow-prisoners. The presence of "a backward element" in a cell impeded the progress of the others.

The mere fact that we all had to spy on one another made any spirit of comradeship in adversity impossible, and it was a travesty of communal life. I was glad I could not speak Chinese, for at least I was spared the humiliating criticism and self-criticism meetings that were held in the cell every week. Solitary confinement had been unbearable, but often I wished I could be alone. I had no link with humanity now: I could not even sing with Bull.

He had company in his cell as well. His pacing had stopped, and I could hear voices instead. I never saw him outside the cell. But sometimes I met Wangda and Dronyer going to the latrines, and we exchanged furtive smiles; it was strictly forbidden to talk.

There were women and children in the prison, and even babies in arms. Once I passed a woman who was obviously in a late stage of pregnancy. I looked at her face—it was Tsering! A moment's glance suddenly unwashed my brain, and I hated the swines and their loathsome, smug clichés. Who had been sitting on poor Tsering's neck, or wasn't she one of the people?

I was now going through a difficult stage in my confession. There were two questions I could not answer satisfactorily: what organization I belonged to, and where I had been trained in espionage.

"Every spy belongs to an organization," said Ho.

I could not make one up, for the Chinese knew more about the British Secret Service than I did.

"How were you paid?" asked Ho.

That was easier. I pointed out that I had been getting a good salary from the Tibetan Government, the assumption being that this was really paid by the British Government. I persisted in saying that the only other agents I contacted were Mr Hopkinson and Fox.

The question of my training was even worse. I had returned to England for six months before returning to Lhasa, and the obvious inference was that I had gone for training. Again I could not invent a school for spies, because the supplementary questions would be bound to catch me out. So I simply said I had already trained as a radio technician, and my masters evidently thought that enough.

"You must think more about this," said Ho. "But now tell me the truth about the death of Geda."

18

Squeezing the Toothpaste

I WAS not going to confess to murder.

I knew that they would not accept anything less than a confirmation of the charges they had published against me, and they had accused me of having "caused the death by poison" of Geda Lama.

To my British way of thinking there still seemed to be the possibility of compromise.

By design or accident—I still do not know which—Fan had put the idea in my mind when he said that my propaganda in Chamdo alone would have made me responsible for Geda's death.

That was the line I took with Ho.

I said I had spread anti-Communist propaganda and made the Tibetans hate the Communists. They had hated them so much that they had killed Geda. Therefore I had indirectly caused his death.

Ho did not like it much. He thought that if I would not admit to having actually administered or even provided the poison I ought at least to say I had incited others to kill Geda. I stood out on this. I admitted that my propaganda had been very strong, but I insisted that I never thought of inciting anyone to murder and that I knew nothing about the affair until after Geda was dead.

Ho questioned me about this again and again. Sometimes, when he became threatening, I thought my whole confession had been in vain. But eventually he stopped pressing, and I won this round. I suspect he was acting under orders from Fan.

I won a few other minor battles. My amateur radio activities were accepted as a harmless hobby, although I had to admit I had used this means of communication to broadcast anti-Communist and separatist propaganda to the rest of the world. Ho also accepted my denial that I had trained Tibetan troops or taken any active part in the defence of the country apart from advising Lhalu to put Bren guns on the hills. But I had to admit that I had incited the Tibetans to rebellion.

The confession was taking much longer than I had expected, and I was still sliding down the slope. When I thought Ho must soon run out of questions he told me to rewrite my life-history from the age of eight.

About the middle of November 1951 Tan and Sun were taken out of the cell, and Huang and I were left alone. We studied furiously. I think I might have liked Huang before his conversion, but such bourgeois sentiments were impossible now. There was not even an unspoken bond between us.

There was no duck for my second Christmas dinner in China; and although I was getting special rations because I was a European, I was beginning to suffer from ill-health. The pains in my toes had now spread to my feet, and a day came when I could not move them.

Never having been seriously ill in my life, I was greatly alarmed. I stayed on my bed, and after two days a medical orderly came and gave me an analgesic. By then my feet were terribly tender, and the pains had spread up to my ankles. I could not diagnose the trouble, which was completely outside my experience, and I had frightening thoughts of paralysis, amputation, and even worse. Then the prison medical officer—who was also a prisoner—came and examined me. He reassured me and said it was only a matter of diet. I realized I had beri-beri.

The doctor gave me a couple of vitamin tablets, and my diet was changed from rice to flour made into a kind of spaghetti. I lay in bed for a month, and for a time the weight of the blankets on my feet caused me so much pain that I could not sleep. I carried on my studies with Huang, and Ho came regularly and continued interrogations in the cell. At last I could get up and hobble about. Then I was taken daily to a courtyard in the middle of the prison, where other prisoners exercised. There I saw some Tibetan clothes—Bull's, I was sure—hanging up to dry.

I was allowed to bath and wash my own clothes now, and I was shaved (with hair-clippers) once a month. All such concessions were pointed out as examples of the people's leniency, and I had to be properly grateful whenever I was given a piece of soap or a needle and thread. It may seem curious, but I felt grateful. I had become so used to not showing resentment, and to not seeing it in others, that I had almost ceased to feel it.

From February copies of *People's China* and *New Times* were brought into the cell for study purposes, and I had to discuss each article with Huang. It was dull, turgid stuff, but almost lively compared with the works of Stalin and Mao. There was also some news. I read that in May of the previous year an agreement had been signed in Peking between the Chinese Government and delegates of "the local Government of Tibet." The Tibetan delegation was "sent by the Dalai Lama" and received personally by Mao Tse-tung, and I was interested to see that the leader was Ngabö Shapé, whom I had last seen kowtowing to General Wang. He seemed to have solved his problem pretty fast.

I was not doing badly myself.

Under the guidance of Ho and with the help of Huang I was constantly recalling fresh crimes I had committed against the people. I was being subjected to the technique of *ch'i fa*, which is perhaps best translated as 'thought-seduction.' By suggestion I was stimulated to remember incidents that I would not have thought of otherwise or that I would not have associated with the charges against me. Most of these incidents were of the order of my ill-treatment of the man whose yak had strayed into my vegetable garden. Many similar actions that I had regarded as harmless came to light as crimes when regarded from the standpoint of the people.

My studies were directed to an understanding of this standpoint. In addition to the text-books we sometimes received a Chinese daily newspaper, which Huang translated for me. He showed me how to relate each item of news to my own problem, and helped me to brush up my style. I was continually rewriting my confession, and Huang had a quick eye for reactionary phraseology.

"What do you mean by 'the Government'?" he asked. "Who put the Government there?" So it became "the people's Government"—no, "the People's Government." Similarly "the British" had to be changed to "the British imperialists"—or, better, "the British imperialist war-mongers"—to distinguish them from the peace-loving but inarticulate mass of the British people.

At the same time Huang helped me to remove all the vagueness and ambiguity from my confession. In my first draft I had said that my anti-Communist propaganda was "an indirect cause" of the murder of Geda; then it became "the main cause"; finally it was simply "the cause."

In April I wrote what might be called the definitive version of my confession, and my photograph was taken when I signed it. It was a

typical Communist-extracted confession, so full of self-abasement
and Party jargon that anyone who knew me would have assumed
from the wording that it had been drafted by some one else. Such
assumptions completely misunderstood the Communist technique.
A confession is never 'ghosted' for a prisoner: he has to find the
right words himself.

My confession was provisionally accepted. How far it was
believed, and by whom, I shall never know.

I think Ho believed it, although I doubt if he would have been
satisfied with the part about Geda if he had not received guidance
from above. I think that Fan knew that my espionage confession
was basically false, and that he was a tacit party to the compromise.
He was too clever to have been fooled by my lame explanations to
the question why I did not belong to any organization and had not
received any training during my six months in England; and he was
too thorough to have accepted my story of the way I had transmitted
information to Fox if he had really wanted me to tell only the
truth. He could have had the story checked by the Chinese monitoring service, which would surely have broken it down.

In the Communist religion absolution does not follow confession
immediately, for first the prisoner must do penance: through study
and labour he must strive to become "a new man." During this
period his whole case may be reopened at any time, and I could see
that Huang, who had confessed long ago, was haunted by this fear.
At this time, the spring of 1952, China was in the throes of a
national drive against corruption, waste, and bureaucracy. Many
cases were reopened in the prisons, usually for further investigation
into corruption; and as a former officer of the Kuomintang Army,
Huang was obviously vulnerable. He never told me his personal
feelings, but after reading the paper he became silent and looked
depressed.

Then, in May, he was released.

We had been fellow-students for nine months, and alone together
in that cell for six; yet we parted without a handshake or a smile,
or even a thought. There was no human feeling between us. I suspect that under the varnish he was a fundamentally decent person;
or he had been, until it had eaten into his soul. He had gone over
to the people and was therefore lost to humanity.

Was the same thing going to happen to me?

Tan came back. He would have been a horrid man in any society, and I loathed him. Once he let out that he had written some of the plays I had seen performed at the Chinese Mission in Lhasa during the VJ Day celebrations. Like a fool I said I had enjoyed them, and he rounded on me at once.

"Can't you see that they were soaked in reactionary thought?" he said. "You haven't made much progress."

And at the next interrogation Ho said he was sorry that I did not seem to be going ahead.

Tan stayed only a month. He was succeeded by Kang, who was worse.

Like Tan, Kang did not speak English but was quite fluent in Tibetan. He also had been in the Chinese Mission in Lhasa and claimed to remember me. He was a probing, nagging man, always digging into my mind. He had reached the depths of self-abasement, and was continually trying to drag me down as well. As my future depended largely on his progress-reports to Ho I had to pretend to go. At first the humiliation was unbearable; then I got used to it, and that was terrifying.

As Kang could not read English the newspapers became the main text-books for my studies, which continued as before. I could now talk Communism with a fair degree of fluency; and, although I was ashamed of my glibness, objective discussions on subjects like the Korean War, or the tour of Russian actors and scientists in China, were not too bad. They were not enough, either.

"You claim that through your studies you have progressed," said Ho. "But you must prove it. You must show that you are sincere by finding more faults in your own conduct. We cannot find them for you. Think over all you have done."

I learnt later that this process was known in the prison as "squeezing the toothpaste." No confession was accepted as complete so long as the prisoner remained in custody. He was expected to go on adding to it, each addition taking him another step nearer the solution of his problem. If he stopped adding to it he was considered to have stopped making progress.

The object of this was partly to collect more information—they never stopped seeking this—and also to test the prisoner's sincerity, to gauge how far his thoughts had been reformed.

I thought I had already been squeezed dry, and even with the help of *ch'i fa* I found it hard to recall any more crimes. Nor could I risk making any up: inventing offences was considered definitely retrogressive. But Ho showed me there was still a great deal for me to say. He pointed out that I had not yet said what I thought of my former associates in crime.

"You are still backward in your outlook," he said. "You still retain a bourgeois loyalty to reactionaries like Hopkinson and Fox and regard them as your friends. They are not your friends—they are your enemies, for they are enemies of the people. You must show which side you are on before you can expect us to believe that you are really progressive. Rewrite your relations with Hopkinson and Fox from this point of view."

This was hateful. It was one thing to abuse Truman and Attlee, whom I had never met; but to have to vilify men like Mr Hopkinson and Fox brought me near to revolt. But, of course, I had gone too far. I had to go on now, and confine my resistance to an effort not to believe what I said.

This was becoming harder, too.

The summer passed. I was glad when the weather became cooler, for I had suffered a good deal from mosquitoes; also I was never quite conditioned to the stench of the latrines. The second anniversary of my capture came and went. How many more years would I have cut out of my life?

Then, in December, I had the biggest setback since I confessed.

"What prison regulations have you broken since you came here?" Ho asked.

I had once forgotten to shout "*Bao Gao!*" when I was summoned for interrogation, and another time when I went to the latrines. I had already confessed these crimes, but I confessed them again. Ho was not satisfied, and I realized he had found out something else.

"Think harder," he kept urging; and I thought like mad. In the cell Kang nagged me unceasingly, until I was willing to confess having broken every regulation there was.

Then Ho gave me a hint.

"Have you ever tried to communicate with a prisoner in another cell?" he asked.

That could only mean one thing. They had found out about my hymn-singing with Bull over a year before.

What had happened was that Bull had been taken along the ground-floor corridor and had looked at my cell as he passed. This was a crime under Regulation No. 3 ("It is strictly forbidden to peer round corners"). It had been investigated, and inevitably the singing came to light. No one had heard us singing, but under their relentless interrogation both Bull and I confessed that we had.

For two weeks I was questioned ceaselessly about my relations with Bull. The only thing that saved me from despair was the knowledge that Bull would also be questioned, and as we had nothing to hide we had only to tell the truth for our stories to agree. But there was still the fact that I had committed a double breach of prison regulations—singing and communicating with another prisoner—and, most important of all, I had not confessed.

"How can you expect us to believe you are sincere?" Ho asked me. "You have told me repeatedly that you had nothing more to confess. If you can conceal such a serious offence as this, how many other crimes are you still hiding from us?" So ended 1952.

Shortly after the New Year I was given an English translation of the speeches by Lysenko to enable me to brush up my knowledge of genetics. The proper nouns in the book were given with their Russian equivalents, and I amused myself by working out the Russian alphabet. This enabled me to understand some of the captions in the illustrated Russian-language magazines that were brought in. In one of these there was a picture of a Chinese delegation in which a woman was wearing a very smart-looking fur coat. I pointed it out to Kang.

"Yes," he said, "after Peking was liberated any woman could buy a fur coat. They were very cheap. The capitalists had left so many behind that it was difficult to sell them at all."

I was still getting old copies of *People's China*, and from these and Kang's translations of the daily newspapers I learnt that several of the Tibetan officials I had known were being taken on conducted tours in China and hospitably received in Chungking and Peking. I saw a photograph of one group including Shiwala Rimpoche and the monk Foreign Minister.

"This shows how the People's Government is respecting Tibetan minority rights and religion," said Kang.

"Yes," I agreed, "and now that they have been liberated from American and British imperialists the Tibetan people are reaping the advantages of reunion with the Motherland."

Evidently the Chinese were ruling through the officials and letting the old feudal system go on. That explained why I had not been guided into following the same line as the Kuomintang prisoners, all of whom confessed that they had been serving a corrupt reactionary clique.

Stalin died, and the Chinese newspapers were edged with black. After watching me closely Kang accused me of looking cheerful. In fact I felt quite indifferent. I had no reason to think Stalin's death would make any difference to me.

A week later Ho told me that the People's Government had decided I should learn Chinese.

"We have not got enough books in English for your studies," he explained. "This is evidently hindering your progress."

Now I was in despair. Since I had been in prison I had picked up some Chinese words, and I would have welcomed the chance to learn the language instead of spending all my time thinking about my problem and continuing my studies. I had not been given the chance. But now, two and a half years after capture and eighteen months after I had begun to confess, I was to start learning to read in an exceptionally difficult language as a prelude to further reform of my thought. I was suddenly robbed of one of my main props— the possibility, however slight, that to-morrow I might be let out.

Kang was appointed my tutor. I was to spend only half my time in learning Chinese: the rest was to be spent on continuing my studies. At first I was not given any grammar-book or dictionary, but just some rice-paper and a writing brush. I used the paper to make cards, on each of which I painted one or two of the most commonly used characters, writing an approximate romanization and the English meaning on the back. In this way I was able to learn about fifty characters a day, and after a few months I had acquired a vocabulary that was reasonable in size and curious in content.

I never learnt the Chinese for 'the pen of my aunt.' My class-reader was the daily newspaper, and the commonest characters were 'the glorious Communist Party,' 'the Peoples' Democracies,' 'imperialist war-mongers,' 'corrupt reactionary clique,' 'the great Chairman Mao Tse-tung,' and other similar political clichés. But this was the language I needed to know. It enabled me to read relatively simple tracts, like *Labour created the World*. It also sufficed for me to discover, from a tiny paragraph on the back page of the daily newspaper, that Queen Elizabeth II had been crowned. I felt unreasonably cheered up.

I had more reason for rejoicing a few days later, when two other prisoners moved in. After fifteen months my confinement with Kang alone had at last come to an end.

One of the newcomers was a former helmsman of a Yangtze

Mass Rally organized by Communists at the foot of the Potala, the Dalai Lama's winter palace in Lhasa

Ngabö Shapé, the Communist-styled "Chief Tibetan Delegate," presents a white scarf to Mao Tse-tung in Peking after the signing of the Agreement for the "peaceful liberation" of Tibet

Ngabö Shapé, the newly appointed Governor-General of Eastern Tibet, sets out for Kham from Lhasa
By courtesy of Heinrich Harrer

river boat, and he was in handcuffs and fetters: a brave and stubborn man. Kang went to work on him, and I was put on a more-or-less equal footing with my fellow-students. Soon I knew enough Chinese to be able to take part in the weekly criticism and self-criticism meetings and the communal group-discussions on current affairs.

After this the population of our cell was continually changing, but Kang always remained. One day I discovered that he was still human.

There were loudspeakers outside the cell, which relayed news bulletins and talks, and sometimes even music, from Radio Chungking. On this occasion we heard the news in Tibetan, read by a woman with a good Lhasa accent. Shortly afterwards I was astonished to see Kang crying.

"Why are you crying?" I asked; not out of sympathy or pity, but because it was my duty to ask.

"I was thinking of my parents," he said, "and how badly I have treated them by supporting a corrupt reactionary régime."

I knew that was not the truth, but it was some time later that I learnt that the Tibetan news-reader was Kang's wife.

I took part in the condemnation of the Americans for germ-warfare, and I joined in the congratulations to Mao for building the New China that I had not seen. I became adept at picking the Party line out of the newspapers and developing it, and especially relating it to my own misdeeds.

But I slipped up over the arrest of Beria. I had not read the paper that day, as Kang well knew when he asked me to open the discussion with my opinion of this event. I did not know what to say. I could hardly say I had always thought Beria was an enemy of the people. So I was vague and evasive, and Kang sneered nastily, and that meant a bad progress-report to Ho. The other prisoners had read the paper, and were well aware that the arrest of a traitor in such a high position showed how vigilant and democratic the Communist Party was.

It showed me that Stalin's death had not ended the era of purges. I knew that the People's Government of the Soviet Union was as lenient to criminals as the Chinese, and I did not like to relate Beria's execution to my own problem. He too had been an agent of the American and British imperialists.

I still feared that one day I would be taken out and shot.

19

Thought Reform

WHAT do you think of Kang?" Ho asked me.

"I am very grateful to him for all the help he has given me," I said. "I think I have made great progress since I began to learn Chinese."

"You have made a little progress," Ho corrected me. "Enough, I think, for you to play a full part in communal life. This will mean separating you from Kang." I bore this blow with fortitude. "You will be moved into another cell."

It was now September 1953. I had hailed the armistice in Korea as a great victory for the peace-loving democracies, and the Russian announcement of the explosion of a hydrogen bomb as fresh evidence of the glorious Soviet Union's desire for peace. I had abused my country and my friends. I had abased myself and plumbed the depths of humiliation.

"Yes, you have made a little progress," said Ho. "Enough for you to realize that you have much more to make. You know that we are not keeping you here because we want to." His was an almost paternal, Puritan style. "As you have freely confessed, you committed great crimes against the people; and it is our duty to help you to change your whole outlook, so that you will not even want to commit such crimes again. It is true that if we let you return home now," he went on, "you would not be able to commit any more crimes against the Chinese people; but our duty to the British people is just as great. For their protection we must keep you here until you have become a new man and are fit to take your place among them and work for them and help them to throw off their imperialist rulers."

I am sure he was completely sincere.

My new cell-leader was a man named Chang, and he had been a

chief of the Kuomintang secret police. If he has solved his problem by now he should be doing well under the new régime. When I first met him his favourite victim was a Chinese Roman Catholic priest. Chang questioned and insulted him mercilessly about his faith, and I got some idea of what Bull must have been going through. The priest spoke fluent English and several other European languages, and when he was not being tormented by Chang he taught me a Chinese phonetic system that helped me a great deal.

Another inmate of the cell was a former general of the Kuomintang Army who had missed the last 'plane to Formosa by half an hour. He was fifty-eight, which meant that he had exactly half a century's errors to clear up. He had the misfortune to be ham-fisted, and soon after I entered the cell he broke a rice-bowl. He apologized for his clumsiness at the next criticism and self-criticism session, and promised to be more vigilant in future. A few days later he broke another. In his next self-criticism he blamed himself for falling back into the old attitude of contempt for the property of the people. This did not satisfy Chang, who accused him of having done it deliberately. The General rashly denied this, and was literally howled at for failing to accept criticism in the spirit in which it was given. After an hour's argument he confessed.

These weekly criticism and self-criticism meetings were my worst penalty for having learnt Chinese. As we were all prisoners it was difficult to find anything concrete to criticize oneself for, and the most popular choice was some minor breach of the prison regulations. This recurred so regularly that it was necessary to invest it with the maximum significance, and often an absurdly petty misdemeanour was exalted to a major crime.

For example, once I confessed that I had gone to the latrines without reporting to the warder. To make more of it I said that I had not only broken prison regulations but had felt angry with the warder, thus showing that I still had bourgeois thoughts of being top-dog.

"Yes," said Chang when I had finished, "but you haven't taken your analysis deep enough. You were resentful not only against the warder but against the prison authorities in general—indeed, against the People's Government. That means you felt resentment against the people."

Each of the others added his piece, and I had to admit all their charges and promise to try not to commit any more serious offences like this. Then the others criticized themselves, and I had to "help" them as they had helped me. It was bad enough having to flagellate myself for some trivial breach of prison regulations which I had to build up into a serious thought-crime; it was even worse having to criticize the others. Especially that poor old General and the Roman Catholic priest.

Thus did I play a full part in communal life.

We rose every day at six, cleaned out our cell, washed, and went to the courtyard for exercise and community singing. We sang the latest popular songs, which had jolly marching tunes and lyrics about American imperialism, the evils of germ warfare, and the democratic peoples' desire for peace. I was glad I did not have to sing them in my mother tongue.

We had our first meal at eight, and began studies at nine. We continued studying until midday, when we had a break of an hour and a half and sometimes another meal. Then we studied until five in the afternoon. Another meal, and a free period till seven; then studies till ten, and bed. In the hot weather there was a compulsory siesta in the afternoon, but we still managed over nine hours' study a day.

Our studies were highly organized. We were given a specific subject, such as the co-operative movement or the transition to socialism, and had to study it in newspapers or magazines; in China all publications of this kind were designed for education, not entertainment. Then we discussed the subject among ourselves, each of us trying to find something to add to what we had read. Finally we drew common conclusions and embodied them in a formal resolution, which our cell-leader wrote down.

The same subject was studied simultaneously throughout the prison, and when we had finished the discussion in our cell we joined four or five other cells in a big room. Each cell-leader gave his report and read his cell's resolution, and then each of us had to speak on the various resolutions before the meeting. Finally a general resolution was drawn up and presented to the prison officials. They compared it with their own conclusions—for they had been spending their own study-time in the same way—and then one of them gave us a talk in which he pointed out the mistakes we had made and the things we had missed. The prison officials always had the advantage, for they had access to more books and magazines than were sent round the cells.

I felt less embarrassment in uttering the Comunist clichés in Chinese than I had in English, and I think I sounded less obviously forced and insincere; also the fact that I was still learning the language gave me some excuse when I became inarticulate.

As usual, we had to relate the general subject to our particular problems, and I became appallingly efficient in developing the Party line. As a Briton I was often called upon to compare New China with my own country, always to the latter's detriment. Thus when we studied the new Chinese Constitution I was asked to compare it with the British Constitution. I created quite a stir when I said that Britain was so backward that it did not have a written Constitution at all. I showed how undemocratic our electoral system was by explaining about the £150 deposit. Similarly when Hungary beat England at football at Wembley I explained how the game was organized in my own country, and compared the professional's maximum wage with his potential transfer fee. I could give other examples of my perfidy, but they are still too distressing to relate.

My increasing fluency and glibness made it easier for me—at a price: I discovered that I was beginning to believe what I was saying.

The chief weakness in my resistance to Communist indoctrination was my inadequate knowledge of the opposite point of view. Balanced judgment depends on knowing both sides. I heard only one, and was relatively ignorant of the other.

I had never studied economics; and if anyone had asked me why there was a Wall Street crash in 1929, and a consequent economic depression throughout the non-Communist world, I would not have been able to answer. Marxism-Leninism answered this question, and many others. It had a neat, apparently logical answer for everything. I could find few flaws. There was no one to point them out.

I was equally ignorant about the history of China. The captured Kuomintang officers doubtless exaggerated, but I could not believe that all their confessions were pure invention. Even in the West the Kuomintang régime had been considered reactionary and corrupt. It did not seem outlandish to consider the Communist victory in the Civil War a triumph for the people.

I was weak on British imperial history in the Far East. I knew almost nothing about the Opium Wars. But I was aware that our own view of our imperial history was not entirely shared by the rest of the world. I knew that even friends of ours, like the Americans, were critical not only of our past but of our present, and even apprehensive about our future aims. Hadn't our staunch ally Roosevelt thought the world had more to fear from post-war British imperialism than from his comrade Stalin? Being British did not make the British point of view right. I had never believed in the gospel of 'my country right or wrong.' I had not read history or politics in terms of black and white. The greys soon became murkier under the influence of one-sided education. Again I failed to see the flaws.

But I was not looking for flaws. I did not study the Party line to find out what was wrong with it: all my mental efforts were devoted to discovering its merits and applying them to my own case. I had a vested interest in demonstrating that Communism was right. That was the only way I could get out.

These were what I might call my chief negative susceptibilities to indoctrination. There were powerful positive ones, too.

I was living in a society where Communism was normal, and an anti-Communist a monstrous and criminal freak. All my fellow-students professed to believe in Communism. Some may have been insincere, but if they could fool the interrogators they could not help but fool me. They did not look sullen and brow-beaten when they stood up and spouted the Party line. Their mood seemed to me to be genuinely enthusiastic, sometimes even exhilarated; at a group meeting I often felt a wave of mob emotionalism, and as I joined in the shouting of slogans it nearly caught me up. I was saved from this by the fact that the basic impulse was patriotism, a fervent belief in the New China, to which I did not belong. But I still had the normal human feeling of not wanting to be the only one out of step.

Besides, I had to join in.

Some philosopher once defended hypocrisy on the grounds that if a man pretends to have a virtue long enough he will eventually acquire it. The same might be said of Communism. And there was also a strong incentive to believe rather than pretend.

The diabolical cleverness of thought reform is that the victim is made to want to believe. Unless he is exceptionally intelligent and a brilliant actor he has no hope of release until he does. If he merely had to listen to propaganda, or even repeat it parrot-fashion himself, he might be able to emerge mentally unscathed. But he has to create and deliver the propaganda himself.

"Anyone can shout slogans," Chang used to say when a prisoner merely repeated the clichés he had read in the newspaper. "Prove that you have progressed."

The method of extracting confessions and the technique of criticism and self-criticism sessions were completely analogous, and
indeed inseparable from the rest. The victim was given guidance,
but everything had to come from him. And everything he said had
to pass the exacting tests of apparent truthfulness, dogmatic con-
formity, and, above all, sincerity.

At the beginning, when I was saying things I did not believe, and
trying to make them ring true, I listened with envy to those who
were obviously converted. All they said sounded so effortless, spontaneous, and natural. It became clear that to sound sincere the easiest
way—perhaps the only possible way—was to be sincere. I know
nothing of psychology, but presumably my unconscious mind took
the hint.

As time went on I achieved a facility of argument and fluency of
speech that earned me the approval of Ho and woke me up in alarm
in the middle of the night. Were they going to succeed in converting
me? Would I go home a dedicated Communist, magnetically
clinched to the Party line? The fact that I was alarmed proved that
they had not succeeded yet; but if I ceased to feel alarm it would
mean it was too late.

Then why wasn't I converted?

I was not guilty of the crimes to which I had been obliged to
confess.

Mr Hopkinson did not get me into Tibetan Government service
as a secret agent of the British Government. I was not a spy. I did
not collect information and send it by secret code to Fox. I did not
incite the Tibetans to "separatism." I did not cause the death of
Geda Lama, not even in the broadest sense of the verb.

These were facts, and I could always come back to them. The
South Koreans might have invaded North Korea, the Americans
might have engaged in germ warfare, capitalism might be evil, and
Mao Tse-tung might be the saviour of China—but I had not spied
or caused anyone's death. And when I stood on this firm base much
else fell into perspective. Tibet had not been liberated from American and British imperialism. The transfer of power in India was not
fictitious; Nehru was not a running dog of Whitehall or a lackey of
Wall Street. It was the North Koreans, after all, who had started
the War. . . .

At that point my unconscious mind solicitously put me to sleep.
Whether I liked it or not, some element of belief in falsehood was

necessary if I was ever to get out. Complete scepticism was a luxury I could not be allowed.

I had one other source of strength. I should like to put it first, but that would be hypocritical. I believed in the Christian Faith. In practice I was a feeble sort of Christian, but I believed; not just out of fear or habit either, for I was an Anglican convert. I was brought up a Methodist, but entered the Church of England while I was in the R.A.F. I had thought about it enough for that. And I was still able to pray.

There was at least one real Christian in that prison besides Bull and the Chinese Roman Catholic priest. This was the American missionary Lovegren, who was captured in Szechwan. I saw him the first morning after I was moved into my new cell, when I went to wash. I did not know who he was—I did not discover his name until after I was released—but his fair skin and features showed me that he was what is called, inaccurately in this case, a European.

We always avoided looking at each other—the prohibition on "peering round corners" was interpreted very broadly—but once his cell was in the same collective study group as mine. The subject for discussion was the exchange of prisoners-of-war in Korea. Some of the Chinese captured by United Nations forces had volunteered to go to Formosa, and the Communists protested that they had all been coerced.

That was the Party line, and at our meeting no one deviated from it by a hair's breadth until Lovegren had to speak. The speaker before him had said that every one of those soldiers wanted to return to China. Lovegren said he doubted if every single one wanted to go back.

"After all," he said, while the rest of us were too stunned to speak, "there was re-education on both sides."

Then the storm broke out, and I thought they were going to lynch him. They ranted and raved like madmen, accusing him of every thought-crime in the counter-revolutionary calendar. The suggestion that even one of the soldiers had not wanted to return home was bad enough, but that was nothing compared with Lovegren's statement that there had been re-education on both sides. "Re-education on our side—only terror on the other" was the well-known Party line.

Lovegren remained silent and unyielding. At last it was decided that the matter would be gone into more thoroughly in his own cell.

I also was silent. When I had to speak I was evasive and deliberately muddled up my Chinese. I felt a coward, and I was rewarded with the worst of both worlds. At the next criticism and self-criticism meeting in my cell Chang let loose on me for failing to join in the attack on Lovegren.

"You are selfish," he said. "It was your duty to criticize him for his own sake: it would have helped him to see his error. That is the object of all criticism."

There were frequent changes in the population of our cell, and now that I could speak Chinese I learnt more about my fellow-prisoners. One was a blacksmith. That was his crime.

When Chungking fell into the hands of the Communists, parties of troops went round the city looking for spies, or special agents, of the Kuomintang. Even under the old régime each street had a leader, and one of these leaders, a very old man, was asked by a patrol if there were any special agents living in his street.

He would not have understood the question even if he had heard it properly; but the soldiers came from northern China, and with their accent the word for 'special agent' sounded very similar to the word for 'blacksmith' commonly used in Szechwan. By chance there were about half a dozen blacksmiths in the street, and they were all taken to gaol. The one in our cell had not only confessed to many crimes but was fully convinced of his guilt.

All the others seemed to be; but then so did I to them. None of us would have dared to sound out any of the others for a spark of mental resistance. With every one a potential informer, anything approaching genuine human contact was impossible.

During the free time in the evening we were allowed to talk, but I thought it was safer to read or play Chinese chess. I was at least improving my knowledge of the language. They gave me some books by Chinese authors, and also translations from the English. Jack London was one of their favourites, and I read and enjoyed *White Fang* and *Call of the Wild* in Chinese. I also did some tailoring, or rather needlework, making a pair of trousers out of my Tibetan robe and a shirt out of some old sheets.

I was still being interrogated from time to time. Ho had been taken off my case, and the emphasis now was almost entirely on re-education. The interrogations were conducted in Chinese.

I was questioned mainly about my thoughts, and often I was asked what I expected my sentence would be when the people decided my case. This was my cue for the usual self-abasement followed by an expression of trust in the people's wisdom and appreciation of their leniency to the truly repentant. By this time I had learnt that what they called lenient treatment was often very harsh. I also knew that I had no reason to expect my case to be settled in the near future. Many of my fellow-students seemed to have made much more progress than I had, and they were still kept in. Most of those that left the prison were sent out to labour.

It was real labour, not sewing mailbags, and the prison was completely self-supporting. Labour parties worked in the fields, in building (they had built the prison itself), in light industries, and even in the mines. The prison had its own factories, running at a profit, where articles like towels and toothpaste were made. The prisoners engaged on such work were continually reminded that its main purpose was for their own good.

I had gained the impression that foreigners were not usually sent out to labour but were deported when they had solved their problems. I could not be sure about this—there was no such thing as a prison grapevine—but the little I had gleaned from casual remarks by interrogators and cell-leaders gave me grounds for hope. On the other hand, I knew that I could be sentenced to life-imprisonment, and I could still not exclude the possibility of execution.

In the end, however, I expected they would deal with me according to political expediency rather than on the merits of my case. Here also I had grounds for hope. The only news I had of the outside world was in the Communist Press, and I did not at first detect much change in the Party line after Stalin's death; but in China, at least, there was less abuse of Britain, I inferred that this was part of a plan to separate us from the United States. I thought it might help me.

In the spring of 1954 we had one or two film shows; for education, of course, not entertainment. The first was about the Chinese Civil War, and we had to discuss it for the next two days. One Kuomintang general daringly criticized the film on the grounds that it was too lenient: he said he had committed much worse crimes against the people than those of the villains on the screen. This went down very well, and in a more modest way I took a similar line. I related the film to my own problem by comparing it with the way I had incited the Tibetans to fight their brothers in the rest of China. This also was quite well received.

I cannot recall to what extent my brain was eventually washed—

my thoughts were always muddled and confused, and my present inclination is to forget rather than remember—but I have a clear recollection of this. I can see myself now, standing up and talking what I knew to be rubbish and struggling to make it sound sincere.

Then, at the beginning of May, I read in the *People's Daily* that American prisoners in China were to be allowed to correspond with their relatives and to receive small parcels. Nothing was said about British prisoners, but I felt sure that this concession would be extended to us.

A few days later a prison officer named Liu told me I could write to my parents.

20

Sentence

AT first I was overjoyed: then I was in a mental turmoil. My letter would be censored, and I would be expected to show how my thoughts had been reformed. If I did not all my efforts would have been wasted. But how would my parents feel about a letter like that?

I would have preferred to send a postcard, saying only that I was alive and in good health. Well, I would keep it short. I spent a sleepless night trying to compose a letter that would satisfy the prison authorities and not cause my parents too much distress.

Eventually I hit upon what looked like a solution. I wrote three paragraphs. The first was short and purely personal, announcing that I was all right. The second was longer and was pure Communist propaganda. The third was short, like the first, and again personal and in my natural style. I hoped my parents would guess that only the first and third paragraphs were sincere and the second written under duress. I hoped still more that this would not be spotted by my captors.

Two days later Liu told me the letter did not show as much progress as he had hoped.

"Write it again," he said. "Stress the leniency of the People's Government, and bring out what it is doing to help you. And tell your parents of the people's democracies' desire for peace. There is no need to say you are in prison," he added. "That would only upset them."

He gave me some more advice, and I rewrote the letter. Let it speak for itself:

14/5/54

MY DEAR MOTHER AND FATHER,

I expect this will come as a great and certainly welcome surprise to you hearing from me after all this time—almost like a voice from the grave. But I can assure you I'm far from being in the grave! I'm very much alive, well, and in good spirits. I know that this is the kind of news you've been waiting to hear for so long.

Since I was captured by the Chinese People's Liberation Army during the liberation of Chamdo in October 1950, what kind of life have I been leading? How have I been treated by the Chinese authorities? These and many other questions you will, of course, want to be answered.

Firstly, I want to explain to you the People's Government of China's lenient policy towards prisoners, and I'm quite sure that after hearing that you will be a lot easier and will not worry so much about how I am.

The New China is a China of the People—a China where the People are masters in their own house, a China where the People have chosen their Government and system. The People and the Government are one. What, then, is the People's policy towards a criminal or prisoner (foreigners included)? It is one of leniency. What does this policy of leniency mean in fact? The criminal must first freely confess his crimes, recognize himself for what he is, and then, on that basis, he can go one step further, through study re-educate himself, remould his ideology, and in doing so become a new man fit to re-enter society.

The object of this policy is to eradicate the basic root causes which made the criminal commit his crimes. It is not simply a policy of shutting a criminal up in a prison for the duration of his sentence and, on its expiration, letting him go free—free to enter society and once more commit the same or even worse crimes. It is not a policy which tries to prevent crimes by relying on the use of fear of the consequences if one commits a crime. It does not resort to the use of physical violence. This policy is one of patiently re-educating the criminal—one of remoulding a criminal, a man shunned by society, into a new man —a new man who, when he returns to society, will not commit further crimes, but will be of use, and who, to atone for his previous misdeeds, will give of his whole strength for the betterment of society.

I think you will now be much clearer as to what this policy of leniency means, and from a brief description of my daily life you will be able to see how it is applied in practice.

Since being captured I have been treated well, and I can assure you there is absolutely nothing to worry about. I get three good wholesome meals a day, with extra special dishes on the various festival days! Special food is provided for foreigners. Medical treatment is provided at once in case of sickness, and we have routine medical examinations. I take part in the daily physical exercises, so you can imagine I'm in good health. All my requirements, including toilet articles, are provided by the Authorities here. There is nothing that I am in need of.

My cultural life is quite a full one. We have quite a good library and I can also listen to the radio programmes, see cinema films, and read the daily newspaper. Are the newspapers, books, etc. in English? No. Then how do I manage? I'm studying Chinese. The People's Government has provided me with English-Chinese and Chinese-English dictionaries, and with their encouragement and the help of my room-mates I've made quite good progress. I can already read the daily newspapers and take part in the study-group discussions we have. I've also learnt quite a number of Chinese songs and also learnt to play Chinese chess. In fact from morning to evening there is hardly a minute to spare.

How is life with you both? I do hope you're both in good health. From the newspapers I gather that England is in a pretty bad state— rising prices and the growing number of unemployed seem to be the order of the day. Naturally under these conditions I am anxious to know how you both are. Such conditions naturally are the outcome of the Government's "Guns before Butter" armaments policy, and the stopping, under America's dictation, of East-West trade. I firmly believe that if Sino-British relations can be improved, and as a result trade developed between the two countries, then the lot of the average working man in England can at once be improved. This (the improvement of Sino-British relations) rests solely with our Government. China's foreign policy is one of friendly co-operation with *all* countries —a policy of peace. China has absolutely no interest in war. The Chinese People are much too busy building their new life and realizing the industrialization of their country. I feel here no enmity for Britain and the British People from China and the Chinese People. The Chinese People hold out the hand of friendship to the Peoples of all countries, Britain included. All this is quite different from what the propaganda of the West would have it.

I hope from these few lines you will be able to understand a little of the kind of life I am leading and my feelings. Do write soon and let me have some news of you both.

In closing I just want to add that, Mother, you have absolutely no need to worry about me. I'm well and in good spirits. My love to you both.

Your ever-loving son,

(*signed*) ROBERT WEBSTER FORD

I was glad they told me to sign my full name. I thought it would help my parents to realize that the letter was not spontaneous, as indeed it did. The Communist literary style, with its rhetorical questions, also helped. But it was not a pleasant letter for them to receive.

I had one from them before they received mine. Unknown to me, they had at last succeeded, with the help of the British Foreign Office, in breaking through the Bamboo Curtain, and I got their letter four weeks after I had written mine. I need not describe my feelings.

In July the Geneva Conference on Indo-China took place, and the *People's Daily* praised the work of Molotov and Eden. I had never before seen two such names bracketed in this way. So my hopes were high when a delegation of the British Labour Party, led by Attlee and Bevan, came to China and was received in Peking.

We discussed this in our study-groups, and agreed that it was a good thing for such persons to learn something about the New China. The fact that they represented the British Labour Party was hardly noticed. If anything, the Chinese Communists despised Labour more than the Conservatives, and Bevanites were regarded as the worst traitors to the working class.

My hopes fell when the delegation reached Hong Kong, and Attlee expressed mixed feelings about the visit and said he thought China and Russia ought to reduce their arms. There was an uproar about this in the prison, and I had to agree that the Labour leaders were two-faced warmongers and lackeys of Wall Street.

I passed the fourth anniversary of my capture, and then my whole case was reopened by an interrogator I had not met before. He went through my life from the age of eight.

I had to do much autobiographical writing, especially on my espionage activities and the events leading to the death of Geda Lama. I gave the same mixture of truth and lies as before. Then I was pressed again to say what organization I belonged to, and where I had been trained in England, and I fell into despair. Fan was cheating: I thought we had got over all that.

This gruelling period lasted about a month. Then, on the morning of December 8, 1954, I was marched out of the prison to a closed car. I had not been told to pick up my belongings, so I assumed I was being taken for an interrogation outside. I hoped so, anyway. A more sinister possibility also occurred to me.

But it was neither interrogation nor execution.

After a drive of about two miles I was taken into a room with a long table down the middle and a neon-lighted bust of Mao above. Five men were seated at the table, all in military uniform, and in front of three of them were small plaques. The middle plaque said "Chief Judge," and each of the others said "Deputy Judge."

I realized that my trial was about to begin.

The only other persons in the room were my escort and the guards at each door, armed with tommy-guns. It was very quiet as the Chief Judge asked me to confirm my name, age, and nationality. Then he stood up and read from a sheet of paper, and I learnt that I was appearing before the South-west Area Military Tribunal and that I had been found guilty of a number of offences against the People's Republic of China.

The charges against me—which I was hearing for the first time —were vaguely worded but did not exceed the crimes I had admitted in my own confessions. I was convicted of illegal entry into the People's Republic of China; of espionage activities endangering its security; of instigating a separatist movement in Tibet; of fomenting rebellion; and of causing the assassination of an official of the People's Government.

It sounded a fearful catalogue.

When the Chief Judge had finished reading, the interpreter repeated it all in English, and it sounded even worse. Then I was told to sign a document ratifying it as a fact. As I did so I wondered if I was signing my death-warrant.

The Chief Judge rose again.

"According to the law for the punishment of counter-revolutionaries," he said, and named the section, "you are hereby sentenced to ten years' imprisonment. You have no right of appeal."

Not death, then; not even life imprisonment. Only ten years. Did the four I had done count? That would leave only six. Only! Or was it right that I should be deported now?

I was taken back to the prison, back to my cell; back to my studies. In the afternoon I was called out by Liu. He asked me what I thought of the sentence.

"The People's Government has been very lenient," I said.

He agreed. Then he told me that in view of my progress the People's Government had decided to deport me.

So I would be out by Christmas!

They moved me into a separate cell for the night, and woke me

The Author's Chinese "dictionary," compiled during imprisonment

A rice-paper book for the study of the formation of Chinese characters

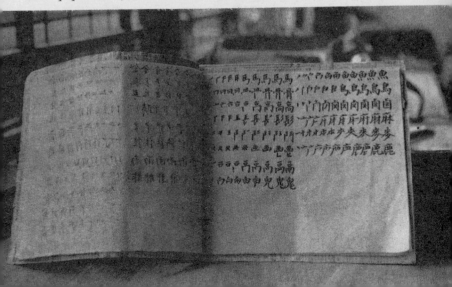

Hong Kong—and freedom

Reunion at London Airport

early next morning and gave me back my watch and gold ring. Then I was put in a jeep and driven through the snow to the airport, where I boarded an old American-built DC3. I was told not to look out of the window, and a quarter of an hour before we landed one of the crew drew all the curtains. When we got out of the aeroplane I learnt that I was in Hankow.

My guards took me to the railway station, and we boarded a train for Canton. I noticed that the carriages were labelled either "soft seats" or "hard seats"—a classless society's euphemisms for first and second class. Our seats were hard, but it was a lovely ride. It took two days.

In Canton I was taken to the Security Bureau. The next morning I was given a brief lecture by a security officer, who warned me not to revert to my former criminal ways when I returned home. He reminded me of the coming world revolution and of the vigilance of the British people. I reminded him that I had become a new man.

I was back in prison now, but that did not worry me. Hong Kong was only a few hours away.

It was nearly six months away.

First they asked me for my passport, and I told them it had been taken off me in Chungking. Then I was left in my cell, in solitary confinement again, with some newspapers and magazines to read. My Christmas dinner was plain rice. Then, to my horror, my re-education was resumed. Nothing more was said about deportation.

I was still alone in the cell, and I spent most of my time staring listlessly at the whitewashed walls. One day I saw some Chinese characters scratched on them. Here is a translation of what they said:

> The sensation of life is a precious gift,
> Love an even dearer emotion;
> But both of these are as naught
> When compared with man's liberty.

No one who has not been in a Communist prison can imagine what courage was needed to scratch out that defiant message. I drew strength from the fact that this bleak cell had been occupied by a brave man.

Early in January I was told I could write to my parents again. I seized on this opportunity to try to find out what my captors' inten-

Q

tions were. I began my letter by saying that I had wonderful news: after being justly sentenced to ten years' imprisonment for my crimes, I had, thanks to the lenient policy of the People's Government, been told that I was going to be deported instead. I hoped to be home again very soon.

After another three months of bad food, solitary confinement, and nagging re-education sessions with a prison official, I was told that my letter was unsuitable and would not be sent.

A few days later I was told to pack up my things.

I would not let my spirits rise, and my caution was justified when I found myself moved into a large prison on the outskirts of Canton. I was put in a cell with another prisoner, interrogated, and given better food, sometimes with even an egg. Then, early in April, I was issued with a new white shirt, new slacks, shoes, and socks—all made of the cheapest materials, but a wonderful wardrobe compared with my patched and tattered rags.

I was sure I was going now. My last doubt vanished when I was allowed to shave myself for the first time since I had been taken prisoner. Then came the loss of an Indian air-liner carrying Chinese delegates to the Afro-Asian Conference at Bandung, and the *People's Daily* told me it was due to sabotage by American agents. I was not released. Cause and effect? I think so. It was an unlucky event for a self-confessed lackey of Wall Street on the verge of release.

I spent nearly two more months in the cell. My fellow-student was the former headmaster of a secondary school in Canton, and we discussed topical events and held weekly criticism and self-criticism meetings. I let him do most of the talking, for I had progressed much further than he had. He had committed the crime of criticizing the Government scheme for "the planned distribution of food." That is Communist jargon for rationing.

So it went on until 11 P.M. on Friday, May 27, when I was woken up and told to go for an interview. I had not been called out so late before since the early interrogations, and my first thought was that they had found out something new and were going to reopen my whole case.

Instead I was told that I was to leave Canton the next morning by the early train for Hong Kong.

I should have to be ready by seven, so if I liked I could shave before I went to bed.

This was the first time I had been given a date for departure, so in spite of the previous false starts I was convinced that this time it was the real thing. I shaved carefully, hardly slept, rose early, put on my new clothes—and was told I was not going.

That was the nearest I ever came to losing my self-control.

These months in Canton, spent mostly in idleness, had been a greater nervous strain than anything since I began my confession. Not only was I in perpetual fear that they would reopen my case, but I found it harder than ever before to profess gratitude for their leniency and to toe the Party line. Now, when I thought that the great moment had come at last, I had to fight to stop myself from shouting abuse.

Slowly I took off my nice new clothes and put on my rags, and sat listlessly in the cell.

Then, at midday, two of the security police came in and told me to dress up. I was not told to pack up my belongings, but was taken out to a car and driven into Canton. On the way my escorts pointed out a new bridge and other landmarks. I could not imagine what had got into them. I had no idea of the purpose of the ride until we stopped at a large department store and the escorts took me round and showed me what people were buying. I was being taken on a conducted tour of Canton!

And I really believe my departure had been delayed for twenty-four hours simply so that I should have the opportunity to tell the people of Britain something of the wonders of New China.

My escorts saw that I kept hitching up my trousers, so they bought me a belt. Then they took me to the Palace of Culture, and bought me cigarettes and a drink. We saw an industrial exhibition, and then rushed through a museum, and sat in a restaurant and had ice-cream. Finally, after only two hours, we returned to the prison.

I left the next morning. Two guards came with me on the train, which lumbered all morning round the swampy Pearl River delta to the Shum Chun frontier. I went into the Communist custom shed, and my two wretched-looking bundles of baggage were prodded and probed. I went out again into the sunlight. One of my guards gave me six Hong Kong dollars and my old passport, and nodded towards the rickety wooden railway bridge.

I began to walk the last fifty yards to freedom.

21

Freedom

A BRITISH police officer was waiting for me at the other end of the bridge, and I went through the unfamiliar ritual of shaking hands. It was true, I thought as I looked at him, that Europeans had long noses. Apart from brief glimpses of Bull and Lovegren I had not seen a European nose since Harrer's, almost exactly six years ago.

I had spoken very little English during those six years, and the words sounded so unfamiliar that I nearly asked the police officer if he spoke Chinese. I was utterly dazed and confused. It was not only that I was still thinking in Chinese: five years of Communist conditioning could not be discarded in five minutes, and I knew that I had other bridges to cross before my spirit could follow my body into freedom.

The police officer's first words seemed almost irreverently casual. "Everest has been climbed," he said when I asked him what had been happening in the world. "We've won back the Ashes."

The startling thing was not merely that non-political events could be considered as news but that he did not invest them with any political significance. Everest had been climbed by a handful of brave individuals, not because a Party was glorious or a Chairman great. England's victory over Australia at cricket was not due to the correct application of Marxist-Leninist principles.

At first I listened in silence, not yet trusting myself to talk without political clichés. I was also inhibited by the fact that he was a police officer, a symbol of the power of the State. For nearly five years I had been tense and guarded in every trifling action, word, and thought. It was not easy to relax. I had received cigarettes and smiles from other men in blue, and when he asked me how I had been treated the old warning signals sounded in my mind. Then I realized that he was not only a police officer but also a human being, that his questions were not designed to produce information but were simply expressions of compassion and fellow-feeling. I crossed another bridge and began to talk. Soon I was revelling in the luxury of saying what I liked without having to choose my words.

As I talked I looked out of the car at this bewildering town of noise and colour, such a complete contrast with the drab uniformity of the New China. The Communists had made a mistake in taking me on the conducted tour of Canton, where men and women alike wore the same sexless boiler suits. I looked at girls in pretty clothes and with made-up faces, and long-suppressed bourgeois emotions began to reappear.

The police officer drove me to the Naval Hospital, where I enjoyed the amazing comforts of good food and a real bed with sheets. But these were minor blessings compared with the feeling of human warmth and friendship. Doctors, nurses, orderlies, and other patients smiled, asked me how I was, treated me as a person, made me feel that I belonged and had a right to be alive.

I spent only two days in the hospital. The doctors found me perfectly fit apart from some cirrhosis of the liver. I knew that my mental rehabilitation was bound to be a longer process, but I soon lost my fears about the result. Merely being in a civilized society again undid much of the work of those years of patient indoctrination, and I knew that nothing of Communism had reached my soul. I began decontamination with the appropriate antidotes of newspapers and magazines.

It was strange to read a paper that was designed to entertain. It was astonishing to read criticism of the Government of the country in which the paper was published. It was wonderful to read human stories about individual men and women without any political slant. It was equally exhilarating to hear idiotic songs on the radio about the moon and June, instead of American imperialism and the democratic peoples' desire for peace. And I enjoyed the first corny film I saw like a kid from school.

I had been advised to go to the Naval Hospital rather than a civilian hospital in order to escape from the Press. When I was discharged I was advised to give a Press Conference, on the grounds that I would have no peace from the journalists until I did. I agreed reluctantly, for I was unable to tell them either what they wanted to hear or what I wanted to say. And I was not prepared to say a word until I knew where every one was.

Most of the news was good. Bull was out, and no other Europeans had been captured in Tibet. Dronyer, Wangda, and Tsering were out, and back in India. On the other hand, I could not find out anything about Sonam Dorje and Sonam Puntso; and Lovegren was still in.

That fact alone made it impossible for me to speak my mind to the Press. I hated the idea of starting life again with further concealment and evasion, but I was not going to say anything that might delay the release of another prisoner by five minutes. If I turned round and cocked a snook at the Communists they might lengthen the period of thought reform for other Europeans.

The Press wanted atrocity stories, and I told them simply that I had not been tortured or subjected to any physical violence. They asked if I thought my arrest and treatment fair and reasonable. I said that from the Communists' point of view they were, but from the Western point of view they were not. "What about your point of view?" one journalist asked. I said I preferred not to answer that question. I must have been a disappointment to the journalists, but they were decent enough to me. After the Press Conference the representative of one very eminent newspaper rang me up to say he understood. I think the word had been passed round.

Meanwhile I was learning more about what had happened to the others. Bull wrote to me as soon as he heard of my release, and the letter arrived while I was still in Hong Kong. I discovered that Harrer had written a best-seller, and it was the first book I read after my release. I was grieved to learn that both Mr Hopkinson and Fox were dead. Fox had not gone back to Lhasa, and after the Communists took over in Tibet he opened a radio school in Kalimpong. He never recovered his health, and died in 1953.

Aufschnaiter had also stayed in India, and he is still working for the Indian Government in Delhi. Nedbailoff had gone to Australia, and he is working there now as an electrical engineer. Dronyer, Wangda, and Tsering (and her baby) were released in December 1951, shortly after I had begun to confess. I like to think that my surrender helped them to get out. I was shocked to learn that Dronyer had been put in irons in an attempt to make him give information about my supposed espionage activities. All three were subjected to a short course of thought reform, and finally they had to sign statements promising to work for Communism in India. They have not hesitated to tell the Indians what they think of Communism.

I stayed in Hong Kong for a week. During that time I began to learn of the repeated efforts that had been made by the British Government to obtain my release. I have no doubt that these representations constituted one of the main factors that led to my being set free. The others were the improvement in Anglo-Chinese relations since the Geneva Conference, and the fact that I had confessed and undergone thought reform. I do not know the proportionate importance of these three factors. I am sure that if I had not confessed I would still be there.

I enjoyed walking round Hong Kong, going where I liked and looking at the people. It was a boom town, and I could not see any sign of the British sitting on the necks of the Chinese. Certainly there were poverty and hardship, for the population was swollen by a million refugees. But there was nothing to stop them from returning to China—except their own preference for freedom. I watched Chinese workers, listened to their conversations, and recalled the study-groups and criticism and self-criticism meetings that were compulsory for all workers in New China. The effects of brainwashing ebbed away.

I went by sea to Singapore, and then was flown to London. My parents met me at the airport, and I cannot describe my joy. The following Sunday I gave thanks to God. Shortly before my release both my mother and father had been admitted to the Church of England, and I was with them at their first Communion.

There were many letters from old friends waiting for me, and soon I saw some of them again. I met Mrs Hopkinson, and we relived the happy days we had spent in Sikkim. I met Harrer when he was making the film of his book, and thanked him for his discretion in his reference to me.

I met Bull at his home in Middlesex. He had been released in September 1953 after an ordeal that must have been worse than mine, for the attack was on his faith. He has now gone to preach the Gospel in Australia. In September 1955 I heard the news that Lovegren and other Americans had been released, and I felt that I could speak more freely. Towards the end of my captivity I had been constantly urged to do something constructive for the peoples of the world when I returned home. I have followed this advice by giving some lectures on a worm's-eye view of Communism.

I met Tagtsher Rimpoche, the Dalai Lama's eldest brother, at the home of a mutual friend in London. He was wearing spectacles and an English lounge suit, and was on his way to the United States. We talked in Chinese, in which I was now more fluent than in Tibetan. He was sincerely distressed about my capture and imprisonment, and apologized repeatedly on behalf of the Tibetan Government and people.

At last I heard that Sonam Puntso and Sonam Dorje were both safe in Sikkim. I wrote to Sonam Puntso, who was now a forestry officer, and he sent me a long letter describing his experiences after the radio station was captured at Dengko.

He and Sonam Dorje were taken to Jyekundo and interrogated for fourteen days. They were bound to posts and beaten and subjected to other forms of physical violence that Sonam Puntso did not define, all in an attempt to make them reveal information about my supposed espionage. Then they were taken to a prison in Sining, the capital of Chinghai. They continued to be interrogated, and were put on building work. They were kept there for eighteen months.

In December 1951 they were taken to Lhasa, where Sonam Puntso succeeded in escaping. He was hidden by friends in the town for three weeks. He got in touch with some Tibetan officials he knew, but they were unable to help him; so he boldly left his hiding-place and made for the Indian Mission. He was recaptured by Chinese soldiers on the way, and taken to a garrison outside the town. He climbed a twelve-foot wall and got away again, and reached the Indian Mission at seven o'clock in the evening. He was given sanctuary, but the next day a party of about a hundred Chinese soldiers went and took him by force. He was bound and beaten with Bren-gun butts, and kept in handcuffs and fetters for another three months. Then he was reunited with Sonam Dorje, and the two were deported to India.

I still read Chinese newspapers sometimes, and from these I learnt that Geda Lama has been ennobled to the status of martyr of the Communist faith. A monument and memorial hall have been erected in his honour in the monastery at Kantze. A delegation of the People's Government of China paid homage at the shrine on June 2, 1956—my own wedding day, as it happened. In reporting the visit the official New China News Agency did not play fair. It concluded a short biography of Geda with the statement that he had been "murdered in Tibet by the British spy, R. W. Ford." The South-west Area Military Tribunal had not convicted me of that.

At my Press Conference in Hong Kong I was asked if I had confessed to the murder of Geda Lama. I replied that I had not and that I was not charged with murder. This aroused some surprise, and after my return to England I discovered why. When I was looking through the files of old newspapers to see how the invasion had been reported I found this in *The Times* of December 5, 1950:

BRITON ACCUSED OF POISONING LAMA

Hong Kong, *December 4*—Mr R. Ford, the British wireless officer who was captured by Chinese Communists in Tibet, was yesterday accused of poisoning a high lama who was deputy chairman of the Sikang Provincial Government, according to the New China News Agency. The agency alleged that Mr Ford destroyed the priest's body to hide the crime, and it accused Mr Ford of being a British secret agent.

The agency alleges that Mr Ford gave the priest poisoned tea and arrested the priest's retainers.

The New China News Agency is the voice of the Communist Government, the Tass of China. This meant that the world had been told I had really killed Geda, and not just caused his death. All my subtle reasoning about the wording of the paragraph I had read in *People's China* had been absolutely wide of the mark, and my idea for a compromise on this charge had been based on a false inference.

But it had worked.

I felt rather pleased. Without realizing I was doing it, I had succeeded in getting the Communists to withdraw a charge—the most serious charge possible—after they had already published it and announced my guilt to the world.

The full irony was revealed when I went to a Communist bookshop in London (incognito) and looked up old copies of *People's China*. In the first January issue, which I had previously seen with the middle pages removed, I found a reproduction of the photograph taken of me outside the radio station at Chamdo, with this caption:

"R. W. Ford, the Englishman arrested in Changtu, charged with the political assassination of the Tibetan leader Geda."

I wonder what I would have done if I had read this instead of the much less definite charge in the previous issue.

I found the reports of the invasion less amusing.

As there had been no Press correspondents in Tibet, all the reports were based on rumours picked up in Kalimpong. Nearly all of them seemed to have been made up there. I read fantastic stories, including one that credited me with having taken command of the frontier defences. That could not have helped my case when the Communists read it. But I was more depressed to read how the Tibetan resistance was belittled. The favourite story was that the Chinese let off some fireworks and the Tibetan troops ran away.

Of course the Lhasa Government was to blame for not letting the world know that Tibet was putting up a genuine fight; and when at last it had the courage to tell the world of the Chinese aggression, and appealed for help to the United Nations, it was already too late.

Not that the Tibetan appeal ever stood a chance. The Kuomintang delegate, while deploring the Communists' use of force, repeated the traditional claim that Tibet was a province of China. The Indian representative, who was the most intimately concerned, said he hoped the matter would be settled peacefully between the two parties. As a result the Salvador request to put the appeal on the agenda was shelved. The United States delegate said that but for the Indian attitude he would have voted for its inclusion. In her desire to appease China, India gave Tibet no help, although it meant having Communist troops stationed along two thousand miles of her northern frontier.

Yet the Tibetans still did not surrender. Their troops barred the only two routes to Lhasa while the Dalai Lama took refuge near the Indian border. The Chinese could have fought their way in and installed the Panchen Lama in his place, but, very wisely, they sought to negotiate a peace instead. Under the terms of the treaty they agreed to leave the internal administration of the country in the hands of the Dalai Lama and to respect the Tibetan religion. The Tibetans had to agree to admit that their country was part of the People's Republic of China and to hand over foreign affairs and defence to Peking. This gave the Chinese the right to keep as many troops in the country as they wished; and that meant they had the power to devour Tibet whenever they considered it digestible.

The Dalai Lama returned to Lhasa, accompanied by almost all the officials who had taken refuge with him. Now they are at the mercy of the Chinese. Through indirect contacts I have heard how some of them are getting on. Tsarong Dzasa is economic adviser to the Government. His son, my old friend George, has been on an official visit to Peking. Pangda Tsang is head of the Government Trade Department, and represents Tibetan traders in conferences at Peking. Pangda Topgye has left his mountain stronghold of Bo for Kangting, where he holds the office of Vice-Chairman of the Provincial People's Congree of Sikang. But the last I heard of Pangda Rapga was that he was at Kalimpong.

Ngabö is now the most powerful lay official, if any Tibetan can be said to hold effective power. He is a Deputy to the National People's Congress of China, a Member of the National Defence Council, and Commander-in-Chief, Tibet, with Chinese as well as Tibetan troops under his command. I have not heard a word of Lhalu or of anyone else I knew in Chamdo. I have no idea what happened to Lobsang and Tashi, or Tenné, Do-Tseten, and Puntso.

Although the Chinese have ruled through the Dalai Lama—but still keeping their candidate for the Panchen Lama up their sleeve—they have not had things all their own way. There has been resistance since the armistice—especially in Kham.

In spite of their betrayal by Ngabö the Khambas continued to resist for a year after the treaty was signed, until the Dalai Lama appealed personally to them to lay down their arms. And in the spring and summer of 1956 there was a definite revolt in East and North-east Tibet, in which Chinese garrisons were massacred. Had guerrillas been organized in 1950 they could have made the invasion immeasurably more difficult. The spirit of independence is still very much alive. How much longer it can last is not so clear. It has been reported that the Chinese propose to raise the population of Tibet from the present two or three million to ten million, and that can only mean large-scale Chinese colonization. Eventually the Tibetans will be outnumbered in their own land.

The Communists have not been hurrying in Tibet. There has been no land reform, and at the moment the feudal system of tenancy still stands. So does the old Upper Yangtze frontier, and, in the new maps drawn by the Communists, Chamdo lies in the "Tibet Autonomous Area." I was right, after all, when I told my amateur radio contacts that Chamdo was in Tibet.

The country has received some spectacular material benefits. The track I rode along from Chamdo to Kantze is now part of the Lhasa-Chungking motor road. A new hydro-electric station has been erected in Lhasa, and aircraft have landed in the Holy City. Agriculture and industry have been developed, and communications improved. New hospitals and schools have been built; and prisons, too. The people are being re-educated, and in time there will be tenancy and social reform. Already the oppressive system of requisitioning transport has been abolished, and no doubt serfdom will go too. But they are all serfs now.

In the past some of our diehard British imperialists, forgetful of the doctrine of eventual self-determination, argued their right to hang on because of the hospitals, schools, roads, and other such benefits they had brought to the subject peoples. Communist imperialists, whose annexations are openly stated to be for ever, make similar capital out of these services. Often non-Communist materialists fall for this line. I have heard it said that countries like China and Tibet needed Communism, just as it was fashionable once to say that Italy needed Fascism. The argument is that a backward country needs a violent revolutionary movement so that it can progress. The argument overlooks the fact that usually the means determine rather than justify the end, and that monstrous crimes can be committed in the name of progress.

Tibet was backward and feudal, but nobody starved. Most of the people were poor, but there was no hunger and much happiness. Material progress was overdue, but it was beginning to come; my own employment was an example of that. Communications were being improved, a new hydro-electric station was under construction, plans were on foot for the development of agriculture and other plans for education. Many of the officials were becoming increasingly progressive—in the civilized sense of the word—in their outlook. Even tenancy and social reform was discussed, under the influence of ideas from the West.

Of course progress was slow. Technical development was in the hands of a few ill-qualified Europeans, working under Tibetan officials who could not even order spare parts. Of course it would have taken us years to accomplish what the Communists did in a few months. No doubt they may raise living standards more quickly than the Tibetans could have raised them on their own. I am not a medievalist, and I think it is extremely important and beneficial that living standards should be raised. But not at that price. Nothing is worth the extinction of the greatest freedom of all, which is freedom of thought. A healthy, well-fed robot is a poor substitute for a human being.

Epilogue

The Occupation

I T is almost forty years since the Chinese occupied Tibet following
their military invasion of October 1950. It has been four decades of
ruthless subjugation coupled with unremitting political indoctrination, relentless religious persecution, and a sustained campaign to
suppress Tibetan culture. The object was to eliminate the Tibetan
identity. It has also been forty years of resistance and opposition by
the Tibetans to preserve their religious freedom and to restore their
independence.

In the first years following the invasion the Chinese proceeded
with caution. Their first priority was to consolidate the military
occupation with Tibetan acquiescence, if not co-operation. A vast
programme of airfield construction and road building to open up
communications between China and Lhasa was begun. With the
completion of this programme in 1954 they were ready to embark
on a more aggressive policy to strengthen their political authority
and impose their foreign Communist ideology. An anti-religious
campaign combined with demands for fundamental changes in the
social structure was launched in the eastern areas of Kham and
Amdo. To the Tibetans' discontent was added deprivation, resulting
from the requirement that they provide supplies for the army of
occupation. It was not long before discontent turned to armed
resistance, and soon the Chinese had a full-scale uprising on their
hands. Retaliation was swift and brutal. Monasteries and villages
were shelled or bombed. The estates of dispossessed landlords were
taken over and the local population terrorized. Meanwhile Chinese
settlers started to arrive in large numbers. All of these events served
to inflame the situation further. In spite of Lhasa's efforts to urge

Publisher's note: It has not been possible to include references to this epilogue in the
index.

restraint, the Khambas took to the mountains and began a guerilla insurrection which was to last for many years.

In Lhasa the Chinese followed a more insidious plan to subvert the Dalai Lama's authority. In April 1956 they set up a so-called Preparatory Committee for the Autonomous Region of Tibet. Whilst appearing Tibetan in its composition it was so constituted as to give effective control to the Chinese, through various nominated collaborating Tibetan groupings. Tibet was divided geographically into three regions. The puppet Panchen Lama and his supporters were given enhanced status. The central authority of the Dalai Lama and his government was considerably weakened.

Celebrations for the 2,500th anniversary of the birth of Buddha were held in India towards the end of 1956. The Chinese allowed the Dalai Lama to participate. He had become very depressed by the tragic events in Tibet and the suffering of his people. He was particularly concerned about the Communist assault on the Buddhist religion. He was above all exasperated by continued Chinese insensitivity and intransigence. He concluded that he could best help his people by remaining in India and so informed Prime Minister Nehru. Nehru in turn obtained what he regarded as satisfactory assurances from Chinese Premier Zhou Enlai regarding Tibetan grievances and urged the Dalai Lama to return. Some semblance of Chinese conciliation was evidenced by their announcement of the postponement of reforms, the withdrawal of some Chinese Communist activists, and assurances of their respect of Tibetan autonomy. The Dalai Lama decided to test their sincerity and returned to Lhasa.

China in its propaganda made much of its willingness to accommodate Tibetan views. It even admitted violence and lawlessness on the part of the army and the Party. But there was no admission that government and Party policy might be flawed. It was only in local application that errors had been made. The myth of party infallibility was thus maintained.

During the next few years dispossessed people and monks swelled the numbers of armed guerilla bands and the activities of these groups became widespread. Ominously the resistance movement, for such it could now be called, spread to other regions of Tibet. Continued attacks on Chinese garrisons and along the vital China–Lhasa highways were so successful that the Chinese were compelled to bring in more and better troops. Politically the demands on the

Dalai Lama and his government were increased. The situation was becoming explosive.

Detailed accounts of China's cruel repression and the widespread and effective nature of Tibet's resistance began to appear in the international media. India, however, remained placatory towards its Chinese neighbour. In parliament Nehru went so far as to deny reports of violence in Tibet. India's attitude was matched by the indifference of Western governments.

Early in 1959 events moved swiftly. The Tibetan uprising in Lhasa, the flight of the Dalai Lama to exile in India, and the subsequent ruthless suppression of Tibetan opposition made headline news around the world. Thousands died in the Lhasa uprising. A countrywide clearance operation to root out every vestige of Tibetan dissent was mounted. Some tens of thousands were killed. More were imprisoned or sent to forced labour camps. Over 60,000 followed their leader to India.

For a brief period the tragedy of Tibet became the focus of world attention as an appeal was made to the United Nations. As in 1950 India, closely concerned with events taking place just over its borders, and Britain, which had enjoyed a special relationship with Tibet, failed to give a lead there. Although much sympathy was expressed for Tibet's plight, governments were not prepared to jeopardize their relations with China by calling for practical measures to ease Tibet's suffering. They contented themselves with a resolution for respect of human rights, Tibetan culture, and religious life.

With the Dalai Lama and the majority of his officials out of the way, the Chinese now abandoned all pretence of working through the local Tibetan authorities. The Preparatory Committee was in effect replaced by a military government. Tibetan participation was limited to a few reliable collaborators like Ngabö and the Panchen Lama. Martial law was declared. A far-reaching and wide-ranging programme aimed at dominating all aspects of Tibetan life was launched. It was implemented with a ferocity to be matched only by the Cultural Revolution some years later.

The first priority was to re-establish firm control throughout the country. The frontier to the south was sealed and all unauthorized movement within Tibet was forbidden. Identity cards for Tibetans were introduced. Army units were reinforced, even in the smallest hamlet. Local committees were set up to control political activity and were increasingly dominated by Chinese party activists. Controls extended down to the family unit. Large numbers of Tibetans from every class, including the poorest, were labelled variously as traitors, counter-revolutionaries, or class enemies, and treated accordingly. Monasteries were looted, ransacked, and emptied of their monks, who were branded as parasites or exploiters. Countless numbers were imprisoned or sent to perform forced labour. Many died. Normal life was completely disrupted. Not a single village was left untouched. A veritable reign of terror was instituted in the name of socialist revolution. More Tibetans fled the country. Chinese immigration continued unabated.

Most insidious was the introduction to the Tibetans of class warfare by means of political indoctrination and struggle sessions. It was the well-tried technique used throughout China after the Communist take-over. It was the same system I had endured in prison. Now Tibet was one huge prison. Struggle meetings and public trials became commonplace. The more important prisoners were called to account before thousands. My old friend Lhalu Shapé, the former Governor-General of Kham, was one of those paraded before huge crowds in Lhasa to be vilified and publicly humiliated before being repeatedly beaten then thrown back into prison. Nothing has been heard of him since.

The clergy were singled out for special attention in the campaign of intimidation and thought reform, since, in the absence of the local authority, they had become the focus of Tibetan unity and dissent. It was imperative, therefore, that they be isolated and their influence destroyed. Society was divided. Peasant was set against landowner, monk against abbot, neighbour against neighbour, and even children against parents. Fear of the Chinese was accompanied by mutual distrust amongst the Tibetans.

So-called democratic reforms in 1960 were followed by land reforms which created havoc with agricultural output. The need to support the army and meet the demands of the increasing numbers of Chinese migrants added to the shortages. Rationing of foodstuffs and other commodities was introduced. Poor harvests in China exacerbated the problem. The famines lasted for three years, by which time thousands more deaths through starvation had been added to those of persecution.

Chinese propaganda meanwhile spoke only of the advance of democracy and lauded the improvements in the economy, education, health, and so on. Certainly there had been improvements, but the main beneficiaries were the Chinese settlers and the army of occupation. Refugees still managed to escape to India, taking with them confirmation of Tibetan suffering and discontent. They also confirmed the continued existence of determined anti-Chinese guerilla forces in the east and south of the country.

Internationally the 1960s were difficult for China. The deterioration in Sino-Soviet relations brought border clashes; relations with India remained strained following border incursions; and China's involvement in the Vietnam war and continued preoccupation with a divided Korea combined to heighten her sense of isolation and feeling of vulnerability.

Internally China was rocked by the Cultural Revolution. In the summer of 1966 the Red Guards reached Lhasa. Soon Tibet, like the whole of China, was embroiled in what was essentially a vicious power struggle within the leadership. Fundamentally it was a battle between two factions within the Communist Party to determine the direction and speed of the country's political and economic development. On the one side were Mao and the Gang of Four advocating a more radical and rapid push towards communism. Opposing them were Liu Shaoqi and Deng Xiaoping favouring a more gradual and less extreme advance. The terror, chaos, death, and destruction lasted for three turbulent years. It was virtual anarchy as activists of both factions and their supporters vied with each other in frenzied clashes over ideology. Mob violence ensued and pitched battles were commonplace as units of the armed forces joined in. Civil war was only narrowly averted.

The conflict within Tibet, still considered politically backward by the party zealots, was particularly fierce. For the most part the Tibetans themselves were confused and innocent victims. All the elements of the class struggle of ten years earlier, the public meetings, and mass demonstrations, were brought into play. The Red Guards concentrated their efforts on the elimination of every aspect of Tibetan culture and customs. The Buddhist religion, already the subject of continuous attack, was targeted for special attention. Nearly all the ancient monasteries and temples remaining in Tibet were systematically looted and their buildings destroyed. Throughout Tibet only a dozen or more were left standing as empty shells. The great monasteries near Lhasa which formerly housed thousands of monks were practically razed to the ground. Anti-religious propaganda was stepped up. Religious worship was now formally forbidden. *Chortens* and *mani* walls were flattened. Tibetan customs were ridiculed and forbidden. The wearing of traditional Tibetan clothes was prohibited. Most degrading of all, Tibetans were forced to witness and participate in this wholesale and wanton destruction.

Communist propaganda indulged in a shrill campaign denigrating the old Tibet. The Dalai Lama, the former aristocracy, and the feudal system were the objects of sustained and virulent abuse. The Panchen Lama was dismissed and imprisoned. Only the puppet Ngabö seems to have been spared. He was taken to Beijing where he remained until 1975 when it was deemed safe for him to return to Lhasa.

By 1970 the influence of the more liberal elements in the Party began to prevail. The excesses of the Cultural Revolution began to subside. Throughout China life began to return to normal, if one can use such a word to describe the absence of conflict. The gradualists headed by Deng made important changes. Some personal freedoms were restored. There was a limited return to individual farming and private industry. A less tense atmosphere was encouraged. Externally China took some trouble to lessen its belligerent stance. She was admitted to the United Nations and relations with the United States were restored.

In Tibet, too, the 1970s saw changes. A road-building programme, mainly implemented by the Army, extended motorable roads throughout Tibet. New settlements were built alongside the old villages and towns. In the south and east large-scale timber cutting began. Small-scale industry was encouraged and livestock and dairy production increased. Mineral exploration and extraction developed. Education and health care were improved. The numbers of Chinese settlers greatly increased and they were the main beneficiaries of these changes. The relative prosperity passed the Tibetans by. Nevertheless, there was some relaxation in the treatment meted out to them. Tibetan was again taught in schools and Tibetans were allowed to wear their national dress. A number of the more important monasteries and shrines in Lhasa and Shigatse were repaired and refurbished, but the number of monks allowed to return to them was minimal. Some semblance of religious freedom was restored but the places of worship had largely disappeared. The changes merely served to accentuate the differences between the Chinese and the Tibetans. They also illustrated the oppressive colonial nature of the occupation. Sporadic armed resistance continued in the countryside.

Mao died in 1976 and the Gang of Four was eliminated. Within two years Deng Xiaoping had assumed full power and the new policy of liberalization proceeded apace. Even the Mao-style tunic was no longer obligatory wear and gaily coloured clothing began to replace drab uniformity in the towns. Political and economic contacts were developed with the outside world. China began to be accepted as a responsible partner in world affairs.

Important initiatives were taken in regard to Tibet. The Panchen Lama, along with other Tibetans of influence, was released from prison and reinstated in local government. More Tibetans were returned from forced labour camps. A general relaxation in Beijing's approach to the problems of Tibet was evident. A high-level Communist delegation, of which Ngabö was a member, visited Lhasa and other areas. Its report, whilst careful not to cast doubt on fundamentals, was highly critical of past implementation of policy and expressed dissatisfaction with conditions generally. Changes in the Chinese leadership in Tibet followed, and the move towards a more liberal regime continued. After decades, the first foreigners were allowed to visit and soon escorted tourist groups were admitted. Most important, contacts, at first secret, were established with the Dalai Lama. Tibetan fact-finding delegations, their composition approved by the Dalai Lama, were allowed to tour Tibet to see conditions for themselves.

The first mission, which included one of the Dalai Lama's brothers, entered in August 1979. A second and third mission to study education followed in May and June 1980. They were able to travel widely, although understandably they were not allowed to visit the militarily sensitive frontier areas or extensive areas of the vast northern plains — the sites of the missile and nuclear testing ranges and of the Gulags. The Chinese were unable to restrict the contacts between members of the missions and their fellow-countrymen. They thus gained an insight into the local conditions and attitudes more revealing than the official briefings arranged for them.

The missions' reports confirmed that after three decades no substantial improvements had been made. Living standards were at subsistence levels. Food, clothing, and other necessities were rationed. Restrictions on movement were still in force and freedom of religion still denied. The sinister system of political indoctrination and surveillance continued. Tibetans were confined to ghettos, their wretched condition contrasting sharply with the superior standards enjoyed by the Chinese who now outnumbered them. Few

Chinese spoke Tibetan or Tibetans Chinese. Tibetans had now become second-class citizens. This is called apartheid in South Africa.

Wherever they travelled the delegates saw encouraging evidence of the tenacity of the Buddhist faith and the widespread reverence attached to the person of the Dalai Lama. Everywhere crowds, running into their thousands in Lhasa, gathered to meet them, to pour out their grievances and above all to express their longing for the return of their God-King. It was a spontaneous and courageous outpouring of devotion and loyalty, desperation, and anger. It signified a total refusal to submit to force and a negation of all Chinese claims. It is not surprising that a fourth mission was postponed and finally, in 1981, cancelled by the Chinese.

During the next few years Deng's authoritarianism was judiciously mixed with pragmatic reformism. A general relaxation in political and economic life continued. Relations with the rest of the world improved. Sadly only limited improvements were evidenced in Tibet. Chinese settlements continued to spread. The oppressive aspects of the occupation remained. Armed resistance by Tibetans on any scale was finally quashed, but passive defiance often exploded into violent rioting. It was firmly dealt with. China continued its indirect and intermittent contacts with the Dalai Lama in the hope of persuading him to return. He resolutely refused to do so whilst self-determination was denied and human rights abused.

Reports by foreign journalists and tourists allowed to travel in Tibet in increasing numbers confirmed the continuing ordeal of the Tibetan people. They also brought to light the extent of the threat to the fragile ecological balance of the Tibetan plateau. Massive deforestation had reduced rich forest areas to barren wasteland. Inefficient and unsuitable farming methods resulting in poor yields added to the problems of the population increase caused by the Chinese influx. Tibet's wildlife, once protected under Buddhism, had been decimated by large-scale hunting and fishing. The vast herds of gazelle, wild ass, and wild yak, a common sight in old Tibet, have disappeared. Geese and duck, once abundant around the lakes and rivers, particularly during the migratory seasons, are no longer seen. Travellers have remarked on the absence of large animals and the paucity in the numbers and variety of birds.

Foreigners were also on hand to witness the uprisings and brutal repression which took place in the autumn of 1987, the spring of 1988, and again in March 1989. The pattern became distressingly familiar. Unarmed demonstrators were indiscriminately fired upon by Chinese troops. Larger crowds gathered and they in turn were brutally dispersed. In March 1989, some 10,000 enraged protesting Tibetans marched through the streets of Lhasa. There were many casualties and arrests. A dusk-to-dawn curfew was imposed and martial law declared. It remains in force almost one year later. Visits by foreign journalists and tourists were banned. Only recently have visits by small guided tourist groups been allowed to resume.

The presence of foreigners during the disturbances ensured world-wide publicity. For the first time in many years there were eye-witness reports of China's brutality. They made the world's headlines. Sadly the widespread sympathy and interest aroused in Tibet's plight was not matched by any parallel move on the part of Western governments other than a mild reprimand for Beijing.

Meanwhile the Dalai Lama continued his efforts to open a meaningful dialogue with the Chinese. In the last resort Tibet does not have the means to throw off Chinese rule. True to his Buddhist approach he continued to hope for some sort of accommodation. The 'one country, two systems' formula to be implemented in the case of Hong Kong seemed at one stage to offer a basis for talks about the future of Tibet, but as Tibet slipped out of the headlines, the Chinese procrastinated. In any event Deng soon had more important forces closer to home threatening his very power base. The student movement for democracy was gaining ground and attracting support outside academic circles. Its accusations of nepotism and corruption gained backing within the party hierarchy. Deng cracked down hard. Martial law was declared in May, followed two weeks later by the massacre of Tiananmen Square. The scenes of brutality that filled our television screens brought home the stark reality of a cynical and ruthless regime prepared to go to any lengths to eradicate any challenge to its authority. The stories of atrocities in Tibet now became entirely believable even to the sceptics. But this was not all. Alarmed by the speed of changes sweeping the Soviet Union and Eastern Europe, the old men of Beijing chose to initiate a return to Communist political orthodoxy and rigid centralized control of the economy — a complete negation of the changes of the past ten years. It does not augur well for Tibet.

It now seems that any changes from Deng's policy reversal will have to await a return to sanity with the emergence of a younger pragmatic leadership. Therein might lie hope for Tibet. A new generation of Chinese rulers might recognize the logic of a stable neutral self-governing buffer in Central Asia. It would also fulfil the dream of all Tibetans simply to be left alone to live their own lives in accordance with their Buddhist beliefs.

ROBERT FORD
1989

Index

Titles marked with an asterisk have restricted rights.